THE SLAVE OF THE LAMP

I0667633

HENRY SETON MERRIMAN

The Slave Of The Lamp

Henry Seton Merriman

© 1st World Library, 2007
PO Box 2211
Fairfield, IA 52556
www.1stworldlibrary.com
First Edition

LCCN: 2007930797

Softcover ISBN: 978-1-4218-4839-6
Hardcover ISBN: 978-1-4218-4742-9
eBook ISBN: 978-1-4218-4936-2

Purchase *"The Slave Of The Lamp"*
as a traditional bound book at:
www.1stWorldLibrary.com/purchase.asp?ISBN=978-1-4218-4839-6

1st World Library is a literary, educational organization
dedicated to:

- Creating a free internet library of downloadable ebooks

- Hosting writing competitions and offering book publishing
scholarships.

Interested in more 1st World Library books? contact:
literacy@1stworldlibrary.com
Check us out at: www.1stworldlibrary.com

1ˢᵗ World Library Literary Society

Giving Back to the World

"If you want to work on the core problem, it's early school literacy."

- James Barksdale, former CEO of Netscape

"No skill is more crucial to the future of a child, or to a democratic and prosperous society, than literacy."

- Los Angeles Times

"Literacy... means far more than learning how to read and write... The aim is to transmit... knowledge and promote social participation."

- UNESCO

"Literacy is not a luxury, it is a right and a responsibility. If our world is to meet the challenges of the twenty-first century we must harness the energy and creativity of all our citizens."

- President Bill Clinton

"Parents should be encouraged to read to their children, and teachers should be equipped with all available techniques for teaching literacy, so the varying needs and capacities of individual kids can be taken into account."

- Hugh Mackay

PREFACE

Henry Seton Merriman published his first novel, "Young Mistley," in 1888, when he was twenty-six years old. Messrs. Bentley's reader, in his critique on the book, spoke of its "powerful situations" and unconventionality of treatment: and, while dwelling at much greater length on its failings, declared, in effect, its faults to be the right faults, and added that, if "Young Mistley" was not in itself a good novel, its author was one who might hereafter certainly write good novels.

"Young Mistley" was followed in quick succession by "The Phantom Future," "Suspense," and "Prisoners and Captives." Some years later, considering them crude and immature works, the author, at some difficulty and with no little pecuniary loss, withdrew all these four first books from circulation in England. Their republication in America he was powerless to prevent. He therefore revised and abbreviated them, "conscious," as he said himself in a preface, "of a hundred defects which the most careful revision cannot eliminate." He was perhaps then, as he was ever, too severe a critic of his own works. But though these four early books have, added to youthful failings, the youthful merits of freshness, vigour and imagination, their author was undoubtedly right to suppress them. By writing them he learnt, it is true, the technique of his art: but no author wishes—or no author should wish—to give his copybooks to the world. It is as well then—it is certainly as he himself desired—that these four books do not form part of the present edition. It may, however, be noted that both "Young Mistley" and "Prisoners and Captives" dealt, as did "The Sowers" hereafter, with Russian subjects: "Suspense" is the story of a war-correspondent in the Russo-Turkish War of 1877: and "The Phantom Future" is the only novel of Merriman's in which the scene is laid entirely in his own country.

In 1892 he produced "The Slave of the Lamp," which had run serially through the *Cornhill Magazine*, then under the editorship of Mr. James Payn.

To Mr. Payn, Merriman always felt that he owed a debt of gratitude for much shrewd and kindly advice and encouragement. But one item of that advice he neglected with, as Mr. Payn always generously owned, great advantage. Mr. Payn believed that the insular nature of the ordinary Briton made it, as a general rule, highly undesirable that the scene of any novel should be laid outside the British Isles.

After 1892 all Merriman's books, with the single exception of "Flotsam," which appeared serially in *Longman's Magazine*, and was, at first, produced in book form by Messrs. Longman, were published by the firm of Messrs. Smith, Elder, & Co.

His long and serene connection with the great and honourable house which had produced the works of such masters of literature as Thackeray, Charlotte Bronte, and Robert Browning, was always a source of sincere pleasure to him. He often expressed the opinion that, from the moment when, as an inexperienced and perfectly unknown author, he sent "Young Mistley" to Messrs. Bentley, until the time when, as a very successful one, he was publishing his later novels with Messrs. Smith, Elder, he had invariably received from his publishers an entirely just and upright treatment.

Also in 1892 he produced "From One Generation to Another": and, two years later, the first of his really successful novels, "With Edged Tools." It is the only one of his books of which he never visited the *mise-en-scene*— West Africa: but he had so completely imbued himself with the scenery and the spirit of the country that few, if any, of his critics detected that he did not write of it from personal experience. Many of his readers were firmly convinced of the reality of the precious plant, Simiacine, on whose discovery the action of the plot turns. More than one correspondent wrote to express a wish to take shares in the Simiacine Company!

"With Edged Tools" was closely followed by "The Grey Lady." Some practical experience of a seafaring life, a strong love of it, and a great fellow-feeling for all those whose business is in great waters, helped the reality of the characters of the sailor brothers and of the sea-scenes generally. The author was for some years, and at the time "The Grey Lady" was written, an underwriter at Lloyd's, so that on the subject of ship insurance—a subject on which it will be remembered part of the plot hinges—he was *en pays de connaissance*. For the purpose of this story, he travelled in the Balearic Islands, having, earlier, made the first of many visits to Spain.

One of the strongest characteristics in his nature, as it is certainly one of the strongest characteristics in his books, was his sympathy with, and, in consequence, his under-standing of, the mind of the foreigner. For him, indeed, there were no alien countries. He learnt the character of the stranger as quickly as he learnt his language. His greatest delight was to merge himself completely in the life and interests of the country he was visiting—to stay at the mean *venta*, or the *auberge* where the tourist was never seen—to sit in the local cafes of an evening and listen to local politics and gossip; to read for the time nothing but the native newspapers, and no literature but the literature, past and present, of the land where he was sojourning; to follow the native customs, and to see Spain, Poland or Russia with the eyes and from the point of view of the Spaniard, the Pole or the Russian.

The difficulties—sometimes there were even serious difficulties—of visiting places where there was neither provision nor protection made for the stranger, always acted upon him not as deterrent but incentive: he liked something to overcome, and found the safe, comfortable, convenient resting-places as uncongenial to his nature as they were unproductive for the purposes of his work.

In 1896 "The Sowers" was published. Merriman's travels in Russia had taken place some years before—before, in fact, the publication of "Young Mistley"—but time had not at all weakened the strong and sombre impression which that great country and its unhappy people had left upon him. The most popular of all his books with his English public, Merriman himself did not consider it his best. It early received the compliment of being banned by the Russian censor: very recently, a Russian woman told the present writers that "The Sowers" is still the first book the travelling Russian buys in the Tauchnitz edition, as soon as he is out of his own country—"we like to hear the truth about ourselves."

In the same year as "The Sowers," Merriman produced "Flotsam." It is not, strictly speaking, a romance: some of its main incidents were taken from the life of a young officer of the 44th Regiment in Early Victorian days. The character of Harry Wylam is, as a whole, faithful to its prototype; and the last scene in the book, recording Harry's death in the Orange Free State, as he was being taken in a waggon to the missionary station by the Bishop of the State, is literally accurate. Merriman had visited India as a boy; so here, too, the scenery is from the brush of an eye-witness.

His next novel, "In Kedar's Tents," was his first Spanish novel—pure and simple: the action of "The Grey Lady" taking place chiefly in Majorca.

All the country mentioned in "In Kedar's Tents" Merriman visited personally—riding, as did Frederick Conyngham and Concepcion Vara, from Algeciras to Ronda, then a difficult ride through a wild, beautiful and not too safe district, the accommodation at Algeciras and Ronda being at that time of an entirely primitive description. Spain had for Merriman ever a peculiar attraction: the character of the Spanish gentleman— proud, courteous, dignified—particularly appealed to him.

The next country in which he sought inspiration was Holland. "Roden's Corner," published in 1898, broke new ground: its plot, it will be remembered, turns on a commercial enterprise. The title and the main idea of the story were taken from Merriman's earliest literary venture, the beginning of a novel—there were only a few chapters of it—which he had written before "Young Mistley," and which he had discarded, dissatisfied.

The novel "Dross" was produced in America in 1899, having appeared serially in this country in a well-known newspaper. Written during a period of ill-health, Merriman thought it beneath his best work, and, true to that principle which ruled his life as an author, to give to the public so far as he could of that best, and of that best only, he declined (of course to his own monetary disadvantage) to permit its publication in England in book form.

Its *mise-en-scene* is France and Suffolk; its period the Second Empire—the period of "The Last Hope." Napoleon III., a character by whom Merriman was always peculiarly attracted, shadows it: in it appears John Turner, the English banker of Paris, of "The Last Hope"; an admirable and amusing sketch of a young Frenchman; and an excellent description of the magnificent scenery about Saint Martin Lantosque, in the Maritime Alps.

For the benefit of "The Isle of Unrest," his next book, Merriman had travelled through Corsica—not the Corsica of fashionable hotels and health-resorts, but the wild and unknown parts of that lawless and magnificent island. For "The Velvet Glove" he visited Pampeluna, Saragossa, and Lerida. The country of "The Vultures"—Warsaw and its neighbourhood—he saw in company with his friend, Mr. Stanley Weyman. The pleasure of another trip, the one he took in western France—Angouleme, Cognac, and the country of the Charente—for the scenery of "The Last Hope," was also doubled by Mr. Weyman's presence. In Dantzig—the Dantzig of "Barlasch of the Guard"—Merriman made a stay in a bitter mid-winter, visiting also Vilna and Koenigsberg; part of the route of the Great Retreat from Moscow he traced himself. He was inclined to consider—and if an author is not quite the worst judge of his own work he is generally quite the best— that in "Barlasch" he reached his high-water mark. The short stories, comprised in the volume entitled "Tomaso's Fortune," were published after his death. In every case, the *locale* they describe was known to Merriman personally. At the Monastery of Montserrat—whence the monk in "A Small World" saw the accident to the diligencia—the author had made a stay of some days. The Farlingford of "The Last Hope" is Orford in Suffolk: the French scenes, as has been said, Merriman had visited with Mr. Weyman, whose "Abbess of Vlaye" they also suggested. The curious may still find the original of the Hotel Gemosac in Paris—not far from the Palais d'Orsay Hotel—"between the Rue de Lille and the Boulevard St. Germain."

"The Last Hope" was not, in a sense, Merriman's last novel. He left at his death about a dozen completed chapters, and the whole plot carefully mapped out, of yet another Spanish book, which dealt with the Spain of the Peninsular War of 1808-14. These chapters, which were destroyed by the author's desire, were of excellent promise, and written with great vigour and spirit. His last trip was taken, in connection with this book, to the country of Sir Arthur Wellesley's exploits. The plot of the story was concerned with a case of mistaken identity; the sketch of a Guerilla leader, Pedro— bearing some affinity to the Concepcion Vara of "In Kedar's Tents"—was especially happy.

It has been seen that Merriman was not the class of author who "sits in Fleet Street and writes news from the front." He strongly believed in the value of personal impressions, and scarcely less in the value of first impressions. In his own case, the correctness of his first impressions—what he himself called laughingly his *"coup d'oeil"*—is in a measure proved by a note-book, now lying before the writers, in which he recorded his views of Bastia and the Corsicans after a very brief acquaintance—that view requiring scarcely any modification when first impressions had been exchanged for real knowledge and experience.

As to his methods of writing, in the case of all his novels, except the four early suppressed ones, he invariably followed the plan of drawing out the whole plot and a complete synopsis of every chapter before he began to write the book at all.

Partly as a result of this plan perhaps, but more as a result of great natural facility in writing, his manuscripts were often without a single erasure for many pages; and a typewriter was really a superfluity.

It is certainly true to say that no author ever had more pleasure in his art than Merriman. The fever and the worry which accompany many literary productions he never knew.

Among the professional critics he had neither personal friends nor personal foes; and accepted their criticisms—hostile or favourable—with perfect serenity and open-mindedness. He was, perhaps, if anything, only too ready to alter his work in accordance with their advice: he always said that he owed them much; and admired their perspicuity in detecting a promise in his earliest books, which he denied finding there himself. His invincible modesty made him ready to accept not only professional criticism but—a harder thing—the advice of critics on the hearth. It was out of compliance with such a domestic criticism that the *denouement* in "The Sowers" was re-written as it now stands, the scene of the attack on the Castle being at first wholly different.

The jealousy and bitterness which are supposed to be inseparable from the literary life certainly never affected Merriman's. He had no trace of such feelings in his nature. Of one who is known to the public exclusively through his writings, it may seem strange—but it is not the less true—to say that his natural bent was not to the life of a literary man, but to a life of action, and that it was fate, rather than inclination, which made him express himself in words instead of deeds. A writer's books are generally his best biography: the "strong, quiet man," whose forte was to do much and say nothing; who, like Marcos Sarrion, loved the free and plain life of the field and the open, was a natural hero for Merriman, "as finding there unconsciously some image of himself."

To any other biography he was strongly opposed. His dislike of the advertisement and the self-advertisement of the interview and the personal paragraph deepened with time. He held strongly and consistently, as he held all his opinions, that a writer should be known to the public by his books, and by his books only. One of his last expressed wishes was that there should be no record of his private life.

It is respect for that wish which here stays the present writers' pen.

E.F.S. S.G.T. *July* 1909.

CONTENTS

CHAPTER I

IN THE RUE ST. GINGOLPHE

It was, not so many years ago, called the Rue de l'Empire, but republics are proverbially sensitive. Once they are established they become morbidly desirous of obliterating a past wherein no republic flourished. The street is therefore dedicated to St. Gingolphe to-day. To-morrow? Who can tell?

It is presumably safe to take it for granted that you are located in the neighbourhood of the Louvre, on the north side of the river which is so unimportant a factor to Paris. For all good Englishmen have been, or hope in the near future to be, located near this spot. All good Americans, we are told, relegate the sojourn to a more distant future.

The bridge to cross is that of the Holy Fathers. So called to-day. Once upon a time—but no matter. Bridges are peculiarly liable to change in troubled times. The Rue St. Gingolphe is situated between the Boulevard St. Germain and Quai Voltaire. One hears with equal facility the low-toned boom of the steamers' whistle upon the river, and the crack of whips in the boulevard. Once across the bridge, turn to the right, and go along the Quay, between the lime-trees and the bookstalls. You will probably go slowly because of the bookstalls. No one worth talking to could help doing so. Then turn to the left, and after a few paces you will find upon your right hand the Rue St. Gingolphe. It is noted in the Directory "Botot" that this street is one hundred and forty-five metres long; and who would care to contradict "Botot," or even to throw the faintest shadow of a doubt upon his statement? He has probably measured.

If your fair and economical spouse should think of repairing to the Bon-Marche to secure some of those wonderful linen pillow-cases (at one franc forty) with your august initial embroidered on the centre with a view of impressing the sleeper's cheek, she will pass the end of the Rue St. Gingolphe on her way—provided the cabman be honest. There! You cannot help finding it now.

The street itself is a typical Parisian street of one hundred and forty-five metres. There is room for a baker's, a cafe, a bootmaker's, and a tobacconist who sells very few stamps. The Parisians do not write many letters. They say they have not time. But the tobacconist makes up for the meanness of his contribution to the inland revenue of one department by a generous aid to the other. He sells a vast number of cigarettes and cigars of the very worst quality. And it is upon the worst quality that the Government makes the largest profit. It is in every sense of the word a weed which grows as lustily as any of its compeers in and around Oran, Algiers, and Bonah.

The Rue St. Gingolphe is within a stone's-throw of the Ecole des Beaux-Arts, and in the very centre of a remarkably cheap and yet respectable quarter. Thus there are many young men occupying apartments in close proximity—and young men do not mind much what they smoke, especially provincial young men living in Paris. They feel it incumbent upon them to be constantly smoking something—just to show that they are Parisians, true sons of the pavement, knowing how to live. And their brightest hopes are in all truth realised, because theirs is certainly a reckless life, flavoured as it is with "number one" tobacco, and those "little corporal" cigarettes which are enveloped in the blue paper.

The tobacconist's shop is singularly convenient. It has, namely, an entrance at the back, as well as that giving on to the street of St. Gingolphe. This entrance is through a little courtyard, in which is the stable and coach-house combined, where Madame Perinere, a lady who paints the magic word "Modes" beneath her name on the door-post of number seventeen, keeps the dapper little cart and pony which carry her bonnets to the farthest corner of Paris.

The tobacconist is a large man, much given to perspiration. In fact, one may safely make the statement that he perspires annually from the middle of April to the second or even third week in October. In consequence of this habit he wears no collar, and a man without a collar does not start fairly on the social race. It is always best to make inquiries before condemning a man who wears no collar. There is probably a very good reason, as in the case of Mr. Jacquetot, but it is to be feared that few pause to seek it. One need not seek the reason with much assiduity in this instance, because the tobacconist of the Rue St. Gingolphe is always prepared to explain it at length. French people are thus. They talk of things, and take pleasure in so doing, which we, on this side of the Channel, treat with a larger discretion.

Mr. Jacquetot does not even wear a collar on Sunday, for the simple reason that Sunday is to him as other days. He attends no place of worship, because he acknowledges but one god— the god of most Frenchmen—his inner man. His pleasures are gastronomical, his sorrows stomachic. The little shop is open early and late, Sundays, week-days, and holidays. Moreover, the tobacconist—Mr. Jacquetot himself—is always at his post, on the high chair behind the counter, near the window, where he can see into the street. This constant attention to business is almost phenomenal, because Frenchmen who worship the god of Mr. Jacquetot love to pay tribute on fete-days at one of the little restaurants on the Place at Versailles, at Duval's, or even in the Palais Royal. Mr. Jacquetot would have loved nothing better than a pilgrimage to any one of these shrines, but he was tied to the little tobacco store. Not by the chains of commerce. Oh, no! When rallied by his neighbours for such an unenterprising love of his own hearth, he merely shrugged his heavy shoulders.

"What will you?" he would say; "one has one's affairs."

Now the affairs of Mr. Jacquetot were, in the days with which we have to do, like many things on this earth, inasmuch as they were not what they seemed.

It would be inexpedient, for reasons closely connected with the tobacconist of the Rue St. Gingolphe, as well as with other gentlemen still happily with us in the flesh, to be too exact as to dates. Suffice it, therefore, to say that it was only a few years ago that Mr. Jacquetot sat one evening as usual in his little shop. It happened to be a Tuesday evening, which is fortunate, because it was on Tuesdays and Saturdays that the little barber from round the corner called and shaved the vast cheeks of the tobacconist. Mr. Jacquetot was therefore quite presentable—doubly so, indeed, because it was yet March, and he had not yet entered upon his summer season.

The little street was very quiet. There was no through traffic, and folks living in this quarter of Paris usually carry their own parcels. It was thus quite easy to note the approach of any passenger, when such had once turned the corner. Some one was approaching now, and Mr. Jacquetot threw away the stump of a cheap cigar. One would almost have said that he recognised the step at a considerable distance. Young people are in the habit of considering that when one gets old and stout one loses in intelligence; but this is not always the case. One is apt to expect little from a fat man; but that is often a mistake. Mr. Jacquetot weighed seventeen stone, but he was eminently intelligent. He had recognised the footstep while it was yet seventy metres away.

In a few moments a gentleman of middle height paused in front of the shop, noted that it was a tobacconist's, and entered, carrying an unstamped letter with some ostentation. It must, by the way, be remembered that in France postage-stamps are to be bought at all tobacconists'.

The new-comer's actions were characterised by a certain carelessness, as if he were going through a formula—perfunctorily—without admitting its necessity.

He nodded to Mr. Jacquetot, and rather a pleasant smile flickered for a moment across his face. He was a singularly well-made man, of medium height, with straight, square shoulders and small limbs. He wore spectacles, and as he looked at one straight in the face there was a singular contraction of the eyes which hardly amounted to a cast— moreover, it was momentary. It was precisely the look of a hawk when its hood is suddenly removed in full daylight. This resemblance was furthered by the fact that the man's profile was birdlike. He was clean-shaven, and there was in his sleek head and determined little face that smooth, compact self-complacency which is to be noted in the head of a hawk.

The face was small, like that of a Greek bust, but in expression it suggested a yet older people. There was that mystic depth of expression which comes from ancient Egypt.

No one feature was obtrusive—all were chiselled with equal delicacy; and yet there was only one point of real beauty in the entire countenance. The mouth was perfect. But the man with a perfect mouth is usually one whom it will be found expedient to avoid. Without a certain allowance of sensuality no man is genial—without a little weakness there is no kind heart. This Frenchman's mouth was not, however, obtrusively faultless. It was perfect in its design, but, somehow, many people failed to take note of the fact. It is so with the "many," one finds. The human world is so blind that at times it would be almost excusable to harbour the suspicion that animals see more. There may be something in that instinct by which dogs, horses, and cats distinguish between friends and foes, detect sympathy, discover antipathy. It is possible that they see things in the human face to which our eyes are blinded—intentionally and mercifully blinded. If some of us were a little more observant, a few of the human combinations which we bring about might perhaps be less egregiously mistaken.

It was probably the form of the lips that lent pleasantness to the smile with which Mr. Jacquetot was greeted, rather than the expression of the velvety eyes, which had in reality no power of smiling at all. They were sad eyes, like those of the women one sees on the banks of the Upper Nile, which never alter in expression—eyes that do not seem to be busy with this life at all, but fully occupied with something else: something beyond to-morrow or behind yesterday.

"Not yet arrived?" inquired the new-comer in a voice of some distinction. It was a full, rich voice, and the French it spoke was not the French of Mr. Jacquetot, nor, indeed, of the Rue St. Gingolphe. It was the language one sometimes hears in an old *chateau* lost in the depths of the country—the vast unexplored rural districts of France—where the bearers of dangerously historical names live out their lives with a

Henry Seton Merriman

singular suppression and patience. They are either biding their time or else they are content with the past and the part played by their ancestors therein. For there is an old French and a new. In Paris the new is spoken—the very newest. Were it anything but French it would be intolerably vulgar; as it is, it is merely neat and intensely expressive.

"Not yet arrived, sir," said the tobacconist, and then he seemed to recollect himself, for he repeated:

"Not yet arrived," without the respectful addition which had slipped out by accident.

The new arrival took out his watch—a small one of beautiful workmanship, the watch of a lady—and consulted it. His movements were compact and rapid. He would have made a splendid light-weight boxer.

"That," he said shortly, "is the way they fail. They do not understand the necessity of exactitude. The people—see you, Mr. Jacquetot, they fail because they have no exactitude."

"But I am of the people," moving ponderously on his chair.

"Essentially so. I know it, my friend. But I have taught you something."

The tobacconist laughed.

"I suppose so. But is it safe to stand there in the full day? Will you not pass in? The room is ready; the lamp is lighted. There is an agent of the police always at the end of the street now."

"Ah, bah!" and he shrugged his shoulders contemptuously. "I am not afraid of them. There is only one thing to be feared,

Citizen Jacquetot—the press. The press and the people, *bien entendu*."

"If you despise the people why do you use them?" asked Jacquetot abruptly.

"In default of better, my friend. If one has not steam one uses the river to turn the mill-wheel. The river is slow; sometimes it is too weak, sometimes too strong. One never has full control over it, but it turns the wheel—it turns the wheel, brother Jacquetot."

"And eventually sweeps away the miller," suggested the tobacconist lightly. It must be remembered that though stout he was intelligent. Had he not been so it is probable that this conversation would never have taken place. The dark-eyed man did not look like one who would have the patience to deal with stupid people.

Again the pleasant smile flickered like the light of a fire in a dark place.

"That," was the reply, "is the affair of the miller."

"But," conceded Jacquetot, meditatively selecting a new cigar from a box which he had reached without moving from his chair, "but the people—they are fools, hein!"

"Ah!" with a protesting shrug, as if deprecating the enunciation of such a platitude.

Then he passed through into a little room behind the shop—a little room where no daylight penetrated, because there was no window to it. It depended for daylight upon the shop, with which it communicated by a door of which the upper half was glass. But this glass was thickly curtained with the material called Turkey-red, threefold.

And the tobacconist was left alone in his shop, smoking gravely. There are some people like oysters, inasmuch as they leave an after-taste behind them. The man who had just gone into the little room at the rear of the tobacconist's shop of the Rue St. Gingolphe in Paris was one of these. And the taste he left behind him was rather disquieting. One was apt to feel that there was a mistake somewhere in the ordering of human affairs, and that this man was one of its victims.

In a few minutes two men passed hastily through the shop into the little room, with scarcely so much as a nod for Mr. Jacquetot.

CHAPTER II

TOOLS

The first man to enter the room was clad in a blouse of coarse grey cloth which reached down to his knees. On his head he wore a black silk cap, very much pressed down and exceedingly greasy on the right side. This was to be accounted for by the fact that he used his right shoulder more than the left in that state of life in which he had been placed. It was not what we, who do not kill, would consider a pleasant state. He was, in fact, a slayer of beasts—a foreman at the slaughter-house.

It is, perhaps, fortunate that Antoine Lerac is of no great prominence in this record, and of none in his official capacity at the slaughter-house. But the man is worthy of some small attention, because he was so essentially of the nineteenth century—so distinctly a product of the latter end of what is, for us at least, the most important cycle of years the world has passed through. He was a man wearing the blouse with ostentation, and glorying in the greasy cap: professing his unwillingness to exchange the one for an ermine robe or the other for a crown. As a matter of fact, he invariably purchased the largest and roughest blouse to be found, and his cap was unnecessarily soaked with suet. He was a knight of industry of the very worst description—a

Henry Seton Merriman

braggart, a talker, a windbag. He preached, or rather he shrieked, the doctrine of equality, but the equality he sought was that which would place him on a par with his superiors, while in no way benefiting those beneath him.

At one time, when he had first come into contact with the dark-eyed man who now sat at the table watching him curiously, there had been a struggle for mastery.

"I am," he had said with considerable heat, "as good as you. That is all I wish to demonstrate."

"No," replied the other with that calm and assured air of superiority which the people once tried in vain to stamp out with the guillotine. "No, it is not. You want to demonstrate that you are superior, and you cannot do it. You say that you have as much right to walk on the pavement as I. I admit it. In your heart you want to prove that you have *more*, and you cannot do it. I could wear your blouse with comfort, but you could not put on my hat or my gloves without making yourself ridiculous. But—that is not the question. Let us get to business."

And in time the butcher succumbed, as he was bound to do, to the man whom he shrewdly suspected of being an aristocrat.

He who entered the room immediately afterwards was of a very different type. His mode of entry was of another description. Whereas the man of blood swaggered in with an air of nervous truculence, as if he were afraid that some one was desirous of disputing his equality, the next comer crept in softly, and closed the door with accuracy. He was the incarnation of benevolence—in the best sense of the word, a sweet old man—looking out upon the world through large tinted spectacles with a beam which could not be otherwise than blind to all motes. In earlier years his face might, perhaps, have been a trifle hard in its contour; but Time, the lubricator, had eased some of the corners, and it was now the seat of kindness and love. He bowed ceremoniously to the first comer, and his manner seemed rather to breathe of fraternity than equality. As he bowed he mentioned the gentleman's name in such loving tones that no greeting could have been heartier.

"Citizen Morot," he said.

The butcher, with more haste than dignity, assumed the chair which stood at the opposite end of the table to that occupied by the Citizen Morot. He had evidently hurried in first in order to secure that seat. From his pocket he produced a somewhat soiled paper, which he threw with exaggerated carelessness across the table. His manner was not entirely free from a suggestion of patronage.

"What have we here?" inquired the first comer, who had not hitherto opened his lips, with a deep interest which might possibly have been ironical. He was just the sort of man to indulge in irony for his own satisfaction. He unfolded the paper, raised his eyebrows, and read.

"Ah!" he said, "a receipt for five hundred rifles with bayonets and shoulder-straps complete. 'Received of the Citizen Morot five hundred rifles with bayonets and shoulder-straps complete.—Antoine Lerac.'"

He folded the paper again and carefully tore it into very small pieces.

"Thank you," he said gravely.

Then he turned in his chair and threw the papers into the

ash-tray of the little iron stove behind him.

"I judged it best to be strictly business-like," said the butcher, with moderately well-simulated carelessness.

"But yes, Monsieur Lerac," with a shrug. "We of the Republic distrust each other so completely."

The old gentleman looked from one to the other with a soothing smile.

"The brave Lerac," he said, "is a man of business."

Citizen Morot ignored this observation.

"And," he said, turning to Lerac, "you have them stored in a safe place? There is absolutely no doubt of that?"

"Absolutely none."

"Good."

"They are under my own eye."

"Very good. It is not for a short time only, but for some months. One cannot hurry the people. Besides, we are not ready. The rifles we bought, the ammunition we must steal."

"They are good rifles—they are English," said the butcher.

"Yes; the English Government is full of chivalry. They are always ready to place it within the power of their enemies to be as well armed as themselves."

The old gentleman laughed—a pleasant, cooing laugh. He invariably encouraged humour, this genial philanthropist.

"At last Friday's meeting," Lerac said shortly, "we enrolled forty new members. We now number four hundred and two in our *arrondissement* alone."

"Good," muttered the Citizen Morot, without enthusiasm.

"And four hundred hardy companions they are."

"So I should imagine" (very gravely).

"Four hundred strong men," broke in the old gentleman rather hastily. "Ah, but that is already a power."

"It is," opined Lerac sententiously, "the strong man who is the power. Riches are nothing; birth is nothing. This is the day of force. Force is everything."

"Everything," acquiesced Morot fervently. He was consulting a small note-book, wherein he jotted down some figures.

"Four hundred and two," he muttered as he wrote, "up to Friday night, in the *arrondissement* of the citizen—the good citizen—Antoine Lerac."

The butcher looked up with a doubtful expression upon his coarse face. His great brutal lips twitched, and he was on the point of speaking when the Citizen Morot's velvety eyes met his gaze with a quiet smile in which arrogance and innocence were mingled.

"And now," said the last-mentioned, turning affably to the old gentleman, "let us have the report of the reverend Father."

"Ah," laughed Lerac, without attempting to conceal the

contempt that was in his soul, "the Church."

The old gentleman spread out his hands in mild deprecation.

"Yes," he admitted, "we are under a shadow. I do not even dare to wear my cassock."

"You are in a valley of shadow, my reverend friend," said the butcher, with visible exultation, "to which the sun will never penetrate now."

The Citizen Morot laughed at this pleasantry, while the old man against whom it was directed bowed his head patiently.

"And yet," said the laugher, with a certain air of patronage, "the Church is of some use still. She paid for those rifles, and she will pay for the ammunition—is it not so, my father?"

"Without doubt—without doubt."

"Not to mention," continued the other, "many contributions towards our general fund. The force that is supplied by the strong right arm of the people is, one finds, a force constantly in need of substantial replenishment."

"But," exclaimed the butcher, emphatically banging his fist down upon the table, "why does she do it? That is what I want to know!"

The old priest glanced furtively towards Morot, and then his face assumed an air of childish bewilderment.

"Ah!" he said guilelessly, "who can tell?"

"Who, indeed!" chimed in Morot.

The butcher was pleased with himself. He sat upright, and, banging the table a second time, he looked round defiantly.

"But," said Morot, in an indifferent way which was frequently characteristic, "I do not see that it matters much. The money is good. It buys rifles, and it places them in the hands of the Citizen Lerac and his hardy companions. And when all is said and done, when the cartridges are burnt and a New Commune is raised, what does it matter whose money bought the rifles, and with what object the money was supplied?"

The old gentleman looked relieved. He was evidently of a timid and conciliatory nature, and would, with slight encouragement, have turned upon that Church of which he was the humble representative, merely for the sake of peace.

The butcher cleared his throat after the manner of the streets—causing Morot to wince visibly—and acquiesced.

"But," he added cunningly, "the Church, see you—Ach! it is deep—it is treacherous. Never trust the Church!"

The Citizen Morot, to whom these remarks were addressed, smiled in a singular way and made no reply. Then he turned gravely to the old man and said—

"Have you nothing to report to us—my father?"

"Nothing of great importance," replied he humbly. "All is going on well. We are in treaty for two hundred rifles with the Montenegrin Government, and shall no doubt carry the contract through. I go to England next week in order to carry out the—the—what shall I say?—the loan of the ammunition."

"Ha, ha!" laughed the butcher.

Morot smiled also, as he made an entry in the little note-book.

"Next week?" he said interrogatively.

"Yes—on Tuesday."

"Thank you."

The butcher here rose and ostentatiously dragged out a watch from the depths of his blouse.

"I must go," he said. "I have committee at seven o'clock. And I shall dine first."

"Yes," said Morot gravely. "Dine first. Take good care of yourself, citizen."

"Trust me."

"I do," was the reply, delivered with a little nod in answer to Lerac's curt farewell bow.

The butcher walked noisily through the shop—heavy with responsibility—weighted with the sense of his own impor-tance to the world in general and to France in particular. Had he walked less noisily he might have overheard the soft laugh of the old priest.

Citizen Morot did not laugh. He was not a laughing man. But a fine, disdainful smile passed over his face, scarce lighting it up at all.

"What an utter fool the man is!" he said impatiently.

"Yes—sir," replied the old man, "but if he were less so it would be difficult to manage him."

"I am not sure. I always prefer to deal with knaves than with fools."

"That is because your Highness knows how to outwit them."

"No titles—my father," said the Citizen Morot quietly. "No titles here, if you please. Tell me, are you quite sure of this scum—this Lerac?"

"As sure as one can be of anything that comes from the streets. He is an excitable, bumptious, quarrelsome man; but he has a certain influence with those beneath him, although it seems hard to realise that there are such."

"Ha! you are right! But a republic is a social manure-heap— that which is on the top is not pleasant, and the stuff below— ugh!"

The manner of the two men had quite changed. He who was called Morot leant back in his seat and stretched his arms out wearily. There is no disguise like animation; when that is laid aside we see the real man or the real woman. In repose this Frenchman was not cheerful to look upon. He was not sanguine, and a French pessimist is the worst thing of the kind that is to be found.

When the door had closed behind the departing Lerac, the old priest seemed to throw off suddenly quite a number of years. His voice, when next he spoke, was less senile, his movements were brisker. He was, in a word, less harmless.

Mr. Jacquetot had finished his dinner, brought in from a neighbouring restaurant all hot, and was slumberously enjoying a very strong-smelling cigar, when the door of the little room opened at length, and the two men went out together into the dimly-lighted street.

CHAPTER III

WITHOUT REST

Half-way down Fleet Street, on the left-hand side, stands the church of St. Dunstan-in-the-West. Around its grimy foundations there seethes a struggling, toiling race of men— not only from morning till night, but throughout the twenty-four hours. Within sound of this church bell a hundred printing-presses throb out their odorous broadsheets to be despatched to every part of the world. Day and night, week in week out, the human writing-machines, and those other machines which are almost human (and better than human in some points) hurry through their allotted tasks, and ignore the saintly shadow cast upon them by the spire of St. Dunstan. This is indeed the centre of the world: the hub from whence spring the spokes of the vast wheel of life. For to this point all things over the world converge by a vast web of wire, railroad, coach road, and steamer track. Upon wings that boast of greater speed than the wind can compass come to this point the voices of our kin in farthest lands. News— news—news. News from the East of events occurring in the afternoon—scan it over and flash it westward, where it will be read on the morning of the same day! News in every tongue to be translated and brought into shape—while the solemn church clock tells his tale in deep voice, audible above the din and scurry.

Henry Seton Merriman

From hurried scribbler to pale compositor, and behold, the news is bawled all over London! Such work as this goes on for ever around the church of St. Dunstan. Scribblers come and scribblers go; compositors come to their work young and hopeful, they leave it bent and poisoned, yet the work goes on. Each day the pace grows quicker, each day some new means of rapid propagation is discovered, and each day life becomes harder to live. One morning, perhaps, a scribbler is absent from his post—"Brain-fever, complete rest; a wreck." For years his writings have been read by thousands daily. A new man takes the vacant chair—he has been waiting more or less impatiently for this—and the thousands are none the wiser. One night the head compositor presses his black hand to his sunken chest, and staggers home. "And time too—he's had his turn," mutters the second compositor as he thinks of the extra five shillings a week. No doubt he is right. Every dog his day.

Nearly opposite to the church stands a tall narrow house of dirty red brick, and it is with this house that we have to do.

At seven o'clock, one evening some years ago—when heads now grey were brown, when eyes now dim were bright—the Strand was in its usual state of turmoil. Carriage followed carriage. Seedy clerks hustled past portly merchants—not their own masters, *bien entendu*, but those of other seedy clerks. Carriages and foot-passengers were alike going westward. All were leaving behind them the day and the busy city—some after a few hours devoted to the perusal of *Times* and *Gazette*; others fagged and weary from a long day of dusty books.

Ah! those were prosperous days in the City. Days when men of but a few years' standing rolled out to Clapham or High-gate behind a pair of horses. Days when books were often represented by a bank-book and a roughly-kept day-book.

What need to keep mighty ledgers when profits are great and returns quick in their returning?

As the pedestrians made their way along the narrow pavement some of them glanced at the door of the tall red-brick house and read the inscription on a brass plate screwed thereon. This consisted of two mystic words: *The Beacon.* There was, however, in reality, no mystery about it. The *Beacon* was a newspaper, published weekly, and the clock of St. Dunstan's striking seven told the end of another week. The publishing day was past; another week with its work and pleasure was to be faced.

From early morning until six o'clock in the evening this narrow doorway and passage had been crowded by a heaving, swearing, laughing mass of more or less dilapidated humanity interested in the retail sale of newspapers. At six o'clock Ephraim Bander, a retired constable, now on the staff of the *Beacon*, had taken his station at the door, in order to greet would-be purchasers with the laconic and discouraging words: "Sold hout!"

During the last two years ex-constable Bander had announced the selling "hout" of the *Beacon* every Tuesday evening.

At seven o'clock Mrs. Bander emerged from her den on the fourth floor, like a portly good-natured spider, and with a broom proceeded to attack the dust shaken from the boots of the journalistic fraternity, with noisy energy. After that she polished the door-plate; and peace reigned within the narrow house.

On the second floor there was a small room with windows looking out into a narrow lane behind the house. It was a singularly quiet room; the door opened and shut without sound or vibration; double windows insured immunity from the harrowing cries of such enterprising merchants as exercised their lungs and callings in the narrow lane beneath. A certain sense of ease and comfort imperceptibly crept over the senses of persons entering this tiny apartment. It must have been in the atmosphere; for some rooms more luxuriously furnished are without it. It certainly does not lie in the furniture—this imperceptible sense of companionship; it does not lurk in the curtains. Some mansions know it, and many cottages. It is even to be met with in the tiny cabin of a coasting vessel.

This diminutive room, despite its lack of sunlight, was such as one might wish to sit in. A broad low table stood in the middle of the floor, and on it lay the mellow light of a shaded lamp. At this table two men were seated opposite to each other. One was writing, slowly and easily, the other was idling with the calm restfulness of a man who has never worked very hard. He was rolling his pencil up to the top of his blotting-pad, and allowing it to come down again in accordance with the rules of gravity.

This was Mr. Bodcry's habit when thoughtful; and after all, there was no great harm in it. Mr. Bodery was editor and proprietor of the *Beacon*. The amusing and somewhat satirical article which appeared weekly under the heading of "Light" was penned by the chubby hand at that moment engaged with the pencil.

Mr. Morgan, sub-editor, was even stouter than his chief. Laughter was his most prominent characteristic. He laughed over "Light" when in its embryo state, he laughed when the *Beacon* sold out at six o'clock on Tuesday evenings. He laughed when the printing-machine went wrong on Monday afternoon, and—most wonderful of all—he laughed at his own jokes, in which exercise he was usually alone. His jokes were not of the first force. Mr. Morgan was the author of the slightly laboured and weighty Parliamentary articles on the first page. He never joked on paper, which is a gift apart.

These two gentlemen were in no way of brilliant intellect. They had their share of sound, practical common-sense, which is in itself a splendid substitute. Fortune had come to them (as it comes to most men when it comes at all) without any apparent reason. Mr. Bodery had supplied the capital, and Mr. Morgan's share of the undertaking was added in the form of a bustling, hollow energy. The *Beacon* was lighted, so to speak. It burnt in a dull and somewhat flickering manner for some years; then a new hand fed the flame, and its light spread afar.

It was from pure good nature that Mr. Bodery held out a helping hand to the son of his old friend, Walter Vellacott, when that youth appeared one day at the office of the *Beacon*, and in an off-hand manner announced that he was seeking employment. Like many actions performed from a similar motive, Mr. Bodery's kindness of heart met with its reward. Young Christian Vellacott developed a remarkable talent for journalistic literature—in fact, he was fortunate enough to have found, at the age of twenty-two, his avocation in life.

Gradually, as the years wore on, the influence of the young fellow's superior intellect made itself felt. Prom the position of a mere supernumerary, he worked his way upwards, taking on to his shoulders one duty after another—bearing the weight, quietly and confidently, of one responsibility after another. This exactly suited Mr. Bodery and his sub-editor. There was very little of the slave in the composition of either. They delighted in an easy, luxurious life, with just enough work to impart a pleasant feeling of self-satisfaction. It suited Christian Vellacott also. In a few weeks he found his level—in a few months he began rising to higher levels.

He was an only son; the only child of a brilliant father whose name was known in every court in Europe as that of a harum-scarum diplomatist, who could have done great things in his short life if he had wished to. It is from only sons that Fortune selects her favourites. Men who have no brothers to share their amusements turn to serious matters early in life. Christian Vellacott soon discovered that a head was required at the office of the *Beacon* to develop the elements of success undoubtedly lying within the journal, and that the owner of such a head could in time dictate his own terms to the easy-going proprietor.

Unsparingly he devoted the whole of his exceptional energies to the work before him. He lived in and for it. Each night he went home fagged and weary; but each morning saw him return to it with undaunted spirit.

Human nature, however, is exhaustible. The influence of a strong mind over a strong body is great, but it is nevertheless limited. The *Beacon* had reached a large circulation, but its slave was worn out. Two years without a holiday—two years of hurried, hard brain-work had left their mark. It is often so when a man finds his avocation too early. He is too hurried, works too hard, and collapses; or he becomes self-satisfied, over-confident, and unbearable. Fortunately for Christian Vellacott he was devoid of conceit, which is like the scaffolding round a church-spire, reaching higher and falling first.

There was also a "home" influence at work. When Christian passed out of the narrow doorway, and turned his face westward, his day's work was by no means over, as will be shown hereafter.

As Mr. Bodery rolled his pencil up and down his blotting-pad, he was slowly realising the fact that something must be done. Presently he looked up, and his pleasant eyes rested on the bent head of his sub-editor.

"Morgan," he said, "I have been thinking—Seems to me Vellacott wants a rest! He's played out!"

Mr. Morgan wiped his pen vigorously upon his coat, just beneath the shoulder, and sat back in his chair.

"Yes," he replied; "he has not been up to the mark for some time. But you will find difficulty in making him take a holiday. He is a devil for working—ha, ha!"

This "ha, ha!" did not mean very much. There was no mirth in it. It was a species of punctuation, and implied that Mr. Morgan had finished his remark.

"I will ring for him now and see what he says about it."

Mr. Bodery extended his chubby white hand and touched a small gong. Almost instantaneously the silent door opened and a voice from without said, "Yess'r." A small boy with a mobile, wicked mouth stood at attention in the doorway.

"Has Mr. Vellacott gone?"

"No—sir!" In a tone which seemed to ask: "Now *is* it likely?"

"Where is he?"

"In the shop, sir."

"Ask him to come here, please."

"Yess'r."

The small boy closed the door. Once outside he placed his hand upon his heart and made a low bow to the handle, retreating backwards to the head of the stairs. Then he proceeded to slide down the banister, to the trifling detriment of his waistcoat. As he reached the end of his perilous journey a door opened at the foot of the stairs, and a man's form became discernible in the dim light.

"Is that the way you generally come downstairs, Wilson?" asked a voice.

"It is the quickest way, sir!"

"Not quite; there is one quicker, which you will discover some day if you overbalance at the top!"

"Mr. Bodery wishes to see you, please sir!" The small boy's manner was very different from what it had been outside the door upstairs.

"All right," replied Vellacott, putting on the coat he had been carrying over his arm. A peculiar smooth rapidity characterised all his movements. At school he had been considered a very "clean" fielder. The cleanness was there still.

The preternaturally sharp boy—sharp as only London boys are—watched the lithe form vanish up the stairs; then he wagged his head very wisely and said to himself in a patronising way:

"He's the right sort, he is—no chalk there!"

Subsequently he balanced his diminutive person full length upon the balustrade, and proceeded to haul himself laboriously, hand over hand, to the top.

In the meantime Christian Vellacott had passed into the editor's room. The light of the lamp was driven downwards upon the table, but the reflection of it rose and illuminated his face. It was a fairly handsome face, with eyes just large enough to be keen and quick without being dreamy. The slight fair moustache was not enough to hide the mouth, which was refined, and singularly immobile. He glanced at Mr. Bodery, as he entered, quickly and comprehensively, and then turned his eyes towards Mr. Morgan. His face was very still and unemotional, but it was pale, and his eyes were deeply sunken. A keen observer would have noticed, in comparing the three men, that there was something about the youngest which was lacking in his elders. It lay in the direct gaze of his eyes, in the carriage of his head, in the small, motionless mouth. It was what is vaguely called "power."

"Sit down, Vellacott," said Mr. Brodery. "We want to have a consultation." After a short pause he continued: "You know, of course, that it is a dull season just now. People do not seem to read the papers in August. Now, we want you to take a holiday. Morgan has been away; I shall go when you come back. Say three weeks or a month. You've been over-working yourself a bit—burning the candle at both ends, eh?"

"Hardly at both ends," corrected Vellacott, with a ready smile which entirely transformed his face. "Hardly at both ends—at one end in a draught, perhaps."

"Ha, ha! Very good," chimed in Mr. Morgan the irrepressible. "At one end in a draught—that is like me, only the draught has got inside my cheeks and blown them out instead of in like yours, eh? Ha, ha!" And he patted his cheeks affectionately.

"I don't think I care for a holiday just now, thanks," he said slowly, without remembering to call up a smile for Mr. Morgan's benefit. Unconsciously he put his hand to his forehead, which was damp with the heat of the printing-office which he had just left.

"My dear fellow," said Mr. Bodery gravely, emphasising his remarks with the pencil, "you have one thing in life to learn yet—no doubt you have many, but this one in particular you must learn. Work is not the only thing we are created for—not the only thing worth living for. It is a necessary evil, that is all. When you have reached my age you will come to look upon it as such. A little enjoyment is good for every one. There are many things to form a brighter side to life. Nature—travelling—riding—rowing—"

"And love," suggested the sub-editor, placing his hand dramatically on the right side of his broad waistcoat instead of the left. He could afford to joke on the subject now that the grass grew high in the little country churchyard where he had laid his young wife fifteen years before. In those days he was a grave, self-contained man, but that sorrow had entirely changed his nature. The true William Morgan only came out on paper now.

Mr. Bodery was right. Christian had yet to learn a great lesson, and unconsciously he was even now beginning to grasp its meaning. His whole mind was full of his work, and out of those earnest grey eyes his soul was looking at the man who was perhaps saving his life.

"We can easily manage it," said the editor, continuing his advantage. "I will take over the foreign policy article. The reviewing you can do yourself, as we can always send you the books, and there is no pressing hurry about them. The general work we will manage somehow—won't we, Morgan?"

"Of course we will; as well as and perhaps better than he could do it himself, eh? Ha, ha!"

"But seriously, Vellacott," continued Mr. Bodery, "things will go on just as well for a time. When I was young I used to make that mistake too. I thought that no one could manage things like myself, but in time I realised (as you will do some day) that things went on as smoothly when I was away. Depend upon it, my boy, when a man is put on the shelf, worn out and useless, another soon fills his place. You are too young to go on the shelf yet. To please me, Vellacott, go away for three weeks."

"You are very kind, sir—" began the young fellow, but Mr. Bodery interrupted him.

"Well, then, that is settled. Shall we say this day week? That will give you time to make your plans."

With a few words of thanks Christian left the room. Vaguely and mechanically he wandered upstairs to his own particular den. It was a disappointing little chamber. The chaos one expects to find on the desk of a literary man was lacking here. No papers lay on the table in artistic disorder. The presiding genius of the room was method—clear-headed, practical method. The walls were hidden by shelves of books, from the last half-hysterical production of some vain woman to the single-volume work of a man's lifetime. Many of the former were uncut, the latter bore signs of having been read and studied. The companionship of these silent friends brought peace and contentment to the young man's spirit. He sat wearily down, and, leaning his chin upon his folded arms, he thought. Gradually there came into his mind pictures of the fair open country, of rolling hills and quiet valleys, of quiet lanes and running waters. A sudden yearning to breathe God's pure air took possession of his faculties. Mr. Bodery had gained the day. In the room below Mr. Morgan wrote on in his easy, comfortable manner. The editor was still thoughtfully playing with his pencil. The sharp little boy was standing on his head in the passage. At last Mr. Bodery rose from his chair and began his preparations for leaving. As he brushed his hat he looked towards his companion and said:

"That young fellow is worth you and me rolled into one."

"I recognised that fact some years ago," replied the sub-editor, wiping his pen on his coat. "It is humiliating, but true. Ha, ha!"

CHAPTER IV

BURDENED

Christian Vellacott soon descended the dingy stairs and joined the westward-wending throng in the Strand. In the midst of the crowd he was alone, as townsmen soon learn to be. The passing faces, the roar of traffic, and the thousand human possibilities of interest around him in no way disturbed his thoughts. In his busy brain the traffic of thought, passing and repassing, crossing and recrossing, went on unaffected by outward things. A modern poet has confessed that his muse loves the pavement—a bold confession, but most certainly true. Why does talent gravitate to cities? Because there it works its best—because friction necessarily produces brilliancy. Nature is a great deceiver; she draws us on to admire her insinuating charms, and in the contemplation of them we lose our energy.

Christian had been born and bred in cities. The din and roar of life was to him what the voice of the sea is to the sailor. In the midst of crowded humanity he was in his element, and as he walked rapidly along he made his way dexterously through the narrow places without thinking of it. While meditating deeply he was by no means absorbed. In his active life there had been no time for thoughts beyond the present, no leisure for dreaming. He could not afford to be absent-minded. Numbers of men are so situated. Their minds are required at all moments, in full working order, clear and rapid—ready, shoes on feet and staff in hand, to go whithersoever they may be called.

Although he was going to the saddest home that ever hung like a mill-stone round a young neck, Christian wasted no time. The glory of the western sky lay ruddily over the river as he emerged from the small streets behind Chelsea and faced the broad placid stream. Presently he stopped opposite the door of a small red-brick house, which formed the corner of a little terrace facing the river and a quiet street running inland from it.

With a latch-key he admitted himself noiselessly—almost surreptitiously. Once inside he closed the door without unnecessary sound and stood for some moments in the dark little entrance-hall, apparently listening.

Presently a voice broke the silence of the house. A querulous, high-pitched voice, quavering with the palsy of extreme age. The sound of it was no new thing for Christian Vellacott. To-night his lips gave a little twist of pain as he heard it. The door of the room on the ground floor was open, and he could hear the words distinctly enough.

"You know, Mrs. Strawd, we have a nephew, but he is always gadding about, I am sure; he has been a terrible affliction to us. A frothy, good-for-nothing boy—that is what he is. We have not set eyes on him for a month or more. Why, I almost forget his name!"

"Christian, that is his name—a most inappropriate one, I am sure," chimed in another voice, almost identical in tone. "Why Walter should have given him such a name I cannot tell. Ah! sister Judith, things are different from what they used to be when we were younger!"

The frothy one outside the door seemed in no great degree impressed by these impartial views upon himself, though the pained look was still upon his lips as he turned to hang up his hat.

"He's coming home to-night, though, Miss Judith," said another voice, in a coaxing, wheedling tone, such as one uses towards petulant children. "He's coming home to-night, sure enough!" It was a pleasant voice, with a strong, capable ring about it. One instinctively felt that the possessor of it was a woman to be relied upon at a crisis.

"Is he now—is he now?" said the first speaker reflectively. "Well, I am sure it is time he did. We will just give him a lesson, eh, sister Hester?—we will give him a lesson, shall we not?"

At this moment the door opened, and a little woman, quiet though somewhat anxious looking, came out. She evinced no surprise at the sight of the good-for-nothing nephew in the dimly-lighted passage, greeting him in a low voice.

"How have they been to-day, nurse?" he asked.

"Oh, they have been well enough, Master Christian," was the reply, in a cheerful undertone.

"Aunt Judith has 'most got rid of her cold. But they've been very trying, sir—just like children, as wilful as could be—the same question over and over again till I was fit to cry. They are quieter now, but—but it's you they're abusing now, Master Chris!"

The young fellow looked down into the little woman's face.

His eyes were sympathetic enough, but he said nothing. With a little nod and a suppressed sigh he turned away from her. He laid his hand upon the door and then stopped.

"As soon as you have brought up tea," he said, looking back, "I will take them for the evening, and you can have your rest as usual."

From the room came, at intervals, the ring of silver, as if some one were moving the spoons and forks from the table. Christian waited until these sounds had ceased before he entered.

"Good evening, Aunt Judith. Good evening, Aunt Hester," he said cheerily.

They were exactly alike, these two old ladies; the same marvellously wrinkled features and silver hair; voluminous caps and white woollen shawls identical. With exaggerated marks of respect he kissed each by turn on her withered cheek.

"May I sit down, Aunt Judith?" he asked, and without waiting for an answer drew a chair towards the fireplace, where a small fire burnt though it was the month of August.

"Yes, Nephew Vellacott, you may take a seat," replied Aunt Judith with chill severity, "and you may also tell us where you have been during the last four weeks."

Poor old human wreck! Only ten hours earlier her nephew had bid her farewell for the day. Christian began an explanation in a weary, mechanical way, like an actor tired of the part assigned to him, but the old ladies would not listen. Aunt Hester interrupted him promptly.

"Your shallow excuses are wasted on us, Nephew Vellacott. You have doubtless been away, enjoying yourself and leaving us—us who support you and deprive ourselves in order to keep a decent coat upon your back—leaving us to the mercy of all the thieves in London. And tell us, pray—what are we to do for spoons and forks to-night?"

"What?" exclaimed Christian with perfunctory interest, "have the spoons gone—?" he almost said "again," but checked himself in time. He turned to look at the table, which had been carefully denuded of every piece of silver.

"There, you see!" quavered Aunt Judith triumphantly; and the two old ladies rubbed their hands, nodded their palsied old heads at each other, and chuckled in utter delight at their nephew's discomfiture, until Aunt Judith was attacked by a violent fit of coughing, which seemed to be tearing her to pieces. Christian watched her with the ready keenness of a sick-nurse.

"How did it occur?" he asked, when the old lady had recovered.

"There, you see," remarked Aunt Hester, with the precise intonation of her accomplice.

"I *am* sure!" panted Aunt Judith triumphantly.

"I *am* sure!" echoed Aunt Hester.

They allowed their nephew's remorse full scope, and then proceeded laboriously to extract the missing articles from the side of Aunt Judith's arm-chair. This farce was rehearsed every night, nearly word for word. A pleasant recreation for an intellectual man, assuredly. The only relief to the monotony was the occasional loss of a spoon in the crevice

Henry Seton Merriman

between the arm and the seat of Aunt Judith's chair. Then followed such a fumbling and a "dear me-ing" until the worthless nephew was perforce called to the rescue, to fish and probe with a paper-knife till the lost treasure was recovered.

"We only wished, Nephew Vellacott, to show you what might have happened during your unconscionable absence. Servants are only too ready to talk to the first comer of their mistresses' wealth and position. They have no discrimination." said Aunt Judith in a reproving tone. The old ladies were very fond of boasting of their wealth and position, whereas, in reality, their nephew was the only barrier between them and the workhouse.

"Well, Aunt Judith," replied Christian patiently, "I will try and stay at home more in future. But you know it is time I was doing something to earn my own livelihood now. I cannot exist on your kindness all my life!"

He had learnt to humour these two silly old women. During the two years which had just passed he had gradually recognised the utter futility of endeavouring to make them realise the true state of their affairs. They spoke grandiloquently of the family solicitor: a man who had been in his grave for nearly a quarter of a century. It was simply impossible to instil into their minds any fact whatever, and such facts as had established themselves there were permanent. They belonged to another generation, and their mode of thought was a remnant of a forgotten and unsatisfactory period. To them Napoleon the First was a living man, Queen Victoria unheard of. The decay of their minds had been slow, and it had been Christian Vellacott's painful task to watch its steady progress. Day by day he had followed the gradual failing of each sense and power.

There is something pathetic about the decay of a mind which has been driven to death by constant work, but there is a compensating thought to alleviate the sadness. It may rattle and grow loose, like some worn-out engine, where the friction presses; but it will work till it collapses totally, and some of the work achieved is good and permanent. It is bound to be so. Infinitely sadder is the sight of a mind which is falling to pieces by reason of the rust that has eaten into its very core. For rust must needs mean idleness—and no human intellect *need* be idle. So it had been with these two old ladies. Born in a wofully unintellectual age, they had never left a certain groove in life. When their brother married Christian Vellacott's grandmother, they had left his house in Honiton to go and live in Bodmin upon a limited but sufficient income. These "sufficient incomes" are a curse; they do not allow of charity and make no call for labour.

When Christian Vellacott arrived in England, an orphan with no great wealth, he made it his first duty to visit the only living relations he possessed. He was just in time to save them, literally, from starvation. It was obvious that he could not make a literary livelihood in Bodmin, so he made a home for the two old wrecks of humanity in London. Their means, like their minds, were simply exhausted. Aunt Judith was ninety-three; Aunt Hester ninety-one. During that vast blank (for blank it was, so far as their lives were concerned) stretching away back into a perspective of time which few around them could gauge—they had never been separated for one day. Like two apples they had grown side by side, until their very contact had engendered disease—a slow, deadly, creeping rot, finding its source at the point of contact, reaching its goal at the heart of each. They had *existed* thus with terrible longevity—lived a mere animal life of sleeping and eating, such as hundreds of women are living around us now.

"Of course, you must learn to make your daily bread, Nephew Vellacott!" answered Aunt Hester. "The desire does you credit; but you should be careful into what society you go without us. Girls are very designing, and many a one would like to marry a nephew of mine—eh, Judith?"

"Yes, that they would," replied the old lady. "The minxes know that they might do worse than catch the nephew of Judith and Hester Vellacott!"

"Look at us," continued Aunt Hester, drawing up her shrunken old form with a touch of pride. "Look at us? We have always avoided marriage, and we are very nice and happy, I am sure!"

She waited for a confirmation of this bold statement, but Christian was not listening. He was leaning forward with his hands clasped between his knees, gazing into the fire. He was recalling the conversation which had passed in the little room in the Strand. Could he leave these two helpless old creatures. Could he get away from it all for a little time—away from the maddening prattle of unguided tongues, from the dread monotony of hopeless watching? He knew that he was wasting his manhood, neglecting his intellectual opportunities, and endangering his career; but his course of duty was marked out with terrible distinctness. He never saw the pathos of it, as a woman would have seen it, gathering perhaps some slight alleviation from the sight. It never entered his thoughts to complain, and he never conceived the idea of drawing comparisons between his position and that of other young men who, instead of being slaves to their relatives, made very good use of them. He merely went on doing his obvious duty and striving not to look forward too eagerly to a release at some future period.

Fortunately, Mrs. Strawd was not long in bringing in the

simple evening meal; and the attention of the old ladies was at once turned to the mystery hidden beneath the dish-cover. What was it, and would there be enough for Nephew Vellacott?

Deftly, Christian poured out the tea. Two cups very weak and one stronger. Then two thin slices of crustless bread had to be buttered. This operation required great judgment and impartiality.

"Excuse me, Nephew Vellacott!" said Aunt Judith, with dangerous severity. "Is that first slice intended for Aunt Hester? It appears to me that the butter is very thick—much thicker than on the second, which is doubtless intended for me!"

"Do you think so, Aunt Judith?" asked Christian in a voice purposely loud in order to drown Aunt Hester's remonstrance. "Then I will take a little off!" He passed the knife harmlessly over the faulty slice, and laid the two side by side upon a plate. Then the old ladies promptly held a survey on them—that declared to be more heavily buttered being awarded to Aunt Judith in recognition of her seniority.

With similar fruitful topics of conversation the meal was pleasantly despatched. The turn of Dick and Mick followed thereon. Dick, the property of Aunt Judith, was a canary of thoughtful temperament. The part he played in the domestic economy of the small household was a contemplative rather than an active one. Mick, Aunt Hester's bird, was of a more lively nature. He had, as a rule, something to say upon all subjects—and said it.

Now Aunt Hester, in her inmost heart, loved a silent bird, and secretly coveted Dick, but as Mick was her property, and Dick the silent was owned by Aunt Judith, she never lost an opportunity of enlarging upon the stupidity and uselessness of silent birds. Aunt Judith, on the other hand, admired a lively and talkative canary; consequently she was weighed down with the conviction that her sister's bird was the superior article. Altogether, birds as a topic of conversation were best avoided. Dick and Mick were housed in cages of similar build—indeed, most things were strictly in duplicate in the whole household. Every evening Christian brought the cages, and Aunt Judith and Aunt Hester carefully placed within the wires a small piece of bread-and-butter, which Nurse Strawd as carefully removed, untouched, the next morning.

When the birds' wants had been attended to, it was Christian's duty to settle the old ladies comfortably in their respective arm-chairs. This he did tenderly and cleverly as a woman, but it was not a pleasant sight to look upon. The man, with his lean, strong face, long jaw, and prominent chin, was so obviously out of place. These peaceful duties were never meant for such as he. His somewhat closely-set eyes were not such as wax tender over drowning flies, for even in repose they were somewhat direct and stern in their gaze. In fact, Christian Vellacott was so visibly created for strife and the forefront of life's battle, that it was almost painful to see him fulfilling a more peaceful avocation.

As a rule he devoted himself to the amusement of his aged relatives for an hour or so; but this evening he sat down to the piano at once, with the deliberate intention of playing them off to sleep. Ten o'clock was their hour for retiring, and before that they would not move, although they dozed in their chairs.

He was no mean musician, this big West-countryman, with a true ear and a touch peculiarly light and tender for a man. He played gently and drowsily for some time, half forgetting that he was not alone in the room. Presently he turned round, letting his fingers rest on the keys. Aunt Judith was asleep, and Aunt Hester made a sign for him to go on playing. Five minutes more, gradually toned down till the very sounds seemed to fall asleep, and Aunt Hester was peacefully slumbering. Silently the player rose, and crossing the room, he resumed his seat at the table from which the white cloth had not yet been removed. Pen, ink, and paper were within reach, and in a few minutes he had written the following note:—

"DEAR SIDNEY,—May I retract the letter I wrote yesterday and accept your invitation? I have been requested to take a holiday, and, rather than offend the powers that be, have given in. I can think of no happier way of spending it than in seeing you all again and recalling the jolly old Prague days. With kind regards, yours ever,

"CHRISTIAN VELLACOTT."

He folded the note and slipped it into an envelope, which he addressed to "Sidney Carew, Esq., St. Mary Western, Dorset." Then he slipped noiselessly out of the room and upstairs to where Mrs. Strawd had a small sitting-room of her own. The little woman heard his footstep on the old creaking stairs, and opened the door of her room before he reached it.

"If I went away for three weeks," he said, "could you do without me?"

"Of course I could," replied the little woman readily. "Just you go away and take a holiday, Master Christian. You need it sorely, that I know. You do indeed. We shall get on splendidly without you. I'll just have my sister to come and stay, same as I did when you had to go to the Paris House of Parliament."

"I have not had much of a holiday, you see, for two years now!"

"Of course you haven't, and you want it. It's only human nature—and you a young man that ought to be in the open air all day. For an old woman like me it's different. We're made differently by the good God on purpose, I think;"

"Well, then, if your sister comes it must be understood, nurse, that I make the same arrangement with her as exists with you. She must simply be a duplicate of you—you understand?"

The little woman laughed, lightly enough.

"Oh, yes, Master Christian, that is all right. But you need not have troubled about that. She never would have thought of such a thing as wages, I'm sure!"

"No," replied he gravely, "I know she would not, but it will be better, I think, to have it understood beforehand. Gratitude is a very nice thing to work for, but some work is worth more than gratitude. If you are going out for your walk, perhaps you will post this letter."

Before Christian went to bed that night he held a candle close to the mirror and looked long and hard at his own reflection. There were dark streaks under his eyes, his small mouth was drawn and dry, his lips colourless. At each temple the bone stood out rather prominently, and the skin was brilliant in its whiteness and reflected the light of the candle. He felt his own pulse. It was beating, at one moment fast and irregular, at the next it was hardly perceptible.

"Yes!" he muttered, with a professional nod—in his training as a journalist he had learnt a little of many sciences—"yes, old Bodery was right."

CHAPTER V

A REUNION

The gentle August night had cooled and soothed the dusty atmosphere. All things looked fair, even in London. The placid Thames glided stealthily down to the sea, as if wishing to speed on unseen, to cast at last his reeking waters into the cool ocean. The bright brown sails, low hulls, and gaily painted spars of the barges dropping down with the stream added to the beauty of the scene.

Such was the morning that greeted Christian Vellacott, as he opened the door of his little Chelsea home and stepped forth a free man. When once he had made up his mind to go, every obstacle was thrown aside, and his determination was now as great as had been his previous reluctance. He had no presentiment that he was taking an important step in life—one of those steps which we hardly notice at the time, but upon which we look back in after years and note how clear and definite it was, losing ourselves in vague conjecture as to what might have been had we held back.

Christian being practical in all things, knew how to travel comfortably, dispensing with rugs and bags and such small packages as are understood to be dear to the elderly single female heart.

Henry Seton Merriman

The smoky suburbs were soon left behind, and the smiling land gave forth such gentle, pastoral odours as only long confinement in cities can teach us to detect. Christian lowered the window, and the warm air played round him as it had not done for two long years. The whizz of the wind past his face brought back the memory of the long, idle, happy days spent with his father in the Mediterranean, when they had been half sailors and wholly Bohemians, gliding from port to port, village to city, in their yacht, as free and careless as the wind. The warm breeze almost seemed to be coming to him from some parched Italian plain instead of pastoral Buckinghamshire.

Then his thoughts travelled still further back to his school-days in Prague, when his father and Mr. Carew were colleagues in a brilliant but unfortunate embassy. Five years had passed since then. The two fathers were now dead, and the children had dropped apart as men and women do when their own personal interests begin to engross them. Now again, in this late summer time, they were to meet. All, that is, who were left. The *debris*, as it were. Three voices there were whose tones would never more be heard in the round of merry jest. Mr. Carew, Walter Vellacott (Uncle Walter, the young ones called him), and little Charlie Carew, the bright-eyed sailor of the family, had all three travelled on. The two former, whose age and work achieved had softened their departure, were often spoken of with gently lowered voice, but little Charlie's name was never mentioned. It was a fatal mistake—this silence—if you will; but it was one of those mistakes which are often made in wisdom. In splendid, solitary grandeur he lay awaiting the end of all things—the call of his Creator—in the grey ice-fields of the North. The darling of his ship, he had died with a smile in his blue eyes and a sad little jest upon his lips to cheer the rough fur-clad giants kneeling at his side. Time, the merciful, had healed, as best he could (which is by no means perfectly), the wound in the younger hearts. It is only the old that are quite beyond his powers; he cannot touch them. Mrs. Carew, a woman with a patient face and a ready smile, was the only representative of the vanishing generation. Her daughters—ay! and perhaps her sons as well (though boys are not credited with so much tender divination)—knew the meaning of the little droop at the side of their mother's smiling lips. They detected the insincerity of her kindly laugh.

Shortly after leaving Exeter, Christian's station was reached. This was an old-fashioned seaport town, whose good fortune it was to lie too far west for a London watering-place, and too far east for Plymouth or Bristol. Sidney Carew was on the platform—a sturdy, typical Englishman, with a certain sure slowness of movement handed down to him by seafaring ancestors. The two friends had not met for many years, but with men absence has little effect upon affection. During the space of many years they may never meet and seldom write, but at the end that gulf of time is bridged over by a simple "Halloa, old fellow!" and a warm grip. Slowly, piece by piece, the history of the past years comes out. Both are probably changed in thought and nature, but the old individuality remains, the old bond of friendship survives.

"Well, Sidney?"

"How are you?"

Simultaneously—and that was all. The changes were there in both, and noted by both, but not commented upon.

"Molly is outside with the dog-cart," said Sidney; "is your luggage forward?"

"Yes, that is it being pitched out now."

It was with womanly foresight that Miss Molly Carew had elected to wait outside with the dog-cart while her brother met Christian on the platform. She feared a little natural embarrassment at meeting the old playfellow of the family, and concluded that the first moments would be more easily tided over here than at the train. Her fears were, as it turned out, unnecessary, but she did not know what Christian might be like after the lapse of years. Of herself she was sure enough, being one of those happy people who have no self-consciousness whatever.

On seeing her, Christian came forward at once, raising his hat and shaking hands as if they had parted the day before.

She saw at once that it was all right. This was Christian Vellacott as she had remembered him. She looked down at him as he stood with one hand resting on the splashboard, and he, looking up to her, smiled in return.

"Christian," she said, "do you know I should scarcely have recognised you. You are so big, and—and you look positively ghastly!" She finished her remark with a little laugh which took away from the spoken meaning of it.

"Ghastly?" he replied. "Thanks: I do not feel like it—only hungry. Hungry, and desperately glad to see a face that does not look overworked."

"Meaning me."

"Meaning you."

She gave a little sarcastic nod, and pursed up a pair of very red lips.

"Nevertheless I am the only person in the house who does

any work at all. Hilda, for instance—"

At this moment Sidney came up and interrupted them.

"Jump up in front, Chris," he said; "Molly will drive, while I sit behind. Your luggage will follow in the cart."

The drive of six miles passed away very pleasantly. Molly's strong little hands were quite accustomed to the reins, and the men were free to talk, which, however, she found time to do as well. The two young people on the front seat stole occasional sidelong glances at each other. The clever, mischievous little girl of Christian's recollection was transformed by the kindly hand of time into a fascinating and capable young lady. The uncertain profile had grown clear and regular. The truant hair was somewhat more under control, which, however, was all that could be said upon that subject. Only her eyes were unchanged, the laughing, fearless eyes of old. Fearless they had been in the times of childish mischief and adventure; fearless they remained in the face of life's graver mischances now.

Christian had been a shy and commonplace-enough boy as she recollected him. Now she found a self-possessed man of the world. Tall and strong of body she saw he was, and she felt that he possessed another strength—a strength of mind and will which, reaching out, can grasp and hold anything or everything.

With practised skill, Molly turned into the narrow gateway at a swinging trot, and then only was the house visible—a low, rambling building of brick and stone uncouthly mixed. Its chief outward characteristic was a promise of inward comfort. The sturdy manner in which its windows faced the scantily-wooded tableland that stretched away unbroken by wall or hedgerow to the sea, implied a certain thickness of wall and woodwork. The doorway which looked inland was singularly broad, and bore signs about its stonework of having once been even broader. The house had originally been a hollow square, with a roofless courtyard in the centre, into which the sheep and cattle were in olden times driven for safety at night against French marauders. This had later on been roofed in, and transformed into a roomy and comfortable hall, such as might be used as a sitting-room. All around the house, except, indeed, upon the sea-ward side, stood gnarled and twisted trees; Scotch firs in abundance, here and there a Weymouth pine, and occasionally a knotted dwarf oak with a tendency to run inland. The garden was, however, rich enough in shrubs and undergrowth, and to the landward side was a gleam of still water, being all that remained of a broad, deep moat.

Mrs. Carew welcomed Christian at the open door. She said very little, but her manner was sufficiently warm and friendly to dispense with words.

"Where is Hilda?" asked Molly, as she leapt lightly to the ground.

"I do not know, dear. She is out, somewhere; in the garden, I expect. You are before your time a little. The train must have been punctual, for a wonder. Had Hilda known, she would have been here to welcome you, I know, Christian."

"I expect she is at the moat," said Molly. "Come along, Christian; we will go and look for her. This way."

In the meantime Sidney had driven the dog-cart round to the stables, kneeling awkwardly upon the back seat.

As Christian followed his fair guide down the little path leading to the moat, he began to feel that it was not so difficult after all to throw off the dull weight of anxiety that lay upon his mind. The thoughts about the *Beacon* were after all not so very absorbing. The anxiety regarding the welfare of the two old ladies was already alleviated by distance. The strong sea air, the change to pleasant and kindly society, were already beginning their work.

Suddenly Molly stopped, and Christian saw that she was standing at the edge of a long, still sheet of water bounded by solid stonework, which, however, was crumbling away in parts, while everywhere the green moss grew in velvety profusion.

"Oh, Christian," said Molly lightly, "I suppose Sidney told you a little of our news. Men's letters are not discursive as a rule I know, but no doubt he told you—something."

He was standing beside her at the edge of the moat, looking down into the deep, clear water.

"Yes," he replied slowly, "yes, Molly; he told me a little in a scrappy, unsatisfactory way."

A pained expression came into her eyes for a moment, and then she spoke, rather more quickly than was habitual with her, but without raising her voice.

"He told you—nothing about Hilda?" she said interrogatively.

He turned and looked down at her.

"No—nothing."

Then he followed the direction of her eyes, and saw approaching them a young man and a maiden whose footsteps had been inaudible upon the moss-grown path. The man was of medium height, with an honest brown face. He was dressed for riding, and walked with a slight swagger, which arose less from conceit than from excessive riding on horseback. The maiden was tall and stately, and in her walk there was an old-fashioned grace of movement which harmonised perfectly with the old-world surroundings. She was looking down, and Christian could not see her face; but as she wore no hat, he saw and recognised her hair. This was of gold—not red, not auburn, not flaxen, but pure and living gold. The sun glinting through the trees shone upon it and gleamed, but in reality the hair gleamed without the aid of sunlight.

CHAPTER VI

BROKEN THREADS

They came forward, and suddenly the girl raised her face. She made a little hesitating movement of non-recognition, and then suddenly her face was transformed by a very pleasant smile. There was something peculiar in Hilda Carew's smile, which came from the fact that her eyelashes were golden, while her eyes were dark blue. The effect suggested a fascinating kitten. In repose her face was almost severe in its refined beauty, and the set of her lips indicated a certain self-reliance which with years might become more prominent if trouble should arrive.

"Christian!" she exclaimed, "I am sorry I did not know you." They shook hands, and Molly hastened to introduce her sister's companion.

"Mr. Farrar," she said; "Mr. Vellacott."

The two men shook hands, and Christian was disappointed. The grip of Farrar's fingers was limp and almost nerveless, in striking contradiction to the promise of his honest face and well-set person.

"Tea is ready," said Molly somewhat hastily; "let us go in."

Hilda and her companion passed on in front while Molly and Christian followed them. The latter purposely lagged behind, and his companion found herself compelled to wait for him.

"Look at the effect of the sunlight through the trees upon that water," said he in a conversational way; "it is quite green, and almost transparent."

"Yes," replied Molly, moving away tentatively, "we see most peculiar effects over the moat. The water is so very still and deep."

He raised his quiet eyes to her face, upon which the ready smile still lingered. As she met his gaze she raised her hand and pushed back a few truant wisps of hair which, curling forward like tendrils, tickled her cheek. It was a movement he soon learned to know.

"Yes," he said absently. He was wondering in an analytical way whether the action was habitual with her, or significant of embarrassment. At length he turned to follow her, but Molly had failed in her object; the others had passed out of earshot.

"Tell me," said Christian in a lowered voice, "who is he?"

"He is the squire of St. Mary Eastern, six miles from here," she replied; "very well off; very good to his mother, and in every way nice."

Christian tore off a small branch which would have touched his forehead had he walked on without stooping. He broke it into small pieces, and continued throwing up at intervals into the air a tiny stick, hitting it with his hand as they walked on.

"And," he said suggestively, "and—"

"Yes, Christian," she replied decisively, "they are engaged. Come, let us hurry; I always pour out the tea. I told you before, if you remember, that I was the only person in the house who did any work."

When Christian opened his eyes the following morning, the soft hum of insects fell on his ear instead of the roar of London traffic. Through the open window the southern air blew upon his face. Above the sound of busy wings the distant sea sang its low dirge. It was a living perspective of sound. The least rustle near at hand overpowered it, and yet it was always there—an unceasing throb to be felt as much as heard. Some acoustic formation of the land carried the noise, for the sea was eight miles away. It was very peaceful; for utter stillness is not peace. A room wherein an old clock ticks is infinitely more soothing than a noiseless chamber.

Nevertheless the feeling that forced itself into Christian Vellacott's waking thoughts was not peaceful. It was a sense of discomfort. Town-people expect too much from the country—that is the truth of it. They quite overlook the fact that where human beings are there can be no peace.

This sudden sense of restlessness annoyed him. He knew it so well. It had hovered over his waking head almost daily during the last two years, and here, in the depths of the country, he had expected to be without it. Moreover, he was conscious that he had not brought the cause with him. He had found it, waiting.

There were many things—indeed there was almost everything—to make his life happy and pleasant at St. Mary Western. But in his mind, as he woke up on this first morning, none of these things found place. He came to his senses thinking of the one little item which could be described as untoward—thinking of Hilda, and Hilda engaged to be married to Fred Farrar. It was not that he was in love with Hilda Carew himself. He had scarcely remembered her existence during the last two years. But this engagement jarred, and Farrar jarred. It was something more than the very natural shock which comes with the news that a companion of our youth is about to be married—shock which seems to shake the memory of that youth; to confuse the background of our life. It is by means of such shocks as these that Fate endeavours vainly to make us realise that the past is irrevocable—that we are passing on, and that that which has been can never be again. And at the same time we learn something else: namely, that the past is not by any means unchangeable. So potential is To-day that it not only holds To-morrow in the hollow of its hand, but it can alter Yesterday.

Christian Vellacott lay upon his bed in unwonted idleness, gazing vaguely at the flying clouds. The window was open, and the song of the distant sea rose and fell with a rhythm full of peace. But in this man's mind there was no peace. In all probability there never would be complete peace there, because Ambition had set its hold upon him. He wanted to do more than there was time for. Like many of us, he began by thinking that Life is longer than it is. Its whole length is in those "long, long thoughts" of Youth. When those are left behind, we settle down to work, and the rest of the story is nothing but labour. Vellacott resented this engagement because he felt that Hilda Carew had stepped out of that picture which formed what was probably destined to be the happiest time of his life—his Youth. For the unhappiness of Youth is preferable to the resignation of Age. He felt that she had willingly resigned something which he would on no account have given up. Above all, he felt that it was a mistake. This was, of course, at the bottom of it. He probably felt that it was a pity. We usually feel so on hearing that a pretty and charming girl is engaged to be married. We think that she might have done so much better for herself, and we grow pensive or possibly sentimental over her lost opportunity when contemplating him in the mirror as he shaves. Like all so-called happy events, an engagement is not usually a matter of universal rejoicing. Some one is, in all probability, left to think twice about it. But Christian Vellacott was not prepared to admit that he was in that position.

He was naturally of an observant habit—his father had been one of the keenest-sighted men of his day—and he had graduated at the subtlest school in the world. He unwittingly fell to studying his fellow-men whenever the opportunity presented itself, and the result of this habit was a certain classification of detail. He picked up little scraps of evidence here and there, and these were methodically pigeon-holed away, as a lawyer stores up the correspondence of his clients.

With regard to Frederick Farrar, Vellacott had only made one note. The squire of St. Mary Eastern was apparently very similar to his fellows. He was an ordinary young British squire with a knowledge of horses and a highly-developed fancy for smart riding-breeches and long boots. He had probably received a fair education, but this had ceased when he closed his last school-book. The seeds of knowledge had been sown, but they lacked moisture and had failed to grow. He was good-natured, plucky in a hard-headed British way, and gentlemanly. In all this there was nothing exceptional— nothing to take note of—and Vellacott only remembered the limpness of Frederick Farrar's grasp. He thought of this too persistently and magnified it. And this being the only mental note made, was rather hard on the young squire of St. Mary Eastern.

Vellacott thought of these things while he dressed, he thought of them intermittently during the unsettled, noisy, country breakfast, and when he found himself walking beside the moat with Hilda later on he was still thinking of them.

They had not yet gathered into their hands the threads which had been broken years before. At times they hit upon a topic of some slight common interest, but something hovered in the air between them. Hilda was gay, as she had always been, in a gentle, almost purring way; but a certain constrained silence made itself felt at times, and they were both intensely conscious of it.

Vellacott was fully aware that there was something to be got over, and so instead of skipping round it, as a woman might have done, he went blundering on to the top of it.

"Hilda," he said suddenly, "I have never congratulated you."

She bent her head in a grave little bow which was not quite English; but she said nothing.

"I can only wish you all happiness," he continued rather vaguely.

Again she made that mystic little motion of the head, but did not look towards him, and never offered the assistance of smile or word.

"A long life, a happy one, and your own will," he added more lightly, looking down into the green water of the moat.

"Thank you," she said, standing quite still beside him.

And then there followed an awkward pause. It was Vellacott who finally broke the silence in the only way left to him.

"I like Farrar," he said. "I am sure he will make you happy. He—is a lucky fellow."

At the end of the walk that ran the whole length of that part of the moat which had been allowed to remain intact, she made a little movement as if to turn aside beneath the hazel trees and towards the house. But he would not let her go. He turned deliberately upon his heel and waited for her. There was nothing else to do but acquiesce. They retraced their steps with that slow reflectiveness which comes when one walks backwards and forwards over the same ground.

There is something eminently conversational in the practice of walking to and fro. For that purpose it is better than an arm-chair and a pipe, or a piece of knitting.

Occasionally Vellacott dropped a pace behind, apparently with a purpose; for when he did so he raised his eyes instantly. He seemed to be slowly detailing the maiden, and he frowned a little. She was exactly what she had promised to be. The singularly golden hair which he had last seen flowing freely over her slight young shoulders had acquired a decorousness of curve, although the hue was unchanged. The shoulders were exactly the same in contour, on a slightly larger scale; and the manner of carrying her head—a manner peculiarly her own, and suggestive of a certain gentle wilfulness—was unaltered.

And yet there was a change: that subtle change which seems to come to girls suddenly, in the space of a week—of one night. And this man was watching her with his analytical eyes, wondering what the change might be.

He was more or less a bookworm, and he possibly thought that this subject—this pleasant young subject walking beside him in a blue cotton dress—was one which might easily be grasped and understood if only one gave one's mind to it. Hence the little frown. It denoted the gift of his mind. It was the frown that settled over his eyes when he cut the pages of a deep book and glanced at the point of his pencil.

He had read many books, and he knew a number of things. But there is one subject of which very little can be learnt in books—precisely the subject that walked in a blue cotton dress by Christian Vellacott's side at the edge of the moat. If any one thinks that book-learning can aid this study, let him read the ignorance of Gibbon, comparing it with the learning of that cheery old ignoramus Montaigne. And Vellacott was nearer to Gibbon in his learning than to Montaigne in his careless ignorance of those things that are written in books.

He glanced at her; he frowned and brought his whole attention to bear upon her, and he could not even find out whether she was pleased to listen to his congratulations, or angry, or merely indifferent. It was rather a humiliating position for a clever man—for a critic who knew himself to be capable of understanding most things, of catching the drift of most thoughts, however imperfectly expressed. He was vaguely conscious of defeat. He felt that he was nonplussed by a pair of soft round eyes like the eyes of a kitten, and the dignified repose of a pair of demure red lips. Both eyes and lips, as well as shoulders and golden hair, were strangely familiar and strangely strange by turns.

With one finger he twisted the left side of his moustache into his mouth, and, dragging at it with his teeth, distorted his face in an unbecoming if reflective manner, which was habitually indicative of the deepest attention.

While reflecting, he forgot to be conversational, and Hilda seemed to be content with silence. So they walked the length of the moat twice without speaking, and might have accomplished it a third time, had little Stanley Carew not appeared upon the scene with the impulsive energy of his thirteen years, begging Christian to bowl him some really swift overhands.

CHAPTER VII

PUPPETS

"Ah! It goes. It goes already!"

The speaker—the Citizen Morot—slowly rubbed his white hands one over the other.

He was standing at the window of a small house in an insignificant street on the southern side of the Seine. He was remarkably calm—quite the calmest man within the radius of a mile; for the insignificant little street was in an uproar. There was a barricade at each end of it. Such a barricade as Parisians love. It was composed of a few overturned omnibuses; for the true Parisian is a cynic. He likes overturned things, and he loves to see objects of peace converted to purposes of war. He is not content that ploughshares be beaten into swords. He prefers altar-rails. And so this little street was blocked at either end by a barricade of overturned omnibuses, of old hampers and empty boxes, of a few loads of second-hand bricks and paving-stones brought from the scene of some drainage operations round the corner.

In the street between the barricades, surged, hooted, and yelled that wildest and most dangerous of

Henry Seton Merriman

incomprehensibles—a Paris mob. Half-a-dozen orators were speaking at once, and no one was listening to them. Here and there amidst the rabble a voice was raised at times with suspicious persistence.

"*Vive le Roi!*" it cried. "Long live the King!"

A few took up the refrain, but the general tone was negative. It was not so much a question of upholding anything as of throwing down that which was already up.

"Down with the Republic!" was the favourite cry. "Down with the President! Down with everything!"

And each man cried down his favourite enemy.

The Citizen Morot listened, and his contemptuous mouth was twisted with a delicate, subtle smile.

"Ah!" he muttered. "The voice of the people. The howling of the wolves. Go on, go on, my braves. Cry 'Long live the King,' and soon you will begin to believe that you mean it. They are barking now. Let them bark. Soon we shall teach them to bite, and then—then, who knows?"

His voice dropped almost to a whisper, and he stood there amidst the din and hubbub—dreaming. At last he raised his hand to his forehead—a prominent, rounded forehead, flat as the palm of one's hand from eyebrow to eyebrow, and curving at either side, sharply, back to deep-sunken temples.

"Ah!" he exclaimed, with a little laugh; and he drew from an inner pocket a delicately scented pocket-handkerchief, with which he wiped his brow. "If I get excited now, what will it be when they begin—to bite?"

All this while the orators were shouting their loudest, and the voices dispersed throughout the crowd raised at intervals their short, sharp cry of—

"Long live the King!"

And the police? There were only two agents attached to the immediate neighbourhood, and they were smoking cigars and drinking absinthe in two separate cellars, with the door locked on the outside. They were prisoners of war of the most resigned type. The room in which stood the Citizen Morot was dark, and wisely so. For the Parisian street politician can make very pretty practice of a lighted petroleum-lamp with an empty bottle or half a brick. The window was wide open, and the wooden shutters were hooked back.

The attitude of the man was interested and slightly self-satisfied. It suggested that of the manager of a theatre looking down from an upper-tier box upon a full house and a faultless stage. At the same time he was keeping what sailors call a very "bright look-out" towards either end of the street. From his elevated position he was able to see over the barricades, and he watched with intense interest the movements of two women (or perhaps men disguised as such) who stood in the centre of the street just beyond each obstruction.

There was something dramatic in the motionless attitude of these two women, standing guard alone in the deserted street, on the wrong side of the barricades.

At times Morot leant well out of the window and listened. Then he stood back again and contemplated the crowd.

Each orator was illuminated by a naphtha "flare," which,

being held in unsteady hands, flickered and wavered, casting strange gleams of light over the evil faces upturned towards it. At times one speaker would succeed in raising a laugh or extracting a groan, and when he did so those listening to his rivals turned and surged towards him. There was plenty of movement. It was what the newspapers call an animated scene—or a disgraceful scene—according to their political bias.

The Citizen Morot could not hear the jokes nor distinguish the cause of the groaning. But he did not seem to mind much. The speeches were not of the description to be given in full in the morning papers. There were, fortunately, no reporters present. It was the frank eloquence of the slaughter-house—the unclad humour of the market.

Suddenly one of the women—she who was posted at the southern end of the street—raised both her arms, and the Citizen leant far out of the window. He was very eager, and his hawk-like eyes blinked perpetually. His hand was raised to his mouth, and the lights of the orators gleamed on something that he held in his fingers—something that looked like silver.

The woman held her two arms straight up into the air for some moments, then she suddenly crossed them twice, turning at the same moment and scrambling over the barricade. A long shrill whistle rang out over the heads of the mob, and its effect was almost instantaneous. The "flares" disappeared like magic. Dark figures swarmed up the lamp-posts and extinguished the feeble lights. The voice of the orator was still. Silence and darkness reigned over that insignificant little street on the southern side of the Seine. Then came the clatter of cavalry—the rattle of horses' feet, and the ominous clank of empty scabbards against spur and buckle. A word of command, and a scrambling halt. Then silence again, broken only by the shuffling of feet (not too well clad) in the darkness between the barricades.

The Citizen Morot leant recklessly out of the window, peering into the gloom. He forgot to make use of the delicately scented pocket-handkerchief now, and the drops of perspiration trickled slowly down his face.

The soldiers shuffled in their saddles. Some of the spirited little Arabs pawed the pavement. One of them squealed angrily, and there was a slight commotion somewhere in the rear ranks—an equine difference of opinion. The officers had come forward to the barricade and were consulting together. The question was—what was there behind that barricade? It might be nothing—it might be everything. In Paris one can never tell. At last one of them determined to see for himself. He scrambled up, putting his foot through the window of an omnibus in passing. Against the dim light of the street-lamp beyond, his slight, straight figure stood out in bold relief. It was a splendid mark for a man with chalked sights to his rifle.

"Ah!" muttered the Citizen, "you are all right this time— master, the young officer. They are only barking. Next time perhaps it will be quite another history."

The officer turned and disappeared. After the lapse of a few moments a dozen words of command were shouted, and upon them followed the sharp click of hilt on scabbard as the sabres fell home.

After a pause it became evident that the barricade was being destroyed. And then lights flashed here and there. In a compact column the cavalry advanced at a trot. The street was empty.

Citizen Morot turned away and sat down on a chair that

happened to be placed near the window. His finely-drawn eyebrows were raised with a questioning weariness.

"Pretty work!" he ejaculated. "Pretty work for—my father's son! So grand, so open, so noble!"

He waited there, in the darkness, until the cavalry had been withdrawn and the local firemen were at work upon the barricade. Then, when order was fully restored, he left the house, walking quietly down the length of the insignificant little street.

Ten minutes later he entered the tobacco-shop in the Rue St. Gingolphe. Mr. Jacquetot was at his post, behind the counter near the window, with the little tin box containing postage-stamps in front of him upon his desk. He was always there—like the poor. He laid aside the *Petit Journal* and wished the new-comer a courteous, though breathless, good evening.

The salutation was returned gravely and pleasantly. The Citizen Morot lingered a moment and remarked that it was a warm evening. He never seemed to be in a hurry. Then he passed on into the little room behind the shop.

There he found Lerac, the foreman of the slaughter-house. The butcher was pale with excitement. His rough clothing was dishevelled; his stringy black hair stood up uncouthly in the centre of his head, while over his temples it was plastered down with perspiration and suet pleasingly mingled.

"Well?" he exclaimed, with triumphant interrogation.

"Good," said Morot. "Very good. It marches, my friend. It marches already."

"Ah! But you are right. The People see you—it is a power!"

"It is," acquiesced Morot fervently.

How he hated this man!

"And you stayed to the last?" inquired Lerac. He was rather white about the lips for a brave man.

"Till the last," echoed Morot, taking up some letters addressed to him which lay on the table.

"And the street was quite clear before they broke through the barrier?"

"Quite—the People did not wait." He seemed to resign himself to conversation, for he put the letters into his pocket and sat down. "Had you," he inquired, "any difficulty in getting them away?"

"Oh no," somewhat loftily and quite unsuspicious of irony. "The passages were narrow, of course; but we had allowed for that in our organisation. Organisation and the People, see you—"

"Yes," replied Morot. "Organisation and the People." Like Lerac, he stopped short, apparently lost in the contemplation of the vast possibilities presented to his mental vision by the mere thought of such a combination.

"Well!" exclaimed the butcher energetically, "I must move on. I have meetings. I merely wished to hear from you that all was right—that no one was caught."

He was bubbling over with excitement and the sense of his own huge importance.

The Citizen Morot raised his secretive eyes.

"Good-night," he said, with an insolence far too fine for the butcher's comprehension.

"Well—good-night. We may congratulate ourselves, I think, Citizen!"

"I congratulate you," said Morot. "Good-night."

"Good-night."

It is probable that, had Lerac looked back, there would have been murder done in the small room behind the tobacco-shop. But the contemptuous smile soon vanished from the face of the Citizen Morot. No smile lingered there long. It was not built upon smiling lines at all.

Then he took up his letters. There were only two of them: one bearing the postmark of a small town in Morbihan, the other hailing from England.

He replaced the first in his pocket unread; the second he opened. It was written in French.

"There are difficulties," it said. "Can you come to me? Cross from Cherbourg to Southampton—train from thence to this place, and ask for Signor Bruno, an Italian refugee, living at the house of Mrs. Potter, a *ci-devant* laundress."

The Citizen Morot rubbed his chin thoughtfully with the back of his hand, making a sharp, grating sound.

"That old man," he said, "is getting past his work. He is losing nerve; and nerve is a thing that we cannot afford to lose."

Then he turned to the letter again.

"Ah!" he exclaimed suddenly; "St. Mary Western. He is there—how very strange. What a singular coincidence!"

He fell into a reverie with the letter before him.

"Carew is dead—but still I can manage it. Perhaps it is just as well that he is dead. I was always afraid of Carew."

Then he wrote a letter, which he addressed to "Signor Bruno, care of Mrs. Potter, St. Mary Western, Dorset."

"I shall come," he wrote, "but not in the way you suggest. I have a better plan. You must not know me when we meet."

He purchased a twenty-five centime stamp from Mr. Jacquetot, and posted the letter with his own hand in the little wall-box at the corner of the Rue St. Gingolphe.

CHAPTER VIII

FALSE METAL

There was, however, no cricket for Stanley Carew that morning. When they came within sight of the house Mrs. Carew emerged from an open window carrying several letters in her hand. She was not hurrying, but walking leisurely, reading a letter as she walked.

"Just think, Hilda dear," she said, with as much surprise as she ever allowed herself. "I have had a letter from the Vicomte d'Audierne. You remember him?"

"Yes," said the girl; "I remember him, of course. He is not the sort of man one forgets."

"I always liked the Viscount," said Mrs. Carew, pensively looking at the letter she held in her hand. "He was a good friend to us at one time. I never understood him, and I like men whom one does not understand."

Hilda laughed.

"Yes," she answered vaguely.

"Your father admired him tremendously," Mrs. Carew went

on to say. "He said that he was one of the cleverest men in France, but that he had fallen in a wrong season, and would not adapt himself. Had France been a monarchy, the Vicomte d'Audierne would have been in a very different position."

Vellacott did not open his own letters. He seemed to be interested in the conversation of these ladies. He was not a reserved man, but a secretive, which is quite a different thing. Reserve is natural—it comes unbidden, and often unwelcome. Secretiveness is born of circumstances. Some men find it imperative to cultivate it, although their soul revolts within them. In professional or social matters it is often merely an expediency—in some cases it almost feels like a crime. There are some secrets which cannot be divulged; there are some deceptions which a certain book-keeper will record upon the credit side of our account.

Like most young men who have got on in their calling, Christian Vellacott held his career in great respect. He felt that any sacrifice made for it carried its own reward. He thought that it levelled scruples and justified deceptions.

He knew this Vicomte d'Audierne by reputation; he wished to hear more of him; and so he feigned ignorance—listening.

"What has he written about?" inquired Hilda.

"To ask if he may come and see us. I suppose he means to come and stay."

Vellacott looked what the French call "contraried."

"When?" asked the girl.

"On Monday week."

And then Mrs. Carew turned to her other letters. Vellacott took the budget addressed to him, and walked away to where an iron table and some chairs stood in the shade of a deodar.

In a few minutes he looked still more put out. He had learnt of the disturbances in Paris, and was reading a rather panic-stricken letter from Mr. Bodery. The truth was that there was no one in the office of the *Beacon* who knew anything whatever about French home politics but Christian Vellacott.

A continuance of these disturbances would necessarily assume political importance, and might even lead to a crisis. This meant an instant recall for Vellacott. In a crisis his presence in London or Paris was absolutely necessary to the *Beacon*.

His holiday had barely lasted twenty-four hours, and there was already a question of recall. It happened also that within that short space a considerable change had come over Vellacott. The subtle influence of a country life, and possibly the low, peaceful song of the distant sea, were already beginning to make themselves felt. He actually detected a desire to sit still and do nothing—a feeling of which he had not hitherto been conscious. He was distinctly averse to leaving St. Mary Western just yet. But there is one task-master who knows no mercy and makes no allowances. Some of us who serve him know it to our cost, and yet we would be content to serve no other. That task-master is the Public.

Vellacott was a public servant, and he knew his position.

Somewhat later in the morning Molly and Hilda found him still seated at the table, writing with that concentrated rapidity which only comes with practice.

"I am sorry," he said, looking up, "but I must send off a telegram. I shall walk in to the station."

"I was just coming," said Hilda, "to ask if you would drive me in. I want to get some things."

"And," added Molly, "there are some domestic commissions—butcher, baker, &c."

Vellacott expressed his entire satisfaction with the arrangement, and by the time he had finished his letter the dog-cart was waiting at the door.

Several of the family were standing round the vehicle talking in a desultory manner, and Vellacott learnt then for the first time that Frederick Farrar had left home that same morning to attend a midland race-meeting.

It was one of those brilliant summer days when it is quite impossible to be pessimistic and exceedingly difficult to compass preoccupation. The light breeze bowling over the upland from the sea had just sufficient strength to blow away all mental cobwebs. Also, Christian Vellacott had suddenly given way to one of those feelings which sometimes come to us without apparent reason. The present was joyous enough without the aid of the ever-to-be-bright future, and Vellacott felt that, after all, French politics and Frederick Farrar did not quite monopolise the world.

Hilda was on this occasion more talkative than usual. There was in her manner a new sense of ease, almost of familiarity, which Vellacott could not understand. He noticed that she spoke invariably in generalities, avoiding all personal matters. Of herself she said no word, though she appeared willing enough to answer any question he might ask. She led him on to talk of himself and his work, listening gravely to his account of the little household at Chelsea. He made the best of this topic, and even treated it in a merry vein; but her smile, though sincere enough, was of short duration and not in itself encouraging. She appeared to see the pathos of it instead of the humour. Suddenly, in the middle of a particularly funny story about Aunt Judith, she interrupted him and changed the conversation entirely. She did not again refer to his home life.

As they were returning in the full glare of the midday sun, they descried in front of them the figure of an old man; he was walking painfully and making poor progress. Carefully dressed in black broadcloth, he wore a soft felt hat of a shape seldom seen in England.

"I believe," said Hilda, as they approached him, "that is Signor Bruno. Yes, it is. Please pull up, Christian. We must give him a lift!"

Christian obeyed her. He thought he detected a shade of annoyance in Hilda's voice, with which he fully sympathised.

On hearing the sound of the wheels, the old man looked up in surprise, as a deaf person might have been expected to do. This movement showed a most charming old face, surrounded by a halo of white hair and beard. The features were almost perfect, and might in former days have been a trifle cold, by reason of their perfection. Now, however, they were softened by the touch of years, and Signor Bruno was the living semblance of guilelessness and benevolence.

"How do you do, Signor Bruno?" said Hilda, speaking rather loudly and very distinctly. "You are back from London sooner than you expected, are you not?"

"Ah! my dear young lady," he replied, courteously removing

his hat and standing bareheaded.

"Ah! now indeed the sun shines upon me. Yes, I am back from London—a most terrible place—terrible—terrible—terrible! As I walked along just now I said to myself: 'The sun is warm, the skies are blue; yonder is the laughing sea, and yet, Bruno, you sigh for Italy.' This is Italy, Miss Hilda—Italy with a northern fairy walking in it!"

Hilda smiled her quick, surprising smile, and hastened to speak before the old gentleman recovered his breath.

"Allow me to introduce to you Sidney's friend, Mr. Vellacott, Signor Bruno!"

Sidney's friend, Mr. Vellacott, was by this time behind her. He had alighted, and was employed in arranging the back seat of the dog-cart. When Signor Bruno looked towards him, he found Christian's eyes fixed upon his face with a quiet persistence which might have been embarrassing to a younger man. He raised his hat and murmured something unintelligible in reply to the Italian's extensive salutation.

"Sidney Carew's friends are, I trust, mine also!" said Signor Bruno, as he replaced his picturesque hat.

Christian smiled spasmodically and continued arranging the seat. He then came round to the front of the cart and made a sign to Hilda that she should move into the right-hand seat and drive. Signor Bruno saw the sign, and said urbanely:

"You will, if you please, resume your seat. I will place myself behind!"

"Oh, no! You must allow me to sit behind!" said Christian.

"But why, my dear sir? That would not be correct. You are Mr. Carew's guest, and I—I am only a poor old Italian runaway, who is accustomed to back seats; all my life I have occupied back seats, I think, Mr. Vell'cott. There is no reason why I should aspire to better things now!"

The old fellow's voice was strangely balanced between pathos and a peculiar self-abnegating humour.

"If we were both to take our hats off again, I think it would be easy to see why you should sit in front!" said Christian with a laugh, which although quite genial, somehow closed the discussion.

"Ah!" replied the old gentleman with outspread hands. "There you have worsted me. After that I am silent, and—I obey!"

He climbed into the cart with a little senile joke about the stiffness of his aged limbs. He chattered on in his innocent, childish way until the village was reached. Here he was deposited on the dusty road at the gate of a small yellow cottage where he had two rooms. The seat was re-arranged, and amidst a volley of thanks and salutations, Hilda and Christian drove away. Presently Hilda looked up and said:

"Is he not a dear old thing? I believe, Christian, in all the various local information I have given you, I have never told you about Signor Bruno. I shall reserve him for the next awkward pause that occurs."

"Yes," replied Christian quietly. "He seems very nice."

Something in his tone seemed to catch her attention. She half turned as if to hear more, but he said nothing. Then she raised her eyes to his face, which was not expressive of anything in particular.

"Christian," she said gravely, "you do not like him?"

Looked upon as a mere divination of thought, this was very quick; but he seemed in no way perturbed. He turned and looked down with a smile at her grave face.

"No," he replied. "Not very much."

"Why?"

"I do not know. There is something wrong about him, I think!"

She laughed and shook her head.

"What do you mean?" she asked. "How can there be anything wrong with him—anything that would affect us, at all events?"

He shrugged his shoulders, still smiling.

"He says he is an Italian?"

"Yes," she replied.

"I say he is a Frenchman," said Christian, suddenly turning towards her. "Italians do not talk English as he talks it."

She looked puzzled.

"Do you know him?" she asked.

"No; not yet. I know his face. I have seen it or a photograph of it somewhere, and at some time. I cannot tell when or where yet, but it will come to me."

"When it does come," said Hilda, with a smile, "you will find that it is some one else. I can assure you Signor Bruno is an Italian, and beyond that he is the nicest old gentleman imaginable."

"Well," replied Christian. "In the meantime I vote that we do not trouble ourselves about him."

The subject was dropped, and not again referred to until after they had reached home, when Hilda informed her mother that Signor Bruno had returned.

"Oh, indeed," was the reply. "I am very glad. You must ask him to dinner to-morrow evening. Is he not a nice old man, Christian?"

"Very," replied Christian, almost before the words were out of her lips. "Yes, very nice." He looked across the table towards Hilda with an absolutely expressionless composure.

During the following day, which he passed with Sidney and Stanley at sea in a little cutter belonging to the Carews, Christian learnt, without asking many questions, all that Signor Bruno had vouchsafed in the way of information respecting himself. It was a short story and an old one, such as many a white-haired Italian could tell to-day. A life, income, and energy devoted to a cause which never had much promise of reward. Failure, exile, and a life closing in a land where the blue skies of Italy are known only by name, where Maraschino is at a premium, and long black cigars almost unobtainable.

Hilda was engaged on this day to lunch and spend the afternoon with Mrs. Farrar, at Farrar Court. Molly and

Christian were to drive over for her in the evening. This programme was carried out, but the young people lingered rather longer at Farrar Court listening to the quaint, old-world recollections of its white-haired hostess than was allowed for. Consequently they were late, and heard the first dinner-bell ringing as they drove up the lane that led in a casual way to their home. (This lane was characteristic of the house. It turned off unobtrusively from the high road at right angles with the evident intention of leading nowhere.) A race upstairs ensued and a hurried toilet. Molly and Christian met on the stairs a few minutes later. Christian had won the race, for he was ready, while Molly struggled with a silver necklace that fitted closely round her throat. Of course he had to help her. While waiting patiently for him to master the intricacies of the old silver clasp, Molly said:

"Oh, Christian, there is one place you have not seen yet. Quite close at hand too."

"Ye—es," he replied absently, as he at length fixed the clasp. "There, it is done!"

As he held open the drawing-room door, he said: "What is the place I have to see?"

Signor Bruno, who was seated at the far end of the room with Mrs. Carew, rose as he heard the door opened, and advanced to meet Molly.

"Porton Abbey," she said over her shoulder as she advanced into the room. "You must see Porton Abbey."

The Italian shook hands with the new-comers and made a clever, laughing reference to Christian's politeness of the previous day. At this moment Hilda entered, and as soon as she had returned Signor Bruno's courteous salutation Molly turned towards her.

"Hilda," she said, "we have never shown Christian Porton Abbey."

"No," was the reply. "I have been reserving it for some afternoon when we do not feel very energetic. Unfortunately, we cannot get inside the Abbey now, though."

"Why?" asked Christian, without looking towards Hilda. He had discovered that Signor Bruno was attempting to keep up a conversation with his hostess, while he took in that which was passing at the other end of the room. The old man was seated, and his face was within the radius of light cast by a shaded lamp. Christian, who stood, was in the shade.

"Because it is a French monastery," replied Molly. "Here," she added, "is a flower for your coat, as you say the button-hole is warped by constant pinning in of stalks."

"Thanks," he replied, stooping a little in order that she could reach the button-hole of his coat. She was in front of him, directly between him and Signor Bruno; but he could see over her head. "What sort of monastery is it?" he continued conversationally. "I did not know that there were any establishments of that sort in England."

Hilda looked up rather sharply from an illustrated newspaper she happened to be studying. She knew that he was not adhering strictly to the truth. From her point of vantage behind the newspaper she continued to watch Christian, and she realised during the minutes that followed, that this was indeed the brilliant young journalist of whose fame Farrar had spoken as already known in London.

Signor Bruno's conversation with Mrs. Carew became at this

moment somewhat muddled.

"There, you see," said Molly vivaciously, "we endeavour to interest him by retailing the simple annals of our neighbourhood, and his highness simply disbelieves us!"

"Not at all," Christian hastened to add, with a laugh. "It simply happened that I was surprised. It shall not occur again. But tell me, what sort of monastery is it? Dominican? Franciscan? Carmelite?—"

"Oh, goodness! I do not know."

"Perhaps," said Christian, advancing towards the Italian— "perhaps Signor Bruno can tell us."

"What is that, Mr. Vell'cott?" asked the old gentleman, making a movement as if about to raise his curved hand to his ear, but restraining himself upon second thoughts.

Hilda noticed that, instead of raising his voice, Christian spoke in the same tone, or even lower, as he said:

"We want some details of the establishment at Porton Abbey, Signor Bruno."

The old gentleman made a little grimace expressive of disgust, at the same time spreading out his hands as if to ward off something hurtful.

"Ach!" he said, "do not ask me. I know nothing of such people, and wish to learn no more. It is to them that my poor country owes her downfall. No, no; leave them alone. I always take care of myself against—against—what you say—*ces gens-la*!"

Henry Seton Merriman

Christian awaited the answer in polite silence, and, when Signor Bruno had again turned to Mrs. Carew, he looked across the room towards Hilda with the same expression of vacant composure that she had noticed on a previous occasion. The accent with which Signor Bruno had spoken the few words of French was of the purest Parisian, entirely free from the harshness which an Italian rarely conquers.

After dinner Hilda went out of the open window into the garden alone. Christian, who had seated himself at a small table in the drawing-room, did not move. Sidney and his mother were talking with the Italian.

The young journalist was stooping over a book, a vase of flowers stood in front of him, but by the movement of his arm it appeared as if he were drawing instead of reading. Presently a faint, low whistle came from the garden. Though soft, the sound was very clear, and each note distinctly given. It was like the beginning of a refrain which broke off suddenly and was repeated. Signor Bruno gave a little start and a quick upward glance.

"What is that?" he asked, with a little laugh, as if at the delicacy of his own nerves.

"Oh," replied Mrs. Carew, "the whistle, you mean. That is our family signal. The children were in the habit of calling each other by that means in bygone years. I expect they are in the garden now, and wish us to join them."

Mrs. Carew knew that Molly was not in the garden, but in making this intentional mistake she showed the wisdom of her kind.

"It seems to me," said Signor Bruno, "that the air—the refrain, one might call it—is familiar."

Christian Vellacott smiled suddenly behind his screen of flowers, but did not move or look up.

"I expect," explained Sidney, "that you have heard the air played upon the bugle. It is the French 'retraite,' played by the patrol in garrison towns at night."

In the meantime Christian had cut the fly-leaf from the book before him, and, after carefully folding it, he placed the paper in his breast-pocket. Then he rose and passed out of the open window into the garden.

Immediately Signor Bruno asked his hostess a few polite questions regarding her guest—what was his occupation, how long he was going to stay, and whether she did not agree with him in considering that their young friend had a remarkably interesting face. In the course of his remarks the old gentleman rose and crossed to the table where Christian had been sitting. There was a flower there which he had not seen in England before. Absently he took up the book which Christian had just been studying, and very naturally turned to the title-page. The fly-leaf was gone! When he laid the volume down again he replaced it in the identical position in which he had found it.

CHAPTER IX

A CLUE

When Christian left the drawing-room he walked quickly down the moss-grown path to the moat. Hilda was standing at the edge of the dark water, and as he joined her she turned and walked slowly by his side.

"You are a most unsatisfactory person," she said gravely after a few moments.

He looked down at her without replying. His eyes softened for a moment into a smile, but his lips remained grave.

"You deliberately set yourself," she continued, "to shatter one illusion after another. You have made me feel quite old and worldly to-night, and the worst of it is that you are invariably right. It is most annoying."

Her voice was only half-playful. There was a shade of sadness in it. Christian must have divined her thoughts, for he said:

"Do not let us quarrel over Signor Bruno. I dare say I am wrong altogether."

She looked slowly round. Her eyes rested on the dark surface of the water, where the shadows lay deep and still; then she raised them to the trees, clearly outlined against the sky.

"I suppose that such practical, matter-of-fact people as you are proof against mere outward influences."

"So I used to imagine, but I am beginning to find that outward things are very important after all. In London it seemed only natural that every one should live in a hurry, with no time for thought, pushing forward and trying to outstrip their neighbours; but in the country it seems that things are different. Intellectual people live quiet, thoughtful, and even dreamy lives. They get through somehow without seeing the necessity for doing something—trying to be something that their neighbours cannot be—and no doubt they are happier for it. I am beginning to see how they are content to go on with their uneventful lives from year to year until the end even comes without a shock."

"But you yourself would never reach that stage, Christian."

"No, no, Hilda. I can understand it in others, but for me it is different. I have tasted too deeply of the other life. I should get restless—"

"You are getting restless already," she interrupted gravely, "and you have not been here two days!"

They were interrupted by Sidney's clear whistle, and a moment later Molly came tripping down the path.

"Come along in," she said; "the old gentleman is going. I was just stealing away to join you when Sidney whistled."

When Signor Bruno reached his home that evening, he threw

Henry Seton Merriman

his hat upon the table with some considerable force. His aged landlady, having left the lamp burning, had retired to bed. He sank into an armchair, and contemplated the square toes of his own boots for some moments. Then he scratched his head thoughtfully.

"Sacre nom d'un chien!" he muttered; "where have I seen that face before?"

Signor Bruno spoke French when soliloquising, which was perhaps somewhat peculiar for an Italian. However proficient a man may be in the mastery of foreign tongues, he usually dreams and talks to himself in the language he learnt at his mother's knee. He may count fluently in a strange tongue, but he invariably works out all mental arithmetic in his own. Likewise he prays—if he pray at all—in one tongue only. On the other hand, it appears very easy to swear in an acquired language. Probably our forefathers borrowed each other's expletives when things went so lamentably wrong over the Tower of Babel. Still muttering to himself, Signor Bruno presently retired to rest with the remembrance of a young face, peculiarly and unpleasantly strong, haunting his dreams.

Shortly after Signor Bruno's departure, Christian happened to be left alone in the drawing room with Hilda. He promptly produced from his pocket the leaf he had cut from a book earlier in the evening. Unfolding the paper, he handed it to her, and said:—

"Do you recognise that?"

She looked at it, and answered without hesitation—

"Signor Bruno!"

The drawing was slight, but the likeness was perfect. The face was in profile, and the reproduction of the intelligent features could scarcely have been more lifelike in a careful portrait. Christian replaced the paper in his pocket.

"You remember Carl Trevetz, at Paris," continued he, "his father belonged to the Austrian Embassy!"

"Yes, I remember him!"

"To-morrow I will send this to him, simply asking who it is."

"Yes—and then?"

"When the answer comes, Hilda, I will write on the outside of the envelope the name that you will find inside—written by Trevetz."

For a moment she looked across the table at him with a vague expression of wonder upon her face.

"Even if you are right," she said, "will it affect us? Will it make us cease to look upon him as a friend?"

"I think so."

"Then," she said slowly, "it has come. You remember now?"

"Yes; I remember now—but it may be a mistake yet. I would rather have my memory confirmed by Trevetz before telling you what I know—or think I know—about Bruno!"

Hilda was about to question him further when Molly entered the room, and the subject was perforce dropped.

The next morning there came a letter for Christian from Mr.

Bodery. It was short, and not very pleasant.

"DEAR VELLACOTT,—Sorry to trouble you with business so early in your holiday, but there has been another great row in Paris, as you will see from the papers I send you. It is hinted that the mob are mere tools in the hands of influential wire-pullers, and the worst of it is that they were armed with English rifles and bayonets of a pattern just superseded by the War Office. How these got into their hands is not yet explained, but you will readily see the gravity of the circumstance in the present somewhat strained state of affairs. Several of the 'dailies' refer to us, as you will see, and express a hope that our 'exceptional knowledge of French affairs' will enable us to throw some light upon the subject. Trevetz is giving us all the information he can gather; but, of course, he is only able to devote a portion of his time to us. He hints that there is plenty of money in the background somewhere, and that a strong party has got up the whole affair—perhaps the Church. We must have something to say (something of importance) next week, and with this in view I must ask you to hold yourself in readiness to go to Paris on receipt of a telegram or letter from me.—Yours,

"C. C. BODERY."

Christian folded the letter, and replaced it in the envelope. Suddenly his attention was attracted to the latter. Upon the back there was a rim round the adhesive portion, and within this the glaze was gone from the paper. The envelope had been tampered with by a skilful manipulator. If Mr. Bodery had been in the habit of using inferior stationery, no trace would have been left upon the envelope.

Christian slipped the letter into his pocket, and, glancing round, saw that his movements had passed unobserved.

"Anything new?" asked Sidney, from the head of the table.

"Well, yes," was the reply. "There has been a disturbance in Paris. I may have to go over there on receipt of a telegram from the office;" he stopped, and looked slowly round the table. Hilda's attention was taken up by her plate, upon which, however, there was nothing. He leant forward, and handed her the toast-rack. She took a piece, but forgot to thank him. "I am sorry," he continued simply, "very sorry that the disturbances should have taken place just at this time."

His voice expressed natural and sincere regret, but no surprise. This seemed to arouse Molly's curiosity, for she looked up sharply.

"You do not seem to be at all surprised," she said.

"No," he replied; "I am accustomed to this sort of thing, you see. I knew all along that there was the chance of being summoned at any time. This letter only adds to the chance— that is all!"

"It is a great shame," said Molly, with a pout. "I am sure there are plenty of people who could do it instead of you."

Christian laughed readily.

"I am sure there are," he replied, "and that is the very reason why I must take the opportunities that fortune offers."

Hilda looked across the table at him, and noted the smile upon his lips, the light of energy in his eyes. The love of action had driven all other thoughts from his mind.

"I suppose," she said conversationally, "that it will in reality be a good thing for you if the summons does come."

"Yes," he replied, without meeting her glance; "it will be a good thing for me."

"Is that consolatory view of the matter the outcome of philosophy, or of virtue?" inquired Molly mischievously.

"Of virtue," replied Christian gravely, and then he changed the subject.

After breakfast he devoted a short time to the study of some newspaper cuttings inclosed in Mr. Bodery's letter. Then he suddenly expressed his determination of walking down to the village post office.

"I wish," he said, "to send a telegram, and to get some newspapers, which have no doubt come by the second post. After that you will be troubled no more about my affairs."

"Until a telegram comes," said Hilda quietly, without looking up from a letter she held in her hand. She received one daily from Farrar.

Christian glanced at her with his quick smile.

"Oh," he said, "I do not expect a telegram. It is not so serious as all that. In fact, it is not worth thinking about."

"You have a most enviable way of putting aside disagreeable subjects," persisted Hilda, "for discussion at a vague future period."

Christian was steadily cheerful that morning, imperturbably practical.

"That," he said, "is the outcome—not of virtue—but of philosophy. Will you come to the post office with Stanley and me? I am sure there is no possible household duty to prevent you."

Together they walked through the peaceful fields. Stanley never lingered long beside them; something was for ever attracting him aside or ahead, and he ran restlessly away. Christian could not help noticing the difference in Hilda's manner when they were alone together. The semi-sarcastic *badinage* to which he had been treated lately was completely dropped, and her earnest nature was allowed to show itself undisguised. Still she was a mystery to him. He was by habit a close observer, but her changing moods and humours were to him unaccountable. At times she would make a remark the direct contradiction of which was shining in her eyes, and at other times she remained silent when mere politeness would seem to demand speech. Who knows? Perhaps at all times and in all things they understood each other. When their lips were exchanging mere nothings—the very lightest and emptiest of conversational chaff—despite averted eyes, despite indifferent manner, their souls may have been drawn together by that silent bond of sympathy which holds through fair and foul, through laughter and tears, through life and beyond death.

Christian was not in the habit of allowing himself to become absorbed by any passing thoughts, however deep they might be. His mind had adapted itself to the work required of it, as the human mind is ever ready to do. No deep meditating was required of it, but a quick grasp and a somewhat superficial treatment. Journalism is superficial, it cannot be otherwise; it must be universal and immediate, and therefore its touch is necessarily light. There is nothing permanent about it except the ceaseless throb of the printing machine and the warm smell of ink. That which a man writes one day may be rendered useless and worthless the next, through no careless-ness of his, but by the simple course of events. He must perforce take up his pen again and write against himself. He may be inditing history, and his words may be forgotten in twelve hours. There is no time for deep thought, even if such were required. He who writes for cursory reading is wise if he writes cursorily.

Mr. Bodery's communication in no manner disturbed Christian. He was ready enough to talk and laugh, or talk and be grave, as Hilda might dictate, while they walked side by side that morning, but she was strangely silent. It thus happened that little passed between them until they reached the post office. There, he was formally introduced to the spry little postmistress, who looked at him sharply over her spectacles.

"I wish, Mrs. Chalder," he said cheerily, as he scribbled off his message to Mr. Bodery, while Hilda made friendly overtures to the official cat, "I wish that you would forget to send me the disagreeable letters, and only forward the pleasant ones. There was one this morning, for instance, which you might very easily have mislaid. Instead of which you carefully sent it rather earlier than usual and spoilt my breakfast."

His voice unconsciously followed the swing of his pencil. It seemed certain that he was making conversation with the sole purpose of entertaining the old woman. With a pleased laugh and a shake of her grey curls she replied:

"Ah, I wish I could, sir. I wish I could burn the bad letters and send on only the good ones—but they're all alike on the outside. It's as hard to say what's inside a letter as it is to tell what's inside a man by lookin' on his face."

"Yes," replied Christian, reading over what he had just written. "Yes, Mrs. Chalder, you are right."

"But the reason of your letter gettin' earlier this morning was that Seen'yer Bruno said he was goin' past the Hall, sir, and would just leave the letters at the Lodge. It is a bit out of the carrier's way, and that man *do* have a long tramp every day, sir."

"Ah, that accounts for it," murmured the journalist, without looking up. He was occupied in crossing his t's and dotting his i's. He felt that Hilda was looking at him, and some instinct told him that she saw the motive of his conversation, but still he played his part and wore his mask of carelessness, as men have done before women, knowing the futility of it, since the world began. She never referred to the incident, and made no remark whatever with a view to his doing so, but he knew that it would be remembered, and in after days he learnt to build up a very castle of hope upon that frail foundation.

Hilda had not been paying much attention to what he was saying until Signor Bruno's name was mentioned. The old man had hitherto occupied a very secondary place in her thoughts. He was no one in her circle of possibly interesting people, beyond the fact of his having passed through a troubled political phase—a fighter on the losing side. Now he had, as it were, assumed a more important *role*. The mention of his name possessed a new suggestion: and all this, forsooth, because Christian Vellacott opined that the benevolent old face was known to him.

She began to entertain exaggerated ideas concerning the young journalist's thoughts and motives. Twice had she obtained a glimpse into the inner chamber of his mind, and on each occasion the result had been a vague suggestion of some mental conflict, some dark game of cross-purposes between him and Signor Bruno. Remembering this, she, in her intelligent simplicity, began to ascribe to Christian's every word and action an ulterior motive which in reality did not perhaps exist. She noted Christian's calm and direct way of reaching the end he desired, and unconsciously she yielded a little to the influence of his strength—an influence dangerously fascinating for a strong woman. Her strength is so different from that of a man that there is no real conflict—it seeks to yield, and glories over its own downfall.

After paying for the telegram, Christian took possession of the bulky packet of newspapers addressed to him, and they left the post office.

CHAPTER X

ON THE SCENT

It appeared to Stanley, on the way home that morning, that the conversation flagged somewhat. He therefore set to himself the task of reviving it.

"Christian," he began conversationally, "is there any smuggling done now? Real smuggling, I mean."

"No, I think not," replied Christian. He evidently did not look upon smuggling as a fruitful topic at that moment.

"Why do you ask?" interposed Hilda goodnaturedly.

"Well, I was just wondering," replied the boy. "It struck me yesterday that our boat had been moved."

"But," suggested Christian, "it should be very easy to see whether it has been dragged over the sand or not."

"Three strong men could carry it bodily into the water and make no marks whatever on the sand," argued little Stanley, determined not to be cheated out of his smugglers.

"Perhaps some one has been out for a row for his own

Henry Seton Merriman

pleasure and enjoyment," suggested Christian, without thinking much of what he was saying.

"Then how did he get the padlock open?"

"Smugglers, I suppose," said Hilda, smiling down at her small brother, "would be provided with skeleton keys."

"Of course," replied Stanley in an awestruck tone.

"I will tell you what we will do, Stanley," said Christian. "To-morrow morning we will go and have a bathe; at the same time I will look at the boat and tell you whether it has been moved."

"Unless," added Hilda, "a telegram comes today."

Christian laughed.

"Unless," he said gravely, "the world comes to an end this evening."

It happened during the precise moments occupied by this conversation, that Mr. Bodery, seated at his table in the little editor's room, opened the flimsy brown envelope of a telegram. He spread out the pink paper, and Mr. Morgan, seated opposite, raised his head from the closely-written sheets upon which his hand was resting.

"It is from Vellacott," said the editor, and after a moment's thought he read aloud as follows:—

"Letter and papers received; believe I have dropped into the clue of the whole affair. Will write particulars."

Mr. Morgan caressed his heavy moustache with the end of

his penholder.

"That young man," he said, "goes about the world with his eyes remarkably wide open, ha-ha!"

Mr. Bodery rolled the telegram out flat with his pencil silently.

*   *   *   *   *

Stanley Carew was so anxious that the inspection of the boat should not be delayed, that an expedition to the Cove was arranged for the same afternoon. Accordingly the five young people walked across the bleak tableland together. Huge white clouds were rolling up from the south-west, obscuring every now and then the burning sun. A gentle breeze blew gaily across the bleak upland—a very different breath from that which twisted and gnarled the strong Scotch firs in winter-time.

"You would not care about climbing *down* there, I should think," observed Sidney, when they had reached the Cove. "It is a very different matter getting up."

He was standing, gazing lazily up at the brown cliffs with his straw hat tilted backwards, his hands in his pockets, and his whole person presenting as fair a picture as one could desire of lazy, quiescent strength—a striking contrast to the nervous, wiry townsman at his side.

"Hardly," replied Christian, gazing upwards at the dizzy height. "It is rather nasty stuff—slippery in parts and soft."

He turned and strolled off by Hilda's side. With a climber's love of a rocky height he looked upwards as they walked, and she noted the direction of his gaze.

Presently they sat on the edge of the boat over which Stanley's sense of proprietorship had been so grievously outraged.

"What do you know, Christian, or what do you suspect about Signor Bruno?" asked Hilda suddenly.

Stanley was running across the sands towards them, and Christian, seeing his approach, avoided the question by a generality.

"Wait a little longer," he said. "Let me have Trevetz's answer to confirm my suspicions, and then I will tell you. Suspicions are dangerous things to meddle with. In imparting them to other people it is so difficult to remember that they *are* suspicions and nothing more."

At this moment Stanley arrived and threw himself down breathlessly on the warm sand.

"Chris!" he exclaimed, "come down here and look at these seams in the boat—the damp is there still."

The boat was clinker-built, and where the planks overlapped a slight appearance of dampness was certainly discernible. Christian lay lazily leaning upon his elbow, sometimes glancing at the boat in obedience to Stanley's accusatory finger, sometimes looking towards Hilda, whose eyes were turned seawards.

Suddenly he caught sight of some words pencilled on the stern-post of the boat, and by the merest chance refrained from calling Stanley's attention to them. Drawing nearer, he could read them easily enough.

Minuit vingt-six.

"It certainly looks," he said rising, "as if the boat had been in the water, but it may be that the dampness is merely owing to heavy dew. The boat wants painting, I think."

He knew well enough that little Stanley's suspicions were correct. There was no doubt that the boat had been afloat quite recently; but Christian knew his duty towards the *Beacon* and sacrificed his strict sense of truth to it.

On the way home he was somewhat pre-occupied—as much, that is to say, as he was in the habit of allowing. The pencil scrawl supplied food enough for conjectural thought. The writing was undoubtedly fresh, and this was the 26th of the month. Some appointment was made for midnight by the words pencilled on the boat, and the journalist determined that he would be there to see. The question was, should he go alone? He watched Sidney Carew walking somewhat heavily along in front of him, and decided that he would not seek aid from that quarter. There was no time to communicate with Mr. Bodery, so the only course open to him was to go by himself.

In a vague manner he had connected the Jesuit party with the disturbances in Paris and the importation of the English rifles wherewith the crowd had been armed. The gay capital was at that time in the hands of the most "Provisional" and uncertain Government imaginable, and the home politics of France were completely disorganised. It was just the moment for the Church party to attempt a retrieval of their lost power. The fire-arms had been recognised by the English authorities as some of a pattern lately discarded. They had been stored at Plymouth, awaiting shipment to the colonies, where they were to be served out to the auxiliary forces, when they had been cleverly removed. The robbery was not discovered until the rifles were found in the hands of a Paris mob, still fresh and brutal from the horrors of a long course of military law.

Some of the more fiery of the French journals boldly hinted that the English Government had secretly sold the firearms with a view to their ultimate gain by the disorganisation of France.

Christian knew as much about affairs in Paris as most men. He was fully aware that in the politics of a disturbed country a deed is either a crime or a heroism according to circumstances, and he was wise enough to await the course of events before thrusting his opinion down the public throat. But now he felt that the crisis had supervened, and unwillingly he recognised that it was not for him to be idle amidst those rapid events.

These thoughts occupied his mind as he walked inland from the Cove, and rendered his answers to Stanley's ceaseless flow of questions upon all conceivable subjects somewhat vague and unreliable. Hilda was walking with them, and divided with Christian the task of supplying her small brother with varied information.

As they were approaching the Hall, Christian discerned two figures upon the smooth lawn, evidently coming towards them. At the same moment Stanley perceived them.

"I see Fred Farrar and Mr. Signor Bruno," he exclaimed.

Christian could not resist glancing over the little fellow's head towards Hilda, though he knew that it was hardly a fair action. Hilda felt the glance but betrayed no sign. She was looking straight in front of her with no change of colour, no glad smile of welcome for her stalwart lover.

"I wonder why she never told me," thought Christian.

Presently he said, in an airy, conversational way: "I did not know Farrar was coming back so—so soon."

He knew that by this early return Farrar was missing an important day of the race-meeting he had been attending, but did not think it necessary to remark upon the fact.

"Yes," replied Hilda. "He does not like to leave his mother for many days together." The acutest ears could have detected no lowering of the voice, no tenderness of thought. She was simply stating a fact; but she might have been speaking of Signor Bruno, so cool and unembarrassed was her tone.

"I am glad he is back," said Christian thoughtlessly. It was a mere stop-gap. The silence was awkward, but he possessed tact enough to have broken it by some better means. Instantly he recognised his mistake, and for a moment he felt as if he were stumbling blindfold through an unknown country. He experienced a sudden sense of vacuity as if his mind were a blank and all words futile. It was now Stanley's turn to break the silence, and unconsciously he did it very well.

"I wonder," he said speculatively, "whether he has brought any chocolate creams?"

Hilda laughed, and the smile was still hovering in her eyes when she greeted the two men. Stanley ran on into the house to open a parcel which Farrar told him was awaiting inspection. It was only natural that Hilda should walk on with the young squire, leaving Bruno and Christian together. The old man lingered obviously, and his companion took the hint readily enough, anticipating some enjoyment.

"To you, Mr. Vellacott," said the Italian, with senile geniality, "to you whose life is spent in London this must be very charming, very peaceful, and—very disorganising, I may perhaps add."

Christian looked at his companion with grave attention.

"It is very enjoyable," he replied simply.

Signor Bruno mentally trimmed his sails, and started off on another tack.

"Our young friends," he said, indicating with a wave of his expressive hand Hilda and Farrar, "are admirably suited to each other. Both young, both handsome, and both essentially English."

"Yes," answered Christian, with a polite display of interest: "and, nevertheless, the Carews were all brought up and educated in France."

"Ah!" observed the old man, stopping to raise the head of a "Souvenir de Malmaison," of which he inhaled the odour with evident pleasure. The little ejaculation, and its accompanying action, were admirably calculated to leave the hearer in doubt as to whether mere surprise was expressed or polite acquiescence in the statement of a known fact.

"Yes," added Christian, deliberately. He also stooped and raised a white rose to his face, thus meeting Signor Bruno upon his own ground. The Italian looked up, and the two men smiled at each other across the rose bush; then they turned and walked on.

"You also know France?" hazarded Signor Bruno.

"Yes; if I were not an Englishman I should choose to be a Frenchman."

"Ah!"

"Yes."

"Now with me," said Signor Bruno frankly, "it is different. If I were not an Italian (which God forbid!) I think—I think, yes, I am sure, I would by choice have been born an Englishman."

"Ah!" observed Christian gravely, and Signor Bruno turned sharply to glance at his face. The young Englishman was gazing straight in front of him earnestly, with no suspicion upon his lips of the incredulous smile which seemed somehow to have lurked there when he last spoke. The Italian turned away dissatisfied, and they walked on a few paces in silence, until he spoke again, reflectively:—

"Yes," he said, "there is a quality in the English character which to me is very praiseworthy. It is a certain directness of purpose. You know what you wish to do, and you proceed calmly to do it, without stopping to consider what your neighbours may think of it. Now with the Gallic races—for I take this virtue of straightforwardness as Teutonic—and in my own country especially, men seek to gain their ends by less open means."

They were now walking up a gentle incline to the house, which was built upon the buried ruins of its ancient predecessor, and Signor Bruno was compelled to pause in order to gain breath.

"But," interposed Christian softly, "you are now talking not so much of the people as of the Church."

Again the Italian looked sharply up, and this time he met his companion's eyes fixed quietly on his face. He shrugged his shoulders deprecatingly and spread out his delicate hands.

"Perhaps you are right," he said, with engaging frankness. "I am afraid you are. But you must excuse a little ill-feeling in a man such as I, with a past such as mine has been, and loving his country as I do."

"I am afraid," continued Christian, "that foreigners find our bluntness very disagreeable and difficult to meet; but I know that they frequently misjudge us on the same account. It is to our benefit, so we cannot complain."

"In what way do we misjudge you?" asked Signor Bruno genially. They were almost on the threshold of the drawing-room window, which stood invitingly open, and from which came the sounds of cups and saucers being mated.

"You give us credit for less intelligence than we in reality possess," said Christian with a smile, as he stood aside to let his companion pass in first.

Whatever influences may have been at work among those congregated at the Hall during the half-hour or so occupied by afternoon tea, no sign appeared upon the surface. Molly as usual led the chorus of laughter. Hilda smiled her sweet "kittenish" smile. Signor Bruno surpassed himself in the relation of innocent little tales, told with a true southern "verve" and spirit, while Fred Farrar's genial laugh filled in the interstices reliably. Grave and unobtrusive, Christian moved about among them. He saw when Molly wanted the hot water, and was invariably the first to detect an empty cup. He laughed softly at Signor Bruno's stories, and occasionally capped them with a better, related in a conciser and equally humorous manner. It was to him that Farrar turned for an encouraging acquiescence when one of his latest Newmarket anecdotes threatened to fall flat, and with it all he found time for an occasional spar with Signor Bruno, just by way of keeping that inquiring gentleman upon his guard.

CHAPTER XI

BURY BLUFF

As Christian walked rapidly across the uneven turf towards the sea at midnight, his thoughts were divided between a schoolboy delight in the adventurous nature of his expedition and an uncomfortable sensation of surreptitiousness. He was not accustomed to this sort of work, and felt remarkably like a thief. If by some mischance his absence was discovered at the Hall, it would be difficult to account for it unless he played the part of a temporary lunatic. Fortunately his window communicated easily enough with the garden by means of a few stone steps, but visitors are not usually in the habit of leaving their bedrooms in order to take the air at midnight. Thinking over these things in his rapid and rather superficial way, he unconsciously quickened his pace.

The night was clear and starlit; the air soft and very pleasant, with a faint breath of freshness from the south-west. The moon, being well upon the wane, would not rise for an hour or more, but the heavens were glowing with the gentler light of stars, and on earth the darkness was of that transparent description which sailors prefer to the brightest moonlight.

Christian Vellacott had worked out most problems in life for himself. Taken as a whole, his solutions had been fairly successful—as successful as those of most men. If his views upon things in general were rather photographic—that is to say, hard, with clearly defined shadows—it was owing to his father's somewhat cynical training and to the absence of a mother's influence. Elderly maiden ladies, with sufficient time upon their hands to manage other people's affairs in addition to their own, complained of his want of sympathy, which may be read in the sense of stating that he neither sought theirs nor asked advice upon questions connected with himself. This self-reliance was the inevitable outcome of his life at home and at the office of the *Beacon*. Admirable as it may be, independence can undoubtedly be carried to an unpleasant excess—unpleasant that is for home life. Women love to see their men-folk a trifle dependent upon them.

Christian was in the midst of a problem as he walked across the tableland that stretched from St. Mary Western to the sea. That problem absorbed more of his attention than the home politics of France; it required a more careful study than any article he had ever penned for the *Beacon*. It gave him greater anxiety than Aunt Judy and Aunt Hester combined. Yet it was comprised in a single word. A single arm could encompass the whole of it. The single word—Hilda.

Leaving the narrow road, he presently struck the little pathway leading to the Cove. Suddenly he stopped, and stood motionless. There—not twenty yards from him—was the still figure of a man. Behind Christian the land rose gradually to some considerable height, so that he stood in darkness, while against the glowing sky the figure of this watcher was clearly defined in hard outline. Instinctively crouching down and seeking the covert of a few low bushes, Christian decreased the intervening distance by a few yards. The faint hope that it might prove to be a coastguard was soon dispelled. The heavy clothing and loose thigh-boots were those of a fisherman. The huge "cache-nez" which lay in coils upon his shoulders and completely protected the neck and throat, was such as is worn by the natives of the Cotes-du-Nord.

The sea boomed forth its melancholy song, far down in the black depths beyond. The tide was high, and the breeze freshening every moment. Christian could have crept up to the man's very feet without being detected. Lying still upon the short, dry grass, he watched for some moments.

From the man's clumsy attitude it was almost possible to divine his slow, mindless nature—for there is expression in the very turn of a man's leg as he stands—and it was easy to see that he was guarding the little path down the cliff to the Cove.

He had been posted there, and evidently meant to stay till called away.

There was only one way, now, to the Cove, and that was down the face of the cliff: the way that Christian had that very afternoon pronounced so hazardous. By day it was dangerous enough; by night it was almost an impossibility.

He crept noiselessly along to the eastward, so that the watcher stood upon the windward side of him, and reaching the brink he peered over into the darkness. Of course he could discern nothing. The sea rose and fell with a monotonous roar; overhead the stars twinkled as merrily as they have twinkled over the strifes of men from century to century.

Quietly he knelt upright and buttoned his coat with some care. Then without a moment's hesitation he crept to the edge and cautiously disappeared into the grim abyss of darkness. Slowly and laboriously he worked his way down, feeling for each foothold in advance. Occasionally he muttered impatiently to himself at the slowness of his progress. He knew that the strata of soft sandstone trended downwards at an easy angle, and with consummate skill took full advantage of his knowledge. Occasionally he was forced to progress sideways with his face to the rock and hands outstretched till his fingers were cramped, and the feeling known as "pins and needles" assailed his arms. Then he would rest for some moments, peering into the darkness below him all the while. Once or twice he dropped a small stone cautiously, holding it at arm's length. When the tiny messenger touched earth soon after leaving his hand, he continued his downward progress. Once, no sound followed for some seconds, and then it was only a distant concussion far down beside the sea. With an involuntary shudder, the climber turned and made his way upwards and sideways again, before venturing to descend once more.

For half an hour he continued his perilous struggle, till his strong arms were stiff and his fingers almost powerless. With marvellous tenacity he held to his purpose. Never since leaving the summit had he been able to rest both hands at once. With a dogged, mechanical endurance which is essentially characteristic of climbers and mountaineers, he lowered himself, inch by inch, foot by foot. Louder and louder sang the sea, as if in derision at his petty efforts, but through his head there rushed another sound infinitely more terrible: a painful, continuous buzz, which seemed to press upon his temples. A dull pain was slowly creeping up the muscles of his neck towards his head. All these symptoms the climber knew. The buzzing in his ears would never cease until he could lie down and breathe freely with every muscle relaxed, every sinew slack. The dull ache would creep up until it reached his brain, and then nothing could save him— no strength of will could prevent his fingers from relaxing their hold.

"Sish—sish, sish—sish!" laughed the waves below. Placidly the stars held on their stately course—each perhaps peopled by millions of its own—young and old, tame and fiery—all pursuing shadows as we do here.

"This is getting serious," muttered Christian, with a pitiful laugh. The perspiration was running down his face, burning his eyes, and dripping from his chin. With straining eyes he peered into the night. Close beneath him there was a ledge of some breadth. It was not flat, but inclined upwards from the face of the cliff, thus forming a shelf of solid stone. For some seconds he stared continuously at this, so as to reduce to a minimum the chance of being mistaken. Then with great caution he slid down the steep incline of smooth stone and landed safely. The glissade lasted but a moment, nevertheless it recalled to his mind a picture which was indelibly stamped in his memory. Years before he had seen a man slide like this, unintentionally, after a false step. Again that picture came to him—unimpressionable as his life had rendered him. Again he saw the glittering expanse of snow, and on it the broad, strong figure of the Vaudois guide sliding down and down, with madly increasing speed—feet foremost, skilful to the last. Again he felt the thrill which men cannot but experience at the sight of a man, or even of a dumb beast, fighting bravely for life. Again he saw the dull gleam of the uplifted ice-axe as the man dealt scientific blow after blow on the frozen snow, attempting to arrest his terrible career. And again in his mind's eye the pure expanse of spotless white lay before him, scarred by one straight streak, marking where the taciturn mountaineer had vanished over the edge of the precipice to his certain doom.

Christian lay like a half-drowned man upon the shelving ledge, slowly realising his position. He calculated that he could not yet be half-way down, and his strength was almost exhausted. Yet, as he lay there, no thought of waiting for daylight, no question of retreat entered his stubborn West-country brain. The exploit still possessed for him the elements of a good joke, to be related thereafter in such a manner as would enforce laughter.

Suddenly—within the softer sound of the sea below—a harsh, grating noise struck his ears. It was to him like the sound made by a nailed boot upon rock. It was as if another were following him down the face of the cliff. In a second he was upon his feet, his weariness a thing forgotten. Overhead, against the starlit sky, he could define the line of rock with its sharp, broken angles and uncouth turns. Not thirty feet above him something was moving. His first feeling was one of intense fear. Every climber knows that it is easier to pass a difficult corner than to stand idle, watching another do it. Slowly the dark form came downwards, and suddenly, with a quick sense of unutterable relief, Christian saw the black line of a tightened rope. When it was barely ten feet above him he saw that the object was no man, but a square case. In a flash of thought he divined what the box contained, and unhesitatingly ran along the ledge towards it. As it descended he seized it with both hands and swung it in towards himself. With pendulum-like motion it descended, and at last touched the rock at his feet. As this took place he grasped the rope with both hands and threw his entire weight upon it, hauling slowly in, hand over hand. So quickly and deftly was this carried out that those lowering overhead were deceived, and continued to pay out the rope slowly. Steadily Christian hauled in, the slack falling in snake-like coils at his feet. Only being able to guess at his position on the cliff, it was no easy matter to calculate how much rope it was necessary to take in in order to carry out the deception.

At length he ceased abruptly, and proceeded to untie the knots round the bale. Then, after the manner of a sailor who is working out of sight with a life-line, he jerked the rope,

Henry Seton Merriman

which immediately began to ascend rapidly and with irregularity. Coil after coil ran easily away, and at last the frayed end passed into the darkness above Christian's head. He stood there watching it, and when it had disappeared he burst into a low hoarse laugh which suddenly broke off into a sickening gurgle, and he fell sideways and backwards on to the box, clutching at it with his nerveless fingers.

When he recovered his faculties his first sensation was one of great cold. The breeze had freshened with the approach of dawn, and blowing full upon him as he lay bathed in perspiration, the effect was like that of a refrigerator. He moved uneasily, and found that he was lying on the stone ledge *outside* the box, from which he had fallen. After a moment, he rose rapidly to his feet as if desirous of dismissing the memory of his own collapse, and turned his attention to the bundle. Beneath the rough covering of canvas, which was not sewn but merely lashed round, it was easy enough to detect the shape of the case.

"What luck—what wonderful luck," he muttered, as he groped round the surface of the bundle.

Indeed it seemed as if everything had arranged itself for his special benefit and advantage.

The three men whose duty it had been to lower the case coiled up their rope and started off on foot inland, after telling the sentinel stationed at the head of the little path to rejoin his boat. This the man was only too willing to do at once. He was a semi-superstitious Breton of no great intelligence, who vastly preferred being afloat in his unsavoury yawl to climbing about unknown rocks in the dark. On the beach, he found his two comrades, to whom he gruffly imparted the information that they were to go on board.

"Had the 'monsieur' said nothing else?"

"No, the 'monsieur' said nothing else."

The Breton intellect is not, as a rule, acute. Like sheep the three men proceeded to carry up from the water's edge Stanley's boat, which was required to carry the heavy case, their own dinghy being too small. This done, they rowed off silently to the yawl, which was rolling lazily in the trough of the sea, a quarter of a mile from the shore. Once on board they were regaled with some choice French profanity from the lips of a large man in a sealskin cap and a dirty woollen muffler. This gentleman they addressed as the "patron," and, with clumsy awe, informed him that they had waited at the same spot as before, but nothing had come, until at length Hoel Grall arrived with instructions from the "monsieur" to go on board. Whereupon further French profanity, followed by unintelligible orders, freely interlarded with embellishments of a forcible tenor.

As the yawl swung slowly round and stood out to sea, Christian turned to climb up Bury Bluff. He found that he had in reality made very little progress in descending. Before leaving the case, he edged it by degrees nearer to the base of the ledge, which would render it invisible from the beach. The ascent was soon accomplished, and after a cautious search he concluded that no one was about, so set off home at a rapid pace.

Before he reached the Hall the light of coming day was already creeping up into the eastern sky. All nature was stirring, refreshed with the balmy dew and coolness of the night. Far up in the higher branches of the Weymouth pines, the wrens were awake, calling to each other with tentative twitter, and pluming themselves the while for another day of sunshine and song.

Henry Seton Merriman

Like a thief Christian hurried on, and creeping into his bedroom window, was soon sleeping the dreamless, forgetful sleep of youth.

By seven o'clock he was awake with all the quick realisation of a Londoner. In the country men wake up slowly, and slowly gather together their senses after an all-sufficing sleep of ten hours. In cities, five, four, or even three are sufficient for the unfatigued body and the restless mind. Men wake up quickly, and are at once in full possession of their faculties. It is, after all, a mere matter of habit.

Christian had slept sufficiently. He rose quite fresh and strong, and presently sat down, coatless to write.

Page after page he wrote, turning each leaf over upon its face as it was completed—never referring back, never hesitating, and only occasionally raising his pen from the paper. Line after line of neat, small writing, quite different from what his friends knew in letters or on envelopes, flowed from his pen. It was his "press" handwriting, plain, rapid, and as legible as print. The punctuation was attended to with singular care: the commas broad and heavy, the colons like the kisses in a child's letter, round and black. Once or twice he smiled as he wrote, and occasionally jerked his head to one side critically as he re-read a sentence.

In less than two hours it was finished. He rose from his seat, and walked slowly to the window. Standing there he gazed thoughtfully across the bare, unlovely tableland towards the sea. He had written many hundreds of pages, all more or less masterly; he had read criticisms upon his own work saying that it was good; and yet he knew that the best—the best he had ever written—lay upon the table behind him. Then he turned and shook the loose leaves together symmetrically. Pensively he counted them. He was young and strong; the world and life lay before him, with their infinite possibilities—their countless opportunities to be seized or left. He looked curiously at the written pages. The writing was his own; the form of every letter was familiar; the heavy punctuation and clean, closely written lines such as the compositor loved to deal with; and while he turned the leaves over he wondered if ever he would do better, for he knew that it was good.

CHAPTER XII

A WARNING WORD

As the breakfast-bell echoed through the house Christian ran downstairs. He met Hilda entering the open door with the letters in her hand.

"Down already?" he exclaimed.

"Yes," she replied incautiously, "I wished to get the letters early."

"And, after all, there is nothing for you?"

"No," she replied. "No, but—"

She stopped suddenly and handed him two letters, which he took slowly, and apparently forgot to thank her, saying nothing at all. There was a peculiar expression of dawning surprise upon his face, and he studied the envelopes in his hand without reading a word of the address. Presently he raised his eyes and glanced at Hilda. She was holding a letter daintily between her two forefingers, cornerwise, and with little puffs of her pouted lips was spinning it round, evidently enjoying the infantile amusement immensely.

He dropped his letters into the pocket of his jacket, and stood aside for her to pass into the house; but she, abruptly ceasing her windmill operations, looked at him with raised eyebrows and stood still.

"Well?" she said interrogatively.

"What?"

"And Mr. Trevetz's answer—I suppose it is one of those letters?"

"Oh yes!" he replied. "I had forgotten my promise."

He took the letters from his pocket, and looked at the addresses again.

"One is from Trevetz," he said slowly, "and the other from Mrs. Strawd."

"Nothing from Mr. Bodery?" asked she indifferently.

He had taken a pencil from his pocket, and, turning, he held Trevetz's letter against the wall while he wrote across it. Without ceasing his occupation, and in a casual way, he replied:—

"No, nothing from Mr. Bodery; so I am free as yet."

"I am very glad," she murmured conventionally.

"And I," he said, turning with a polite smile to hand her the letter.

She took the envelope, and holding it up in both hands examined it critically.

"M-a-x," she read; "how badly it is written! Max—Max Talma—is that it?"

"Yes," he answered gravely, "that is it."

With a little laugh and a shrug of her shoulders she proceeded to open the envelope. It contained nothing but the sketch made upon the fly-leaf of a novel. Christian was watching her face. She continued to smile as she unfolded the paper. Then she suddenly became grave, and handed the open sketch to him. At the foot was written:—

"Max Talma—look out! Avoid him as you would the devil!

"In haste, C.T."

Christian read it, laughed carelessly, and thrust the paper into his pocket. "Trevetz writes in a good forcible style," he said, turning to greet Molly, who came, singing, downstairs at this moment. For an instant her merry eyes assumed a scrutinising, almost anxious look as she caught sight of her sister and Christian standing together.

"Are you just down?" she asked carelessly.

"Yes," answered Christian, still holding her hand.

"I have just come down."

As usual the day's pleasure was all prearranged. A groom rode to the station at Christian's request with a large envelope on which was printed Mr. Bodery's name and address. This was to be given to the guard, who would in his turn hand it to a special messenger at Paddington, and the editor of the *Beacon* would receive it by four o'clock in the afternoon.

The day was fine, with a fresh breeze, and the programme of pleasure was satisfactorily carried out. But with sunset the wind freshened into a brisk gale, and heavy clouds rolled upwards from the western horizon. This was the first suggestion of autumn, the first sigh of dying summer. The lamps were lighted a few minutes earlier that night, and the family assembled in the drawing-room soon after dark, although the windows were left open for those who wished to pass in and out.

Mrs. Carew's grey head was, as usual, bent over some simple needlework, while Molly sat near at hand. According to her wont she also was busy, while around her the work lay strewed in picturesque disorder. Sidney was reading in his own room—reading for a vague law examination which always appeared to have been lately postponed till next October.

Christian was seated at the piano, playing by snatches and turning over the brown leaves of some very old music, unearthed from a lumber-room by Mrs. Carew for his benefit. He waited for no thanks or comment; sometimes he read a few bars only, sometimes a page. He appeared to have forgotten that he had an audience. Presently he rose, leaving the music in disorder. Hilda had been called away some time before by an old village woman requiring medicaments for unheard-of symptoms. Christian looked slowly round the room, then raising his hand he dexterously caught a huge moth which had flown past his face.

As he crossed the room towards the open window, with a view of liberating the moth, a low whistle reached his ear. The refrain was that of the familiar "retraite." Hilda had evidently gone out to the moat by another door. Bowing his head, he passed between the muslin curtains and disappeared in the darkness. The sound of his footsteps died away almost immediately amidst the rustle of branch and leaf already crisp with approaching change.

It was Stanley's bed-time. Mechanically, Molly kissed her brother, continuing to work thoughtfully.

In a few minutes the door opened and Hilda entered the room. She came up to the table, and standing there with her hands resting upon some pieces of Molly's work, she gave a graphic description of the old woman's complaints and maladies. She stood quite close to Molly, and told her story to Mrs. Carew merrily, failing to notice that her sister had ceased sewing, and was listening with a surprised look in her eyes. When the symptoms had been detailed and laughed over, Hilda turned quietly and passed out into the garden. With fearless familiarity she ran lightly down the narrow pathway towards the moat, but no signal-whistle greeted her. The leaves rustled and whispered overhead; the water lapped and gurgled at her feet, but there was no sign or sound of life.

Silent and motionless she stood, a tall fair form clad in white, amidst the universal, darkness. So silent and so still that it might have been the shade of some fair maid of bygone years mourning the loss of her true knight, who in all the circumstances of war had crossed that same moat never to return.

Presently a sudden feeling of loneliness, a new sense of fear, came over Hilda. All around was so forbidding. The water at her feet was so black and mysterious. She gave a soft low whistle identical with that which had called Christian out twenty minutes before, but it remained unanswered, and through the rustling leaves she sped towards the house. From the open window a glow of rosy light shone forth upon the flowers, imparting to all alike a pallid pink, and dimly defining the grey tree-trunks across the lawn. As Hilda stepped between the curtains, the servants entered the drawing-room in solemn Indian file for evening prayers.

Mrs. Carew looked up from the Bible which lay open before her, and said to Hilda:—

"Where is Christian?"

"I don't know, mother; he is not in the garden," answered the girl, crossing the room to her own particular chair.

Sidney rose from his seat, and going to the window, sent his loud clear whistle away into the night. His broad figure remained motionless for some minutes, almost filling up the window; then he silently resumed his seat.

Mrs. Carew smoothed down the silken book-marker, and began reading in a low voice. It is to be feared that the Psalmist's words of joy were not heard with understanding ears that night. A short prayer followed; softly and melodiously Mrs. Carew asked for blessings upon the bowed heads around her, and the servants left the room.

"Have you not seen Christian since you went to see Mrs. Sender, Hilda?" asked Molly, at once.

"No," replied Hilda, arranging the music into something like order upon the piano.

"He went out about half an hour ago, in answer to your whistle."

Hilda turned her head as if about to reply hastily, but checked herself, and resumed her task of setting the music in order.

"How could I whistle," she asked gently, "when I was in the kitchen doling out medicated cotton-wool to Mrs. Sender?"

Molly looked puzzled.

"Did *you* whistle, Sidney?" she asked.

"I—no; I was half-asleep over a law-book in my own room."

"I expect he has gone for a stroll, and forgotten the time," suggested Mrs. Carew reassuringly, as she sat down to work again.

"But what about the whistle; are you sure you heard it, Molly?" asked Hilda, speaking rather more quickly than was habitual with her. She walked towards the window and drew aside the curtain, keeping her back turned towards the room.

"Yes," answered Molly uneasily. "Yes—I heard it, and so did he, for he went out at once."

Sidney stood awkwardly with his shoulder against the mantelpiece, listening in a half-hearted way to his sisters' conversation. With a heavy jerk he threw himself upright and slowly crossed the room. He stood for some moments immediately behind Hilda without touching her. Then he raised his hand and with gentle, almost caressing pressure round her waist, he made her step aside so that he could pass out. He was a singularly undemonstrative man, rarely giving way to what he considered the weakness of a caress. Fortunately, however, for their own happiness, his women-folk understood him, and especially between himself and Hilda there existed a peculiar unspoken sympathy.

In the ordinary way he would have mumbled—

"Le'mme out!"

On this occasion he touched her waist gently, and the caress almost startled her. It seemed like a confession that he shared the vague anxiety which she concealed so well.

With the charity of maternal love, which is by no means so blind as is generally supposed, Mrs. Carew often said of Sidney that he invariably rose to the occasion; and Mrs. Carew's statements were as a rule correct. His slowness was partly assumed; his indifference was a mere habit. The assumption of the former saved him infinite worry and responsibility; the habit of indifference did away with the necessity of coming to a decision upon general questions. This state of mind may, to townsmen, be incomprehensible. Certain it is that such as are in that condition are not found among the foremost dwellers in cities. But in the country it is a different matter. Such cases are only too common, and (without breath of disparagement) they are usually to be found in households where one man finds himself among several women—be the latter mother and sisters, or wife and sisters-in-law.

The man may be a thorough sportsman, he may be an excellent landlord and a popular squire, but within his own doors he is overwhelmed. Chivalry bids him give way to the wishes and desires of some woman or other, and if he be a sportsman he is necessarily chivalrous. When one is tired after a long day in the saddle or with a gun, it is so much easier to acquiesce and philosophically persuade oneself that the matter is not worth airing an adverse opinion over. This is the beginning, and if any beginning can look forward to great endings it is that of a habit.

It would appear that Sidney Carew's occasion had come at last, for once outside the window he changed to a different being. The lazy slouch vanished from his movements, his eyes lost their droop, and he held his head erect.

He made his way rapidly to the stable, and there, without the knowledge of the grooms, he obtained a large hurricane-lamp, lighted it, and returned towards the house. From the window Hilda saw him pass down a little path towards the moat, with the lamp swinging at his side, while the shadows waved backwards and forwards across the lawn.

The mind is a strange storehouse. However long a memory may have been warehoused there, deep down beneath piles of other remembrances and conceits, it is generally to be found at the top when the demand comes, ready for use—for good or evil. A dim recollection was resuscitated in Sidney's mind. An unauthenticated nursery tale of a departing guest leaving with a word of joy upon his lips and warm comfort in his heart, turning from the glowing doorway and walking down the little pathway straight into the moat.

Christian, however, was an excellent swimmer; he knew every inch of the pathway, every stone round the moat. That he should have been drowned in ten feet of clear water, with an easy landing within ten yards, seemed the wildest impossibility. Of course such things have happened, but Christian Vellacott was essentially wide awake, and unlikely to come to mishap through his own carelessness. Of all these things Sidney thought as he walked rapidly towards the moat, and in particular he pondered over Molly's statement that she had heard Hilda whistle. This had met with flat denial from Hilda, and Sidney, with brotherly candour, could only arrive at the conclusion that Molly had been mistaken. He would not give way to the least suggestion of anxiety even in his own mind. After all Christian would probably come in with some simple explanation and a laugh for their fears. It often happens thus, as we must all know. The moments so long and dreary for the watcher, whose imagination gains more and more power as the time passes, slip away unheeded by the awaited, who treats the matter with a laugh or, at the most, a few conventional words of sympathy.

Sidney stood at the edge of the water and threw the beams of light across the rippling surface. Mechanically he followed the ray as it swept from end to end of the moat, and presently, without heeding, he turned his attention to the stones at his feet. A gleam of reflected light caught his passing gaze, and he stooped to examine the cause more closely.

The smooth stonework was wet; in fact the water was standing in little pools upon it. Round these there were circles of dampness, showing that evaporation was taking place. The water had not lain there long. A man falling into the moat would have thrown up splashes such as these; in no other way could they be plausibly accounted for. Sidney stood erect. Again he held the lamp over the gleaming water, half fearing to see something. His lips had quite suddenly become dry and parched, and there was an uncomfortable throb in his throat. Suddenly he heard a rustle behind him, and before he could draw back Hilda was at his side. She slipped her hand through his arm, and by the slightest pressure drew him away from the moat.

"You know—Sid—he could swim perfectly," she said persuasively.

He made no answer, but walked slowly by her side, swinging the lamp backwards and forwards as a schoolboy swings his satchel. Thus he gained time to moisten his lips and render speech possible.

Henry Seton Merriman

Together they went round the grounds, but no sign or vestige of Christian did they discover. A pang of remorse came to Hilda as she touched her brother's strong arm. Ever since Christian's arrival she remembered that Sidney had been somewhat neglected, or only remembered when his services were required. Christian had indeed been attentive to him, but Hilda felt that their friendship was not what it used to be. The young journalist in his upward progress had left the slow-thinking country squire behind him. All they had in common belonged to the past; and, for Christian, the past was of small importance compared to the present. She recollected that during the last fortnight everything had been arranged with a view to giving pleasure to herself, Molly, and Christian, without heed to Sidney's inclinations. By word or sign he had never shown his knowledge of this; he had never implied that his existence or opinion was of any great consequence. She remembered even that such pleasures as Christian had shared with Sidney—pleasures after his own heart, sailing, shooting, and fishing—had been undertaken at Christian's instigation or suggestion, and eagerly welcomed by Sidney.

And now, at the first suspicion of trouble, she turned instinctively to her brother for the help and counsel which were so willingly and modestly accorded.

"Sidney," she said, "did he ever speak to you of his work?"

"No," he replied slowly; "no, I think not."

"He has been rather worried over those disturbances in Paris, I think, and—and—I suppose he has never said anything to you about Signor Bruno?"

"Signor Bruno!" said Sidney, repeating the name in some surprise. "No, he has never mentioned his name to me."

"He does not like him—"

"Neither do I."

"But you never told me—Sid!"

"No," he replied simply: "there was nothing to be gained by it!"

This was lamentably true, and Hilda felt that it was so, although her brother had no thought of posing as a martyr.

"Christian," she continued softly, "distrusted him for some reason. He knows something of his former life, and told me a short time ago that Bruno was not his name at all. This morning Christian received a letter from Carl Trevetz, whom we knew in Paris, you will remember, saying that Signor Bruno's real name was Max Talma, also warning Christian to avoid him."

"Is this all you know?" asked Sidney, in a peculiarly quiet tone.

"That is all I know," she replied. "But it has struck me that—that this may have something to do with Signor Bruno. I mean—is it not probable that Christian may have discovered something which caused him to go away suddenly without letting Bruno know of his departure?"

Sidney thought of the water at the edge of the moat. The incident might prove easy enough of explanation, but at the moment it was singularly unreconcilable with Hilda's comforting explanation. And again, the recollection of the signal-whistle heard by Molly was unwelcome.

"Yes," he replied vaguely. "Yes, it may."

He was, by nature and habit, a slow thinker, and Hilda was running away from him a little; but he was, perhaps, surer than she.

"I am convinced, Sidney," she continued, "that Christian connects Signor Bruno in some manner with the disturbances in France. It seems very strange that an old man buried alive in a small village should have it in his power to do so much harm."

"A man's power of doing harm is practically unlimited," he said slowly, still wishing to gain time.

"Yes, but he has always appeared so childlike and innocent."

"That is exactly what I disliked about him," said Sidney.

"Then do you think he has been deliberately deceiving us all along?" she asked.

"Not necessarily," was the tolerant reply. "You must remember that Christian is essentially a politician. He does not suspect Bruno of anything criminal; his suspicions are merely political; and it may be that Bruno's doings, whatever they appear to be now, may in the future be looked upon as the actions of a hero. Politics are impersonal, and Signor Bruno is only known to us socially."

Hilda could not see the matter in this light. No woman could have been expected to do so.

"I suppose," she said presently, "that Signor Bruno is a political intriguer."

"I expect so," replied her brother.

They were walking slowly up the broad path towards the house, having given up the idea of searching for Christian or calling him.

"Then," continued Sidney, "you think it is likely that he has gone off to see Bruno, or to watch him?"

"I think so."

"That is the only reasonable explanation I can think of," he said gravely and doubtfully, for he was still thinking of the moat.

They entered the house, and to Mrs. Carew and Molly their explanation was imparted. It was received somewhat doubtfully, especially by Molly. However, the farce had to be kept up—and do we not act in similar comedies every day?

CHAPTER XIII

A NIGHT WATCH

Cheerfulness is, thank goodness, infectious. The watchers at the Hall that night made a great show of light-heartedness. Sidney had risen to the occasion. He laughed at the idea of anything serious having happened to Christian, and his confidence gradually spread and gained new strength. Molly, however, was apparently beyond its influence. With her perpetual needle-work in her hands she sat beneath the lamp and worked rapidly. Occasionally she glanced towards Hilda, but contributed nothing to the explanations forthcoming from all quarters.

Hilda was also working; slowly, however, and with marvellous care. She was engaged upon a more artistic production than ever came from Molly's work-basket. Once she consulted Mrs. Carew about the colour of a skein of wool, but otherwise showed no inclination to avoid topics in any manner connected with Christian, despite the fact that these were obviously distasteful to her family. In all that she said, indifference was blended in a singular way with imperturbable cheerfulness.

Thus they waited until after midnight, pretending bravely to work and read as if there were no such feeling as suspense in the human heart. Then Mrs. Carew persuaded the young people to go to bed. She had letters to write, and would not be ready for hours. If Christian did not appear by the time that she was sleepy, she would wake Sidney. After all, she acted her part better than they. She was old at it—they were new. She was experienced in stage-craft and made her points skilfully; above all, she did not over-act.

The three young people kissed their mother and left the room, assuring each other of their conviction that they would find Christian at the breakfast table next morning. Molly's room was at the head of the stairs. With a smile and a nod she closed her door while Hilda and Sidney walked slowly down the long passage together. Arrived at the end, Sidney kissed his sister. She turned the handle of her door and stood with her back to him for a few moments without entering the room, as if to give him an opportunity of speaking if he had aught to say. He stood awkwardly behind her, gazing mechanically at her hair, which reflected the light from the candle that he was holding all awry, while the wax dripped upon the carpet.

"It will be all right, Hilda," he said unevenly, "never fear!"

"Yes, dear, I know it will," she replied.

And then she passed into the room without closing the door, and he walked on with loudly-creaking shoes.

Hilda crossed her room and set the candle upon the dressing-table. She waited there till Sidney's footsteps had ceased, and then she turned and walked uprightly to the door, which she closed. She looked round the room with a strange, vacant look in her eyes, and then she made her way unsteadily towards the bed, where she lay staring at the wavering candle and its reflection in the mirror behind until daylight came to make its flame grow pale and yellow.

There were four watchers in the house that night. Downstairs, Mrs. Carew sat by the shaded lamp in her upright armchair. She was not writing, but had re-opened the large black Bible. Molly was courting sleep in vain, having resolutely blown out her candle. Sidney made no pretence. He was fully dressed, and seated at his rarely-used writing-table. Before him lay a telegraph-form bearing nothing but the address –

C.C. BODERY, *Beacon* Office, Fleet St., London.

He was gazing mechanically at the blank spaces waiting to be filled in, and through his mind was passing and repassing the same question that occupied the thoughts of his mother and sisters. What could be the explanation of the whistle heard by Molly? The want of this alone sufficed to overthrow the most ingenious of consolatory explanations. All four looked at it from different points of view, and to each the signal-whistle calling Christian into the garden was an insurmountable barrier to every explanation.

Before it was wholly light Hilda moved wearily to the window. She threw it open, and sat with arms resting on the sill and her chin upon her hands, mechanically noting the wonders of the sunrise. A soft white mist was rising from the thick pasture, wholly obscuring the sea and filling the atmosphere with a damp chill. Seated there in her thin evening dress, she showed no sign of feeling the cold. At times physical pain is almost a pleasure. The glistening damp rested on every blade of grass, on every leaf and twig, while the many webs stood whitely against the shadows, some hanging like festoons from tree to tree, others floating out in mid-air without apparent reason or support. In and among the branches lingered little secret deposits of mist waiting the sun's warmth to melt them all away.

The suppressed creak of Sidney's door attracted Hilda's attention, but she did not move, merely turning to look at her own door as her brother passed it with awkward caution. A dull instinct told her that he was going to the moat again. Presently he passed beneath her window and across the dewy lawn, leaving a trailing mark upon the grass. The whole picture seemed suddenly to be familiar to her. She had lived through it all before—not in another life, not in years gone by, not in a dream, but during the last few hours.

The air was very still, and she could hear the clank of the chain as Sidney unmoored the old punt, rarely used except by the gardener to clean the moat when the weeds died down in autumn. The quiet was rendered more remarkable by the suddenness of its advent. All night it had been blowing a wild gale, which dropped at dawn, and from the soft land the mist rose instantly.

Prompted by a vague desire to be doing something, Hilda presently turned from the window, and, after a moment's indecision, chose from the shelf a novel fresh from the brain of the king of writers. With it she returned to her low chair and listlessly turned over the leaves for some moments. She raised her head and sought in vain the tiny form of a lark trilling out his morning hymn far up in the blue sky. Then she resolutely commenced to read uninterruptedly.

She read on until Sidney's firm step upon the gravel beneath the window roused her. A minute later he knocked softly at her door. The water was glistening on his rough shooting-boots as he entered the room, and upon the brown leather gaiters there was a deeper shade showing where the wet grass had brushed against his legs. His honest, immobile face showed but little surprise at the sight of Hilda still in evening dress, but she saw that he noticed it.

She rose from her low chair and laid aside the book, but no sort of greeting passed between them.

"I have been all round again," he said quietly, "by daylight, and—and of course there is no sign."

She nodded her head, but did not speak.

"I have been thinking," he continued somewhat shyly, "as to what is to be done. First of all, no one must be told. Mother, Molly, you, and I know it, and we must keep it to ourselves. We will tell Stanley that Christian has gone off suddenly in connection with his work, and the same excuse will do for the neighbours and servants. I will telegraph this morning to Mr. Bodery, the editor of the *Beacon*, and await his instructions. I think that is all that we can do in the meantime."

She was standing close to him, with one hand on the table, resting upon the closed volume of "Vanity Fair," but instead of looking at her brother she was gazing calmly out of the window.

"Yes," she murmured, "I think that is all that we can do in the meantime."

Sidney moved awkwardly as if about to leave the room, but hesitated still.

"Have you nothing to suggest?" he asked. "Do you think I am acting rightly?"

She was still looking out of the window—still standing motionless near the table with her hand upon Thackeray's "Vanity Fair."

"Yes," she replied; "everything you suggest seems wise and prudent."

"Then will you see mother and Molly in their rooms and forewarn them to say nothing—nothing that may betray our anxiety?"

"Yes, I will see them."

Sidney walked heavily to the door. Grasping the handle, he turned round once more.

"It is nearly half-past seven," he said, with more confidence in his tone, "and Mary will soon be coming to awake you. It would not do for her to see you in that dress."

Hilda turned and raised her eyes to his face.

"No," she said, with a sudden smile; "I will change it at once."

Henry Seton Merriman

CHAPTER XIV

FOILED

When Mr. Bodery opened the door of the room upon the second floor of the tall house in the Strand that morning, he found Mr. Morgan seated at the table surrounded by proof-sheets, with his coat off and shirt-sleeves tucked up. The subeditor of the *Beacon* was in reality a good hard worker in his comfortable way, and there was little harm in his desire that the world should be aware of his industry.

"Good morning, Morgan," said the editor, hanging up his hat.

"Morning," replied the other genially, but without looking up. Before Mr. Bodery had seated himself, however, the sub-editor laid his hand with heavy approval upon the odoriferous proof-sheet before him, and looked up.

"This article of Vellacott's is first-rate," he said. "By Jove! sir, he drops on these holy fathers—lets them have it right and left. The way he has worked out the thing is wonderful, and that method of putting everything upon supposition is a grand idea. It suggests how the thing *could* be done upon the face of it, while the initiated will see quickly enough that it means to show how the trick was in reality performed—ha, ha!"

"Yes," replied Mr. Bodery absently. He was glancing at the pile of letters that lay upon his desk. There were among them one or two telegrams, and these he put to one side while he took up each envelope in succession to examine the address, throwing it down again unopened. At length he turned again to the telegrams, and picked up the top one. He was about to tear open the envelope when there was a sharp knock at the door.

"'M'in!" said Mr. Morgan sharply, and at the same moment the silent door was thrown open. The diminutive form of the boy stood in the aperture.

"Gentleman to see you, sir," he said, with great solemnity.

"What name?" asked Mr. Bodery.

"Wouldn't give his name, sir—said you didn't know it, sir."

Even this small office-boy was allowed his quantum of discretionary power. It rested with him whether an unknown visitor was admitted or politely dismissed to a much greater extent than any one suspected. Into his manner of announcing a person he somehow managed to convey his opinion as to whether it was worth the editor's time to admit him or not, and he invariably received Mr. Bodery's "Tell him I'm engaged" with a little nod of mutual understanding which was intensely comprehensive.

On this occasion, his manner said, "Have him in have him in, my boy, and you will find it worth your while'"

"Show him in," said Mr. Bodery.

The nameless gentleman must have been at the door upon the boy's heels, for no sooner had the words left Mr.

Bodery's lips than a tall, dark form slid into the room. So noiseless and rapid were this gentleman's movements that there is no other word with which to express his mode of progression.

He made a low bow, and shot up erect again with startling rapidity. He then stood quietly waiting until the door had closed behind the small boy, who, after having punctiliously expectorated upon a silver coin which had found its way into the palm of his hand, proceeded to slide down the balustrade upon his waistcoat.

It often occurred that strangers addressed themselves to Mr. Morgan when ushered into the little back room, under the impression that he was the editor of the *Beacon*. Not so, however, this tall, clean-shaven person. He fixed his peculiar light-blue eyes upon Mr. Bodery, and, with a slight inclination, said suavely—

"This, sir, is, I believe, your printing day?"

"It is, sir, and a busy day with us," replied the editor, with no great warmth of manner.

"Would it be possible now," inquired the stranger conversationally, "at this late hour, to remove a printed article and substitute another?"

At these words Mr. Morgan ceased making some pencil notes with which he was occupied, and looked up. He met the stranger's benign glance and, while still looking at him, deliberately turned over all the proof-sheets before him, leaving no printed matter exposed to the gaze of the curious.

Mr. Bodery had in the meantime consulted his watch.

"Yes," he replied, with dangerous politeness. "There would still be time to do so if necessary—at the sacrifice of some hundredweight of paper."

"How marvellously organised your interesting paper must be!"

Dead silence. Most men would have felt embarrassed, but no sign of such feeling was forthcoming from any of the three. It is possible that the dark gentleman with the sky-blue eyes wished to establish a sense of embarrassment with a view to the furtherance of his own ends. If so, his attempt proved lamentably abortive. Mr. Bodery sat with his plump hands resting on the table, and looked contemplatively up into the stranger's face. Mr. Morgan was scribbling pencil notes on a tablet.

"The truth is," explained the stranger at length, "that a friend of mine, who is unfortunately ill in bed this morning—"

(Mr. Bodery did not look in the least sympathetic, though he listened attentively.)

" ... has received a telegram from a gentleman who I am told is on the staff of your journal—Mr. Vellacott. This gentleman wishes to withdraw, for correction, an article he has sent to you. He states that he will re-write the article, with certain alterations, in time for next week's issue."

Mr. Bodery's face was pleasantly illegible.

"May I see the telegram?" he asked politely.

"Certainly!"

The stranger produced and handed to the editor a pink paper

Henry Seton Merriman

covered with faint black writing.

"You will see at the foot this—Mr. Vellacott's reason for not wiring to you direct. He wished my friend to be here before the printers got to work this morning; but owing to this unfortunate illness—"

"I am afraid you are too late, sir," interrupted Mr. Bodery briskly. "The press is at work—"

"My friend instructed me," interposed the stranger in his turn, "to make you rather a difficult proposition. If a thousand pounds will compensate for the loss incurred by the delay of issue, and defray the expense of paper spoilt—I—I have that amount with me."

Mr. Bodery did not display the least sign of surprise, merely shaking his head with a quiet smile. Mr. Morgan, however, laid aside his pencil, and placed his elbow upon the proof-sheets before him.

The stranger then stepped forward with a sudden change of manner.

"Mr. Bodery," he said, in a low, concentrated voice, "I will give you five hundred pounds for a proof copy of Mr. Vellacott's article."

A dead silence of some moments' duration followed this remark. Mr. Morgan raised his head and looked across the table at his chief. The editor made an almost imperceptible motion with his eyebrows in the direction of the door.

Then Mr. Morgan rose somewhat heavily from his chair, with a hand upon either arm, after the manner of a man who is beginning to put on weight rapidly. He went to the door, opened it, and, turning towards the stranger, said urbanely:

"Sir—the door!"

This kind invitation was not at once accepted.

"You refuse my offers?" said the stranger curtly, without deigning to notice the sub-editor.

Mr. Bodery had turned his attention to his letters, of which he was cutting open the envelopes, one by one, with a paper-knife, without, however, removing the contents. He looked up.

"To-morrow morning," he said, "you will be able to procure a copy from any stationer for the trifling sum of sixpence."

Then the stranger walked slowly past Mr. Morgan out of the room.

"A curse on these Englishmen!" he muttered, as he passed down the narrow staircase. "If I could only see the article I could tell whether it is worth resorting to stronger measures or not. However, that is Talma's business to decide, not mine."

Mr. Morgan closed the door of the small room and resumed his seat. He then laughed aloud, but Mr. Bodery did not respond.

"That's one of them," observed Mr. Morgan comprehensively.

"Yes," replied the editor, "a dangerous customer. I do not like a blue-chinned man."

"I was not much impressed with his diplomatic skill."

"No; but you must remember that he had difficult cards to play. No doubt his information was of the scantiest, and—we are not chickens, Morgan."

"No," said Mr. Morgan, with a little sigh. He turned to the revision of the proof-sheets again, while the editor began opening and reading his telegrams.

"This is a little strong," exclaimed Mr. Morgan, after a few moments of silence, broken only by the crackle of paper. "Just listen here:—

"'It simply comes to this—the General of the Society of Jesus is an autocrat in the worst sense of the word. He holds within his fingers the wires of a vast machine moving with little friction and no noise. No farthest corner of the world is entirely beyond its influence; no political crisis passes that is not hurried on or restrained by its power. Unrecognised, unseen even, and often undreamt of, the vast Society does its work. It is not for us who live in a broad-minded, tolerant age to judge too harshly. It is not for us to say that the Jesuits are unscrupulous and treacherous. Let us be just and give them their due. They are undoubtedly earnest in their work, sincere in their belief, true to their faith. But it is for us to uphold our own integrity. We are accused—as a nation—of stirring up the seeds of rebellion, of crime and bloodshed in the heart of another country. Our denial is considered insufficient; our evidence is ignored. There remains yet to us one mode of self-defence. After denying the crime (for crime it is in humane and political sense) we can turn and boldly lay it upon those whom its results would chiefly benefit: the Roman Catholic Church in general—the Society of Jesus in particular. We have endeavoured to show how the followers of Ignatius Loyola could have brought about the present crisis in France; the extent to which they would benefit by a religious reaction is patent to the most casual observer; let the Government of England do the rest.'"

Mr. Bodery was, however, not listening. He was staring vacantly at a telegram which lay spread out upon the table.

"What is the meaning of this?" he exclaimed huskily.

The sub-editor looked up sharply, with his pen poised in the air. Then Mr. Bodery read:

"Is Vellacott with you? Fear something wrong. Disappeared from here last night."

Mr. Morgan moved in his seat, stretching one arm out, while he pensively rubbed his clean-shaven chin and looked critically across the table.

"Who is it from?" he asked.

"Sidney Carew, the man he is staying with."

They remained thus for some moments; the editor looking at the telegram with a peculiar blank expression in his eyes; Mr. Morgan staring at him while he rubbed his chin thoughtfully with outspread finger and thumb. In the lane beneath the window some industrious housekeeper was sweeping her doorstep with aggravating monotony; otherwise there was no sound.

At length Mr. Morgan rose from his seat and walked slowly to the window. He stood gazing out upon the smoke-begrimed roofs and crooked chimneys. Between his lips he held his pen, and his hands were thrust deeply into his trouser pockets. It was on that spot and in that attitude that he usually thought out his carefully written weekly article upon "Home Affairs." He was still there when the editor touched a small gong which stood on the table at his side. The silent door instantly opened, and the supernaturally sharp boy stood on the threshold grimly awaiting his orders.

"Bradshaw."

"Yess'r," replied the boy, closing the door. His inventive mind had conceived a new and improved method of going downstairs. This was to lie flat on his back upon the balustrade with a leg dangling on either side. If the balance was correct, he slid down rapidly and shot out some feet from the bottom, as he had, from an advantageous point of view on Blackfriars Bridge, seen sacks of meal shoot from a Thames warehouse into the barge beneath. If, however, he made a miscalculation, he inevitably rolled off sideways and landed in a heap on the floor. Either result appeared to afford him infinite enjoyment and exhilaration. On this occasion he performed the feat with marked success.

"Guv'nor's goin' on the loose—wants the railway guide," he confided to a small friend in the printing interest whom he met as he was returning with the required volume.

"Suppose you'll be sitten' upstairs now, then," remarked the black-fingered one with fine sarcasm. Whereupon there followed a feint—a desperate lunge to one side, a vigorous bob of the head, and a resounding bang with the railway guide in the centre of the sarcastic youth's waistcoat.

Having executed a strategic movement, and a masterly retreat up the stairs, the small boy leant over the banisters and delivered himself of the following explanation:

"I 'it yer one that time. Don't do it agin. *Good* morning, sir."

Mr. Bodery turned the flimsy leaves impatiently, stopped,

looked rapidly down a column, and, without raising his eyes from the railway guide, tore a telegraph form from the handle of a drawer at his side. Then he wrote in a large clear style:

"Will be with you at five o'clock. Invent some excuse for V.'s absence. On no account give alarm to authorities."

The sharp boy took the telegram from the editor's hand with an expression of profound respect upon his wicked features.

"Go down to Banks," said Mr. Bodery, "ask him to let me have two copies of the foreign policy article in ten minutes."

When the silent door was closed, Mr. Morgan wheeled round upon his heels, and gazed meditatively at his superior.

"Going down to see these people?" he asked, with a jerk of his head towards the West.

"Yes, I am going by the eleven-fifteen."

"I have been thinking," continued the sub-editor, "we may as well keep the printing-office door locked to-day. That slippery gentleman with the watery eyes meant business, or I am very much mistaken. I'll just send upstairs for Bander to go on duty at the shop door to-day as well as to-morrow; I think we shall have a big sale this week."

Mr. Bodery rose from his seat and began brushing his faultless hat.

"Yes," he replied; "do that. It would be very easy to get at the machinery. Printers are only human!"

"Machinery is ready enough to go wrong when nobody

wishes it," murmured Mr. Morgan vaguely, as he sat down at the table and began setting the scattered papers in order.

Mr. Bodery and his colleagues were in the habit of keeping at the office a small bag, containing the luggage necessary for a few nights in case of their being suddenly called away. This expedient was due to Christian Vellacott's forethought.

The editor now proceeded to stuff into his bag sundry morning newspapers and a large cigar case. Telegraph forms, pen, ink, and foolscap paper were already there.

"I say, Bodery," said the sub-editor with grave familiarity, "it seems to me that you are taking much too serious a view of this matter. Vellacott is as wide awake as any man, and it always struck me that he was very well able to take care of himself."

"I have a wholesome dread of men who use religion as a means of justification. A fanatic is always dangerous."

"A sincere fanatic," suggested the sub-editor.

"Exactly so; and a sincere fanatic in the hands of an agitator is the very devil. That is whence these fellows got their power. Half of them are fanatics and the other half hypocrites."

Mr. Bodery had now completed his preparations, and he held out his plump hand, which the subeditor grasped.

"I hope," said the latter, "that you will find Vellacott at the station to meet you—ha, ha!"

"I hope so."

"If," said Mr. Morgan, following the editor to the door—"if he turns up here, I will wire to Carew and to you, care of the station-master."

CHAPTER XV

BOOKS

The London express rolled with stately deliberation into Brayport station. Mr. Bodery folded up his newspapers, reached down his bag from the netting, and prepared to alight. The editor of the *Beacon* had enjoyed a very pleasant journey, despite broiling sun and searching dust. He knew the possibilities of a first-class smoking-carriage—how to regulate the leeward window and chock off the other with a wooden match borrowed from the guard.

He stepped from the carriage with the laboured sprightliness of a man past the forties, and a moment later Sidney Carew was at his side.

"Mr. Bodery?"

"The same. You are no doubt Mr. Carew?"

"Yes. Thanks for coming. Hope it didn't inconvenience you?"

"Not at all," replied the editor, breaking his return ticket.

"D—n!" said Sidney suddenly.

He was beginning to rise to the occasion. He was one of those men who are usually too slack to burthen their souls with a refreshing expletive.

"What is the matter?" inquired Mr. Bodery gravely.

"There is a man," explained Sidney hurriedly, "getting out of the train who is coming to stay with us. I had forgotten his existence. *Don't* look round!"

Mr. Bodery was a Londoner. He did not look round. Nine out of ten country-bred people would have indulged in a stare.

"Is this all your luggage?" continued Sidney abruptly. He certainly was rising.

"Yes."

"Then come along. We'll bolt for it. He'll have to get a fly, and that means ten minutes' start if the porter is not officious and mulls things."

They hurried out of the station and clambered into the dog-cart. Sidney gathered up the reins.

"Hang it," he exclaimed. "What bad luck! There is a fly waiting. It is never there when you want it."

Mr. Bodery looked between the shafts.

"You need not be afraid of that fly," he said.

"No—come up, you brute!"

Mr. Bodery turned carelessly to put his bag in the back of

the cart.

"Let him have it," he exclaimed in a low voice. "Your friend sees you, but he does not know that you have seen him. He is pointing you out to the station-master."

As he spoke the cart swung round the gate-post of the station yard, nearly throwing him out, and Sidney's right hand felt for the whip-socket.

"There," he said, "we are safe. I think I can manage that fly."

Mr. Bodery settled himself and drew the dust-cloth over his chubby knees.

"Now," he said, "tell me all about Vellacott."

Sidney did so.

He gave a full and minute description of events previous to Christian Vellacott's disappearance, omitting nothing. The relation was somewhat disjointed, somewhat vague in parts, and occasionally incoherent. The narrator repeated himself—hesitated—blurted out some totally irrelevant fact, and finished up with a vague supposition (possessing a solid basis of truth) expressed in doubtful English. It suited Mr. Bodery admirably. In telling all about Vellacott, Sidney unconsciously told all about Mrs. Carew, Molly, Hilda, and himself. When he reached the point in his narration telling how Vellacott had been attracted into the garden, he became extremely vague and his style notably colloquial. Tell the story how he would, he felt that he could not prevent Mr. Bodery from drawing his own inferences. Young ladies are not in the habit of whistling for youthful members of the opposite sex. Few of them master the labial art, which perhaps accounts for much. Sidney Carew was conscious that his style lacked grace and finish.

Mr. Bodery did draw his own inferences, but the countenance into which Sidney glanced at intervals was one of intense stolidity.

"Well, I confess I cannot make it out—at present," he said; "Vellacott has written to us only on business matters. We publish to-morrow a very good article of his purporting to be the dream of an overworked *attache*. It is very cutting and very incriminating. The Government cannot well avoid taking some notice of it. My only hope is that he is in Paris. There is something brewing over there. Our Paris agent wired for Vellacott this morning. By the way, Mr. Carew, is there a monastery somewhere in this part of the country?"

"Down that valley," replied Sidney, pointing with his whip.

"In Vellacott's article there is mention of a monastery—not too minutely described, however. There are also some remarkable suppositions respecting an old foreigner living in seclusion. Could that be the man you mentioned just now—Signor Bruno?"

"Hardly. Bruno is a harmless old soul," replied Sidney, pulling up to turn into the narrow gateway.

There was no time to make further inquiries.

Sidney led the way into the drawing-room. The ladies were there.

"My mother, Mr. Bodery—my sister; my sister Hilda," he blurted out awkwardly.

Mrs. Carew shook hands, and the two young ladies bowed.

They were all disappointed in Mr. Bodery. He was too calm and comfortable—also there was a suggestion of cigar smoke in his presence, which jarred.

"I am sorry," said the Londoner, with genial self-possession, "to owe the pleasure of this visit to such an unfortunate incident."

Molly felt that she hated him.

"Then you have heard nothing of Christian?" said Mrs. Carew.

"Nothing," replied Mr. Bodery, removing his tight gloves. "But it is too soon to think of getting anxious yet. Vellacott is eminently capable of taking care of himself—he is, above all things, a journalist. Things are disturbed in Paris, and it is possible that he has run across there."

Mrs. Carew smiled somewhat incredulously.

"It was a singular time to start," observed Hilda quietly.

Mr. Bodery turned and looked at her.

"Master mind in *this* house," he reflected.

"Yes," he admitted aloud.

He folded his gloves and placed them in the pocket of his coat. The others watched him in silence.

"Do you take sugar and cream?" inquired Hilda sweetly, speaking for the second time.

"Please—both. In moderation."

"I say," interrupted Sidney at this moment, "the Vicomte d'Audierne is following us in a fly. He will be here in five minutes."

Mrs. Carew nodded. She had not forgotten this guest.

"The Vicomte d'Audierne," said Mr. Bodery, with considerable interest, turning away from the tea-table, cup in hand. "Is that the man who got out of my train?"

"Yes," replied Sidney; "do you know him?"

"I have heard of him." Mr. Bodery turned and took a slice of bread and butter from a plate which Hilda held.

At this moment there was a rumble of carriage wheels.

"By the way," said the editor of the *Beacon*, raising his voice so as to command universal attention, "do not tell the Vicomte d'Audierne about Vellacott. Do not let him know that Vellacott has been here. Do not tell him of my connection with the *Beacon*."

The ladies barely had time to reconsider their first impression of Mr. Bodery when the door was thrown open, and a servant announced M. d'Audierne.

He who entered immediately afterwards—with an almost indecent haste—was of middle height, with a certain intrepid carriage of the head which appeals to such as take pleasure in the strength and endurance of men. His face, which was clean shaven, was the face of a hawk, with the contracted myope vision characteristic of that bird. It is probable that from the threshold he took in every occupant of the room.

"Mrs. Carew," he said in a pleasant voice, speaking almost

faultless English, "after all these years. What a pleasure!"

He shook hands, turning at the same time to the others.

"And Sid," he said, "and Molly—wicked little Molly. Never mind—your antecedents are safe. I am silent as the grave."

This was not strictly true. He was as deep, and deeper than the resting-place mentioned, but his method was superior to silence.

"And Hilda," he continued, "thoughtful little Hilda, who was always too busy to be naughty. Not like Molly, eh?"

"Heavens! How old it makes one feel!" he exclaimed, turning to Mrs. Carew.

The lady laughed.

"You are not changed, at all events," she said. "Allow me to introduce Mr. Bodery—the Vicomte d'Audierne."

The two men bowed.

"Much pleasure," said the Frenchman.

Mr. Bodery bowed again in an insular manner, which just escaped awkwardness, and said nothing.

Then Molly offered the new-comer some tea, and the party broke up into groups. But the Vicomte's personality in some subtle manner pervaded the room. Mr. Bodery lapsed into monosyllables and felt ponderous. Monsieur d'Audierne had it in his power to make most men feel ponderous when the spirit moved him in that direction.

As soon as tea was finally disposed of Mrs. Carew proposed an adjournment to the garden. She was desirous of getting Mr. Bodery to herself.

It fell to Hilda's lot to undertake the Frenchman. They had been great friends once, and she was quite ready to renew the pleasant relationship. She led her guest to the prettiest part of the garden—the old overgrown footpath around the moat.

As soon as they had passed under the nut-trees into the open space at the edge of the water, the Vicomte d'Audierne stopped short and looked round him curiously. At the same time he gave a strange little laugh.

"*Hein—hein—c'est drole,*" he muttered, and the girl remembered that in the old friendship between the brilliant, middle-aged diplomatist and the little child they had always spoken French. She liked to hear him speak his own language, for in his lips it received full justice: it was the finest tongue spoken on this earth. But she did not feel disposed just then to humour him. She looked at him wonderingly as his deep eyes wandered over the scene.

While they stood there, something—probably a kestrel—disturbed the rooks dwelling in the summits of the still elms across the moat, and they rose simultaneously in the air with long-drawn cries.

"Ah! Ah—h!" said the Vicomte, with a singular smile.

And then Hilda forgot her shyness.

"What is it?" she inquired in the language she had always spoken to this man.

He turned and walked beside her, suiting his steps to hers,

for some moments before replying.

"I was not here at all," he said at length, apologetically; "I was far away from you. It was impolite. I am sorry."

He intended that she should laugh, and she did so softly. "Where were you?" she inquired, glancing at him beneath her golden lashes.

Again he paused.

"There is," he said at length, "an old *chateau* in Morbihan—many miles from a railway—in the heart of a peaceful country. It has a moat like this—there are elms—there are rooks that swing up into the air like that and call—and one does not know why they do it, and what they are calling. Listen, little girl—they are calling something. What is it? I think I was *there*. It was impolite—I am sorry, Miss Carew."

She laughed again sympathetically and without mirth; for she was meant to laugh.

He looked back over his shoulder at times as if the calling of the rooks jarred upon his nerves.

"I do not think I like them—" he said, "now."

He was not apparently disposed to be loquacious as he had been at first. Possibly the rooks had brought about this change. Hilda also had her thoughts. At times she glanced at the water with a certain shrinking in her heart. She had not yet forgotten the moments she had passed at the edge of the moat the night before. They walked right round the moat and down a little pathway through the elm wood without speaking. The rooks had returned to their nests and only called to each other querulously at intervals.

"Has it ever occurred to you, little girl," said the Vicomte d'Audierne suddenly, "to doubt the wisdom of the Creator's arrangements for our comfort, or otherwise, here below?"

"I suppose not," he went on, without waiting for an answer, which she remembered as an old trick of his. "You are a woman—it is different for you."

The girl said nothing. She may have thought differently; one cannot always read a maiden's thoughts.

They walked on together. Suddenly the Vicomte d'Audierne spoke.

"Who is this?" he said.

Hilda followed the direction of his eyes.

"That," she answered, "is Signor Bruno. An old Italian exile. A friend of ours."

Bruno came forward, hat in hand, bowing and smiling in his charming way.

Hilda introduced the two men, speaking in French.

"I did not know," said Signor Bruno, with outspread hands, "that you spoke French like a Frenchwoman."

Hilda laughed.

"Had it," she said, with a sudden inspiration, "been Italian, I should have told you."

There was a singular smile visible, for a moment only, in the eyes of the Vicomte d'Audierne, and then he spoke.

"Mademoiselle," he said, "learnt most of it from me. We are old friends."

Signor Bruno bowed. He did not look too well pleased.

"Ah—but is that so?" he murmured conversationally.

"Yes; I hope she learnt nothing else from me," replied the Vicomte carelessly.

Hilda turned upon him with a questioning smile.

"Why?"

"I do not imagine, little girl," replied d'Audierne, "that you could learn very much that is good from me."

Hilda gave a non-committing little laugh, and led the way through the nut-trees towards the house. The Vicomte d'Audierne followed, and Signor Bruno came last. When they emerged upon the lawn in view of Mrs. Carew and Mr. Bodery, who were walking together, the Vicomte dropped his handkerchief. Signor Bruno attempted to pick it up, and there was a slight delay caused by the interchange of some Gallic politeness.

Before the two foreigners came up with Hilda, who had walked on, Signor Bruno found time to say:

"I must see you to-night, without fail; I am in a very difficult position. I have had to resort to strong measures."

"Where?" inquired the Vicomte d'Audierne, with that pleasant nonchalance which is so aggravating to the People.

"In the village, any time after nine; a yellow cottage near

the well."

"Good!"

And they joined Hilda Carew.

CHAPTER XVI

FOES

It is only when our feelings are imaginary that we analyse them. When the real thing comes—the thing that only does come to a few of us—we can only feel it, and there is no thought of analysis. Moreover, the action is purely involuntary. We feel strange things—such things as murder—and we cannot help feeling it. We may cringe and shrink; we may toss in our beds when we wake up with such thoughts living, moving, having their being in our brains—but we cannot toss them off. The very attempt to do so is a realisation, and from consciousness we spring to knowledge. We know that in our hearts we are thieves, murderers, slanderers; we know that if we read of such thoughts in a novel we should hold the thinker in all horror; but we are distinctly conscious all the time that these thoughts are our own. This is just the difference existing between artificial feelings and real: the one bears analysis, the other cannot.

Hilda Carew could not have defined her feelings on the evening of the arrival of Mr. Bodery and the Vicomte d'Audierne. She was conscious of the little facts of everyday existence. She dressed for dinner with singular care; during that repast she talked and laughed much as usual, but all the while she felt like any one in all the world but Hilda Carew.

At certain moments she wondered with a throb of apprehension whether the difference which was so glaringly patent to herself could possibly be hidden from others. She caught strange inflections in her own voice which she knew had never been there before—her own laughter was a new thing to her. And yet she went on through dinner and until bedtime, acting this strange part without break, without fault—a part which had never been rehearsed and never learnt: a part which was utterly artificial and yet totally without art, for it came naturally.

And through it all she feared the Vicomte d'Audierne. Mr. Bodery counted for nothing. He made a very good dinner, was genial and even witty in a manner befitting his years and station. Mrs. Carew was fully engaged with her guests, and Molly was on lively terms with the Vicomte; while Sidney, old Sidney—no one counted him. It was only the Vicomte who paused at intervals during his frugal meal, and looked across the table towards the young girl with those deep, impenetrable eyes—shadowless, gleamless, like velvet.

When bedtime at length arrived, she was quite glad to get away from that kind, unobtrusive scrutiny of which she alone was aware. She went to her room, and sitting wearily on the bed she realised for the first time in her life the incapacity to think. It is a realisation which usually comes but once or twice in a lifetime, and we are therefore unable to get accustomed to it. She was conscious of intense pressure within her brain, of a hopeless weight upon her heart, but she could define neither. She rose at length, and mechanically went to bed like one in a trance. In the same way she fell asleep.

In the meantime Mr. Bodery, Sidney Carew, and the Vicomte d'Audierne were smoking in the little room at the side of the porch. A single lamp with a red shade hung from the ceiling in the centre of this room, hardly giving enough light to read by. There were half-a-dozen deep armchairs, a divan, and two or three small tables—beyond that nothing. Sidney's father had furnished it thus, with a knowledge and appreciation of Oriental ways. It was not a study, nor a library, nor a den; but merely a smoking-room. Mr. Bodery had lighted an excellent cigar, and through the thin smoke he glanced persistently at the Vicomte d'Audierne. The Vicomte did not return this attention; he glanced at the clock instead. He was thinking of Signor Bruno, but he was too polite and too diplomatic to give way to restlessness.

At last Mr. Bodery opened fire from, as it were, a masked battery; for he knew that the Frenchman was ignorant of his connection with one of the leading political papers of the day. It was a duel between sheer skill and confident fore-knowledge. When Mr. Bodery spoke, Sidney Carew leant back in his chair and puffed vigorously at his briar pipe.

"Things," said the Englishman, "seem to be very unsettled in France just now."

The Vicomte was engaged in rolling a cigarette, and he finished the delicate operation before looking up with a grave smile.

"Yes," he said. "In Paris. But Paris is not France. That fact is hardly realised in England, I think."

"What," inquired Mr. Bodery, with that conversational heaviness of touch which is essentially British, "is the meaning of this disturbance?"

Sidney Carew was enveloped in a perfect cloud of smoke.

For a moment—and a moment only—the Vicomte's profound gaze rested on the Englishman's face. Mr. Bodery was evidently absorbed in the enjoyment of his cigar. The smile that lay on his genial face like a mask was the smile of a consciousness that he was making himself intensely pleasant, and adapting his conversation to his company in a quite phenomenal way.

"Ah!" replied the Frenchman, with a neat little shrug of bewilderment. "Who can tell? Probably there is no meaning in it. There is so often no meaning in the action of a Parisian mob."

"Many things without meaning are not without result."

Again the Vicomte looked at Mr. Bodery, and again he was baffled.

"You only asked me the meaning," he said lightly. "I am glad you did not inquire after the result; because there I should indeed have been at fault. I always argue to myself that it is useless to trouble one's brain about results. I leave such matters to the good God. He will probably do just as well without my assistance."

"You are a philosopher," said Mr. Bodery, with a pleasant and friendly laugh.

"Thank Heaven—yes! Look at my position. Fancy carrying in France to-day a name that is to be found in the most abridged history. One needs to be a philosopher, Mr. Bodery."

"But," suggested the Englishman, "there may be changes. It may all come right."

The Vicomte sipped his whisky and water with vicious emphasis.

"If it began at once," he said, "it would never be right in my time. Not as it used to be. And in the meantime we are in the present—in the present France is governed by newspaper men."

Sidney drew in his feet and coughed. Some of his smoke had gone astray.

Mr. Bodery looked sympathetic.

"Yes," he said calmly, "that really seems to be the case."

"And newspaper men," pursued the Vicomte, "what are they? Men of no education, no position, no sense of honour. The great aim of politicians in France to-day is the aggrandisement of themselves."

Mr. Bodery yawned.

"Ah!" he said, with a glance towards Sidney.

Perhaps the Frenchman saw the glance, perhaps he was deceived by the yawn. At all events, he rose and expressed a desire to retire to his room. He was tired, he said, having been travelling all the previous night.

Mr. Bodery had not yet finished his cigar, so he rose and shook hands without displaying any intention of following the Vicomte's example.

Sidney lighted a candle, one of many standing on a side table, and led the way upstairs. They walked through the long, dimly lighted corridors in silence, and it was only when they had arrived in the room set apart for the Vicomte d'Audierne that this gentleman spoke.

"By the way," he said, "who is this person—this Mr. Bodery? He was not a friend of your father's." Sidney was lighting the tall candles that stood upon the dressing-table, and the combined illumination showed with remarkable distinctness the reflection of his face in the mirror. From whence he stood the Frenchman could see this reflection.

"He is the friend of a great friend of mine; that is how we know him," replied Sidney, prizing up the wick of a candle. He was still rising to the occasion—this dull young Briton. Then he turned. "Christian Vellacott," he said; "you knew his father?"

"Ah, yes: I knew his father."

Sidney was moving to the door without any hurry, and also without any intention of being deterred.

"His father," continued the Vicomte, winding his watch meditatively, "was brilliant. Has the son inherited any brain?"

"I think so. Good night."

"Good night."

When the door was closed the Vicomte looked at his watch. It was almost midnight.

"The Reverend Father Talma will have to wait till to-morrow morning," he said to himself. "I cannot go to him to-night. It would be too theatrical. That old gentleman is getting too old for his work."

In the meantime, Sidney returned to the little smoking-room at the side of the porch. There he found Mr. Bodery smoking with his usual composure. The younger man forbore asking any questions. He poured out for himself some whisky, and opened a bottle of soda-water with deliberate care and noiselessness.

"That man," said Mr. Bodery at length, "knows nothing about Vellacott."

"You think so?"

"I am convinced of it. By the way, who is the old gentleman who came to tea this afternoon?"

"Signor Bruno, do you mean?"

"I suppose so—that super-innocent old man with the white hair who wears window-glass spectacles."

"Are they window-glass?" asked Sidney, with a little laugh.

"They struck me as window-glass—quite flat. Who is he—beyond his name, I mean?"

"He is an Italian refugee—lives in the village."

Mr. Bodery had taken his silver pencil from his waistcoat pocket, and was rolling it backwards and forwards on the table. This was indicative of the fact that the editor of the *Beacon* was thinking deeply.

"Ah! And how long has he been here?"

"Only a few weeks."

Mr. Bodery looked up sharply.

"Is *that* all?" he inquired, with an eager little laugh.

"Yes."

"Then, my dear sir, Vellacott is right. That old man is at the bottom of it. This Vicomte d'Audierne, what do you know of him?"

"Personally?"

"Yes."

"He is an old friend of my father's. In fact, he is a friend of the family. He calls the girls by their Christian names, as you have heard to-night."

"Yes; I noticed that. And he came here to-day merely on a friendly visit?"

"That is all. Why do you ask?" inquired Sidney, who was getting rather puzzled.

"I know nothing of him personally—except what I have learnt to-day. For my own part, I like him," answered Mr. Bodery. "He is keen and clever. Moreover, he is a thorough gentleman. But, politically speaking, he is one of the most dangerous men in France. He is a Jesuit, an active Royalist, and a staunch worker for the Church party. I don't know much about French politics—that is Vellacott's department. But I know that if he were here, and knew of the Vicomte's presence in England, he would be very much on the alert."

"Then," asked Sidney, "do you connect the presence of the Vicomte here with the absence of Vellacott?"

"There can be little question about it, directly or indirectly. Indirectly, I should think, unless the Vicomte d'Audierne is a scoundrel."

Sidney thought deeply.

"He may be," he admitted.

"I do not," pursued Mr. Bodery, with a certain easy deliberation, "think that the Vicomte is aware of Vellacott's existence. That is my opinion."

"He asked who you were—if you were a friend of my father's."

"And you said—"

"No! I said that you were a friend of a friend, and mentioned Vellacott's name. He knew his father very well."

"Were you"—asked Mr. Bodery, throwing away the end of his cigar and rising from his deep chair—"were you looking at the Vicomte when you answered the question?"

"Yes."

"And there was no sign of discomfort—no flicker of the eyelids, for instance?"

"No; nothing."

Mr. Bodery nodded his head in a businesslike way, indicative of the fact that he was engaged in assimilating a good deal of useful information.

"There is nothing to be done to-night," he said presently, as he made a movement towards the door, "but to go to bed. To-morrow the *Beacon* will be published, and the result will probably be rather startling. We shall hear something before to-morrow afternoon."

Sidney lighted Mr. Bodery's candle and shook hands.

"By the way," said the editor, turning back and speaking more lightly, "if any one should inquire—your mother or one of your sisters—you can say that I am not in the least anxious about Vellacott. Good night."

CHAPTER XVII

A RETREAT

It was quite early the next morning when the Vicomte d'Audierne left his room. As he walked along the still corridor and down the stairs it was noticeable that he made absolutely no sound, without, however, indulging in any of those contortions which are peculiar to late arrivals in church. It would seem that Nature had for purposes of her own made his footfall noiseless—if, by the way, Nature can be credited with any purpose whatever in her allotment of human gifts and failings.

In the hall he found a stout cook armed for assault upon the front-door step.

"Good morning," he said. "Can you tell me the breakfast-hour? I forgot to inquire last night."

"Nine o'clock, sir," replied the servant, rather taken aback at the thought of having this visitor dependent upon her for entertainment during the next hour and a half.

"Ah—and it is not yet eight. Never mind. I will go into the garden. I am fond of fruit before breakfast."

He took his hat and lounged away towards the kitchen-garden which lay near the moat.

"And now," he said to himself, looking round him in a searching way, "where is this pestilential village?"

The way was not hard to find, and as the church clock struck eight the Vicomte d'Audierne opened the little green gate of the cottage where Signor Bruno was lodging.

The old gentleman must have been watching for him; for he opened the door before the Vicomte reached it.

He turned and led the way into a little room on the right hand of the narrow passage. A little room intensely typical: china dogs, knitted antimacassars of a brilliant tendency, and horse-hair covered furniture. There was even the usual stuffy odour as if the windows, half-hidden behind muslin curtains and scarlet geraniums, were never opened from one year's end to another.

Signor Bruno closed the door before speaking. Then he turned upon his companion with something very like fury glittering in his eyes.

"Why did you not come last night?" he asked. "I am left alone to contend against one difficulty on the top of another. Read that!"

He drew from his pocket a thin and somewhat crumpled sheet of paper, upon which there were two columns of printed matter.

"That," he said, "cost us two thousand francs." The Vicomte d'Audierne read the printed matter carefully from beginning to end. He had approached the window because the light was bad, and when he finished he looked up for a few minutes, out of the little casement, upon the quiet village scene.

"The *Beacon*," he said, turning round, "what is that?"

"A leading weekly newspaper."

"Published—?

"To-day," snapped Signor Bruno.

The Vicomte d'Audierne made a little grimace.

"Who wrote this?" he inquired.

"Christian Vellacott, son of *the* Vellacott, whom you knew in the old days."

"Ah!"

There was something in the Vicomte's expressive voice that made Signor Bruno look at him sharply with some apprehension.

"Why do you say that?"

The Vicomte countered with another question.

"Who is this Mr. Bodery?"

He gave a little jerk with his head in the direction of the house he had just left.

"I do not know."

"I was told last night that he was a friend of this Christian

Vellacott—a protector."

The two Frenchmen looked at each other in silence. Signor Bruno was evidently alarmed—his lips were white and unsteady. There was a smile upon the bird-like face of the younger man, and behind his spectacles his eyes glittered with an excitement in which there was obviously no fear.

"Do you know," he asked in a disagreeably soft manner, "where Christian Vellacott is?"

Across the benevolent old face of Signor Bruno here came a very evil smile.

"You will do better not to ask me that question," he replied, "unless you mean to run for it—as I do."

The Vicomte d'Audierne looked at his companion in a curious way.

"You had," he said, "at one time no rival as a man of action—"

Signor Bruno shrugged his shoulders.

"I am a man of action still."

The Vicomte folded the proof-sheet carefully, handed it back to his companion, and said:

"Then I understand that—there will be no more of these very clever articles?"

Bruno nodded his head.

"I ask no questions," continued the other. "It is better so. I shall stay where I am for a few days, unless it grows too hot—unless I think it expedient to vanish."

"You have courage?"

"No; I have impertinence—that is all. There will be a storm—a newspaper storm. The embassies will be busy; in the English Parliament some pompous fool will ask a question, and be snubbed for his pains. In the *Chambre* the newspaper men will rant and challenge each other in the corridors; and it will blow over. In the meantime we have got what we want, and we can hide it till we have need of it. Your Reverence and I have met difficulties together before this one."

But Signor Bruno was not inclined to fall in with these optimistic views.

"I am not so sure," he said, "that we have got what we want. There has been no acknowledgment of receipt of the last parcel—in the usual way—the English *Standard*."

"What was the last parcel?"

"Fifty thousand cartridges."

"But they were sent?"

"Yes; they were despatched in the usual way; but, as I say, they have not been acknowledged. There may have been some difficulty on the other side. Our police are not so easy-going as these coastguard gentlemen."

"Well," said the aristocrat, with that semi-bantering lightness of manner which sometimes aggravated, and always puzzled, his colleagues, "we will not give ourselves trouble over that:

the matter is out of our hands. Let us rather think of ourselves. Have you money?"

"Yes—I have sufficient."

"It is now eight o'clock—this newspaper—this precious *Beacon* is now casting its light into some dark intellects in London. It will take those intellects two hours to assimilate the information, and one more hour to proceed to action. You have, therefore, three hours in which to make yourself scarce."

"I have arranged that," replied the old man calmly. "There is a small French potato-ship lying at Exmouth. In two hours I shall be one of her crew."

"That is well. And the others?"

"The others left yesterday afternoon. They cross by this morning's boat from Southampton to Cherbourg. You see how much I have had to do."

"I see also, my friend, how well you have done it."

"And now," said Signor Bruno, ignoring the compliment, "I must go. We will walk away by the back garden across the fields. You must remember that you may have been seen coming here."

"I have thought of that. One old man saw me, but he did not look at me twice. He will not know me again. And your landlady—where is she?"

"I have sent her out on a fool's errand."

As they spoke they left the little cottage by the back door, as

Henry Seton Merriman

Signor Bruno had proposed, through the little garden, and across some low-lying fields. Presently they parted, Signor Bruno turning to the left, while the Vicomte d'Audierne kept to the right.

"We shall meet, I suppose," were the last words of the younger man, "in the Rue St. Gingolphe?"

"Yes—in the Rue St. Gingolphe."

For so old a man the pace at which Signor Bruno breasted the hill that lay before him was somewhat remarkable. The Vicomte d'Audierne, on the other hand, was evidently blessed with a greater leisure. He looked at his watch and strolled on through the dew-laden meadows, wrapt in thought as in a cloak that hid the sweet freshness of the flowery hedgerows, that muffled the broken song of the busy birds, that killed the scent of ripening hay. Thus these two singular men parted—and it happened that they were never to meet again. These little things *do* happen. We meet with gravity; we part with a smile; perhaps we make an appointment; possibly we speak of the pleasure that the meeting seems to promise: and the next meeting is put off; it belongs to the great postponement.

Often we part with an indifferent nod, as these two men parted amidst the sylvan peace of English meadow on that summer morning. They belonged to two different stations in life almost as far apart as two social stations could be, even in a republic. They were not, in any sense of the word, friends; they were merely partners, intensely awake, as partners usually are, to each other's shortcomings.

The Vicomte d'Audierne probably thought no more of Signor Bruno from the moment that he raised his hat and turned. A few moments later his thoughts were evidently far away.

"The son of Vellacott," he muttered, as he took a cigarette from a neat silver case. "How strange! And yet I am sorry. He might have done something in the world. That article was clever—very clever—curse it! He cannot yet be thirty. But one would expect something from the son of a man like Vellacott."

It was not yet nine o'clock when the Vicomte entered the dining-room by the open window. Only Hilda was there, and she was busy with the old leather post-bag. Among the letters there were several newspapers, and the Vicomte d'Audierne's expression underwent a slight change on perceiving them. His thin, mobile lips were closely pressed, and his chin—a very short one—was thrust forward. Behind the gentle spectacles his eyes assumed for a moment that singular blinking look which cannot be described in English, for it seemed to change their colour. In his country it would have been called *glauque.*

"Ah, Hilda!" he said, approaching slowly, "do I see newspapers? I love a newspaper!"

She handed him the *Times* enveloped in a yellow wrapper, upon which was printed her brother's name and address.

"Ah," he said lightly, "the *Times*—estimable, but just a trifle opaque. Is that all?"

His eyes were fixed upon two packets she held in her hand.

"These are Mr. Bodery's," she replied, looking at him with some concentration.

"And what newspaper does Mr. Bodery read?" asked the Frenchman, holding out his hand.

She hesitated for a moment. His position with regard to her was singular, his ascendency over her had never been tried. It was an unknown quantity; but the Vicomte d'Audierne knew his own power.

"Let me look, little girl," he said quietly in French.

She handed him the newspapers, still watching his face.

"The *Beacon*," he muttered, reading aloud from the ornamented wrapper, "a weekly journal."

He threw the papers down and returned to the *Times*, which he unfolded.

"Tell me, Hilda," he said, "is Mr. Bodery connected with this weekly journal, the *Beacon*?"

Her back was turned towards him. She was hanging up the key of the post-bag on a nail beside the fireplace.

"Yes," she replied, without looking round.

"Is he the editor?"

"Yes."

The Vicomte d'Audierne turned the *Times* carelessly.

"Ah!" he muttered, "the phylloxera has appeared again."

For some time he appeared to be absorbed in this piece of news, then he spoke again.

"I knew something of a man who writes for that news-paper—the *Beacon*. I knew his father very well."

"Yes."

The Vicomte glanced at her.

"Christian Vellacott," he said.

"We know him also," she answered, moving towards the bell. He made a step forward as if about to offer to ring the bell for her, but she was too quick.

When the butler entered the room, Hilda reminded him of some small omission in setting out the breakfast-table. The item required was in the room, and the man set it upon the table with some decision and a slightly aggrieved cast of countenance.

The Vicomte d'Audierne raised his eyes, and then he looked very grave. He was a singular man in many ways, but those who worked with him were aware of one peculiarity which by its prominence cast others into the shade. He possessed a very useful gift rarely given to men—the gift of intuition. It was dangerous to *think* when the eyes of the Vicomte d'Audierne were upon one's face. He had a knack of knowing one's thoughts before they were even formulated. He looked grave—almost distressed—on this occasion, because he knew something of which Hilda herself was ignorant. He knew that she was engaged to be married to one man while she loved another.

CHAPTER XVIII

AN EMPTY NEST

In the middle of breakfast a card was handed to Sidney Carew. He glanced at it, nodded his head as a signal to the servant that he need not wait, and slipped the card into his pocket. Mr. Bodery and the Vicomte d'Audierne were watching him.

Presently he rose from the table and left the room. Mrs. Carew became suddenly lively, and the meal went on unconcernedly. It was not long before Sidney came back.

"Do you want," he said to his mother, "some tickets for a concert at Brayport on the 4th of next month?"

"What sort of a concert?"

Sidney consulted the tickets.

"In aid," he read, "of an orphanage—the Police Orphanage."

"We always take six tickets," put in Miss Molly, and her mother began to seek her pocket.

"Mr. Bodery," said Sidney, at this moment, "you have nothing to eat. Let me cut you some ham."

He moved towards the sideboard, but Mr. Bodery rose from his seat.

"I prefer to carve it myself," he replied, proceeding to do so.

Sidney held the plate. They were quite close together, and Hilda was talking persistently and gaily to the Vicomte d'Audierne.

"The London police are here already," whispered Sidney; "shall I say anything about Vellacott?"

"No," replied Mr. Bodery, after a moment's reflection.

"I am going to ride over to Porton Abbey with them now."

"Right," replied the editor, returning to the table with his plate.

Sidney left the room again, and the Vicomte d'Audierne detected the quick, anxious glance directed by Hilda at his retreating form. A few minutes later young Carew rode away from the house in company with two men, while a fourth horseman followed closely.

He who rode on Sidney's left hand was a tall, grizzled man, with the bearing of a soldier, while his second companion was fair and gentle in manner. The soldier was Captain Pharland, District Inspector of Police; the civilian was the keenest detective in London.

"Of course," said this man, who sat his hired horse with perfect confidence. "Of course we are too late, I know that."

He spoke softly and somewhat slowly; his manner was essentially that of a man accustomed to the entire attention of his hearers.

"The old Italian," he continued, "who went under the name of Signor Bruno, disappeared this morning. It is just possible that he will succeed in getting out of the country. It all depends upon who he is."

"Who do you suppose he is?" asked Captain Pharland. He was an upright old British soldier, and felt ill at ease in the society of his celebrated *confrere*.

"I don't know," was the frank reply; "you see this is not a criminal affair, it is entirely political; it is hardly in my line of country."

They rode on in silence for a space of time, during which Captain Pharland lighted a cigar and offered one to his companions. Sidney accepted, but the gentleman from London refused quietly, and without explanation. It was he who spoke first.

"Mr. Carew," he said, "can you tell me when this monastery was first instituted at Porton Abbey?"

"Last autumn."

The thin flaxen eyebrows went up very high, until they were lost to sight beneath the hat brim.

"Did they—ah—deal with the local tradesmen?"

"No," replied Sidney, "I think not. They received all their stores by train from London."

"And you have never seen any of the monks?"

"No, never."

The fair-haired gentleman gave a little upward jerk of the head and smiled quietly for his own satisfaction.

He did not speak again until the cavalcade reached Porton Abbey. The old place looked very peaceful in the morning light, standing grimly in the midst of that soft lush grass which only grows over old habitations.

One side of the long, low building was in good repair, while the other half had been allowed to crumble away. The narrow Norman windows had been framed with unpainted wood and cheap glass. The broad doorway had been partly filled in with unseasoned deal, and an inexpensive door had been fitted up.

The bell-knob was of brass, new and glaring in the morning sun. The gentleman from London, having alighted, took gently hold of this and rang. A faint tinkle rewarded him. It was the peculiar sound of a bell ringing in an empty house. After a moment's pause he wrenched the bell nearly out of its socket, and a long peal was the result. At last this ceased, and there was no sound in the house. The fair man looked back over his shoulder at Captain Pharland.

"Gone!" he said tersely.

Then he took from his breast pocket a little bar in the shape of a lever. He introduced the bent end of this between the door and the post, just above the keyhole, and gave a sharp jerk. There was a short crack like that made by the snapping of cast iron, and the door flew open.

Without a moment's hesitation the man went in, followed closely by Sidney and Captain Pharland.

The birds had flown. As mysteriously as they had come, the devotees had vanished. Bare walls met the eyes of the searchers. Porton Abbey stood empty again after its brief return to life and warmth, and indeed it scarcely looked habitable. The few personal effects of the simple monks had been removed; the walls and stone floors were rigidly clean; the small chapel showed signs of recent repair. There was an altar-cloth, a crucifix, and two brass candlesticks.

The gentleman from London noted these items with a cynical smile. He had instinctively removed his hat; it is just possible that there was another side to this man's life—a side wherein he dealt with men who were not openly villains. He may have been a churchwarden at home.

"Clever beggars!" he ejaculated, "they were ready for every emergency."

Captain Pharland pointed to the altar with his heavy riding-whip.

"Then," he said, "you think this all humbug?"

"I do. They were no more monks than we are."

The search did not last much longer. Only a few rooms had been inhabited, and there was absolutely nothing left—no shred of evidence, no clue whatever.

"Yes," said the fair-haired man, when they had finished their inspection, "these were exceptional men; they knew their business."

As they left the house he paused, and closed the door again, remaining inside.

"You see," he said, "there is not even a bolt on the door. They knew better than to depend on bolts and bars. They knew a trick worth two of that."

At the gate they met a small, inoffensive man, with a brown beard and a walking-stick. There was nothing else to say about him; without the beard and the walking-stick there would have been nothing left to know him by.

"That is my assistant," announced the London detective quietly. "He has been down to the cliff."

The two men stepped aside together, and consulted in an undertone for some time. Then the last speaker returned to Captain Pharland and Sidney, who were standing together.

"That newspaper," he said, "the *Beacon*, is word for word right. My assistant has been to the spot. The arms and ammunition have undoubtedly been shipped from this place. The cases of cartridges mentioned by the man who wrote the article as having been seen, in a dream, half-way down the cliff, are actually there; my assistant has seen them."

Captain Pharland scratched his honest cavalry head. He was beginning to regret that he had accepted the post of district inspector of the police. Sidney Carew puffed at his pipe in silence.

"Of course," said the detective, "the newspaper man got all this information through the treachery of one of the party. I should like to get hold of that traitor. He would be a useful man to know."

Henry Seton Merriman

In this the astute gentleman from London betrayed his extremely limited knowledge of the Society of Jesus. There are no traitors in that vast corporation.

Sidney and Captain Pharland rode home together, leaving the two detectives to find their way to Brayport Station.

They rode in silence, for the Captain was puzzled, and his companion was intensely anxious.

Sidney Carew was beginning to realise that the events of the last three days had a graver import than they at first promised to conceal. The now celebrated article in the *Beacon* opened his eyes, and he knew that the writer of it must have paid very dearly for his daring. It seemed extremely probable that the head and hands which had conceived and carried out this singular feat were both still for ever. Vellacott's own written tribute to the vast powers of the Jesuits, and their immovable habit of forcing a way through all obstacles to the end in view, was scarcely reassuring to his friends.

Sidney knew and recognised the usual fertility of resource possessed by his friend; but against him were pitted men of greater gifts, of less scruple, and of infinitely superior training in the crooked ways of humanity. That he should have been so long without vouchsafing word or sign was almost proof positive that his absence was involuntary; and men capable of placing fire-arms into the hands of a maddened mob were not likely to hesitate in sacrificing a single life that chanced to stand in their path.

As the young fellow rode along, immersed in meditation, he heard the sound of carriage-wheels, and, looking up, recognised his own grey horse and dog-cart. Mr. Bodery was driving, and driving hard. On seeing Sidney he pulled up, somewhat recklessly, in a manner which suggested that he had not always been a stout, middle-aged Londoner.

"Been telegraphed for," he shouted, "by the people at the office. Government is taking it up. Just time to catch the train."

And the editor of the *Beacon* disappeared in a cloud of dust.

The Vicomte d'Audierne was thus left in full possession of the field.

CHAPTER XIX

FOUL PLAY

When Christian Vellacott passed out of the drawing-room window in answer to what he naturally supposed to be a signal-whistle from Hilda or Sidney, he turned down the narrow, winding pathway that led to the moat. The extreme darkness, contrasting suddenly with the warm light of the room he had just left, caused him to walk slowly with outstretched hands. Floating cobwebs broke across his face, and frequently he stopped to brush the clinging fibre away. The intense darkness was somewhat relieved when he reached the edge of the moat, and the clear sky was overhead instead of interlocked branches. He could just discern that Hilda was not at her usual seat upon the rustic bench farther towards the end of the moat, and he stopped short, with a sudden misgiving, at the spot where the path met, at right angles, the broader stone walk extending the full length of the water.

He was on the point of whistling softly the familiar refrain, when there was a rustle in the bushes behind him. A rush, a sudden shock, and a pair of muscular hands were closed round his throat, dragging him backwards. But Christian stood like a rock. Quick as thought he seized the two wrists, which were small and flat, and wrenched them apart. Then, stepping back with one foot in order to obtain surer leverage, he lifted his assailant from the ground, swung him round, and literally let him fly into the moat—with a devout hope that it might be Signor Bruno. The man hurtled through the darkness, without a cry or sound, and fell face foremost into the water, five yards from the edge, throwing into the air a shower of spray.

Christian Vellacott was one of those men whose litheness is greater than their actual muscular force; but a lithe man possesses greater powers of endurance than a powerful fellow whose muscles are more highly developed. The exertion of lifting his assailant and swinging him away into the darkness was great, although the man's weight was nothing very formidable, and Christian staggered back a few paces without, however, actually losing his balance. At this moment two men sprang upon him from behind and dragged him to the ground. He felt at once that this was a very different matter. Either of these two could have overpowered him singly. Their thick arms encompassed him like the coils of a snake, and there was about their heavy woollen clothing a faint odour of salt water. He knew that they were sailors. Recognising that it was of no avail, he still fought on, as Englishmen do. One of the men had wound a large woollen scarf round his mouth, the other was slowly but very surely succeeding in pinioning his arms. Then a third assailant came, and Christian knew by the wet hand (for he used one arm only) that it was the smallest of the three, who had suffered for his temerity.

"Quick, quick!" this man whispered in French. With his uninjured hand he twisted the scarf tighter and tighter until Christian gasped for breath.

Still the Englishman struggled and writhed upon the ground, while the hard breathing of the two sailors testified that it was no mean resistance. Suddenly the one-armed man loosened the scarf, but before Christian could recover his breath a handkerchief was pressed over his lips, and a sweet, pungent odour filled his nostrils.

"Three to one," he gasped, and quite suddenly his head fell forward, while his clutch relaxed.

"He is a brave man," said the dripping leader of the attack, as he stood upright and touched his damaged shoulder gently and tentatively. "Now quick to the carriage with him. You have not managed this well, my friends, not at all well."

The speaker raised his cold hand to his forehead, which was wet, less perhaps from past exertion than from the agony he was enduring.

"But, monsieur," grumbled one of the sailors in humble self-defence, "he is made of steel!"

* * * * *

The pale light of a grey dawn was stealing slowly up into the riven sky, lighting up the clouds which were flying eastward on the shoulder of a boisterous wind. The heavy grey sea, heaving, surging, and hissing, threw itself upwards into broken spray, which flew to leeward at a sharp angle, blown from the summit of the wave like froth from an over-filled tankard. After a night of squally restlessness, accompanied by a driving rain that tasted brackish, things had settled down with the dawn into a steady, roaring gale of wind. In the growing light sea-gulls rose triumphantly with smooth breasts bravely facing the wind.

In the midst of this a dripping vessel laboured sorely. The green water rushed from side to side over her slippery, filthy deck as she rolled, and carried with it a tangled mass of ropes, a wooden bucket, a capstan bar, and—ominous sign—a soaking, limp fur cap. The huge boom, reaching nearly the whole length of the little vessel, swung wildly from side to side as the yawl dipped her bulwarks to the receding wave. It was certain death for a man to attempt to stand upright upon the sopping deck, for the huge spar swung shoulder high. The steersman, crouching low by his strong tiller, was doing his best to avoid a clean sweep, but only a small jib and the mizzen were standing with straining clews and gleaming seams. Crouching beneath the weather bulwarks, with their feet wedged against the low combing of the hatch, three men were vainly endeavouring to secure the boom, and to disentangle the clogged ropes. Two were huge fellows with tawny, washed-out beards innocent of brush or comb, their faces were half hidden by rough sou'-westers, and they were enveloped from head to foot in oilskins from which the water ran in little rills. The third was Christian Vellacott, who looked very wet indeed. The water was dripping from his cuffs and running down his face. His black dress-clothes were clinging to him with a soppy hindrance, while the feet firmly planted against the combing of the hatch were encased in immaculate patent-leather shoes, and the salt water ran off silk socks. It would have been very funny if it were not that Fortune invariably mingles her strokes of humour most heedlessly with sadder things. Christian Vellacott was apparently unconscious of the humour of the situation. He was working patiently and steadily, as men must needs work when fighting Nature, and his half-forgotten sea-craft was already coming back. Beneath his steady hands something akin to order was slowly being achieved; he was coiling and disentangling the treacherous rope, of which the breaking had cast the boom adrift, laying low a good seaman.

Farther forward upon the hatch lay the limp body of a very big man. His matted head was bare, and the dead, brown face, turned upward to its Maker, jerked from side to side as the vessel heaved. The stalwart legs were encased in greasy sea-boots, deeply wrinkled, and the coils of a huge scarf of faded purple lay upon his broad breast, where they had been dragged down by a hasty hand in order to see more clearly the still features.

At the dead man's side knelt upon the deck a small, spare figure clad in black and wearing his left arm in a sling. With his right hand he held a crucifix to the blue lips that would never breathe a prayer to the Virgin again. The small mouth and refined features of the praying man were strangely out of keeping with his tempestuous surroundings. Unmindful, however, of wind and waves alike, he knelt and prayed audibly. Each lurch of the vessel threw him forward, so that, in order to save himself from falling, he was obliged to press heavily upon the dead man's throat and breast; but this he heeded not. His girlish blue eyes were half closed in an ecstasy of religious fervour, and the pale, narrow face wore a light that was not reflected from sea or sky. This was the man who had unhesitatingly attacked Vellacott, had dared to pit his small strength, more of nerve than of muscle, against the young Englishman's hardened sinews. Violence in itself was most abhorrent to him; it had no part in his nature; and consequently, by the strange tenets of Ignatius Loyola's disciples, he was condemned to a course of it. Any objectionable duty, such as this removal of Vellacott, was immediately assigned to him in the futile endeavour of subjecting the soul to the brain. A true Jesuit must have no nature of his own and no individuality. He is simply a machine, with likes and dislikes, conscience and soul subject to the will of his superior, whose mind is also under the same arbitrary control; and so on to the top. If at the head there were God, it would be well; but man is there, and consequently the whole society is a gigantic mistake. To be a sincere member of it, a man must be a half-witted fool, a religious fanatic, or a rogue for whom no duplicity is too scurrilous, even though it amount to blasphemy.

Rene Drucquer, the man kneeling on the slimy deck, was as nearly a religious fanatic as his soft, sweet nature would allow. With greater bodily strength and attendant greater passions, he would have been a simple monomaniac. In him the passion for self-devotion was singularly strong, and contact with men had cooled it down into an unusually deep sense of duty.

Personally courageous, his bravery was of a high order, if the spirit of self-devotion called it into existence. In this his courage was more akin to that of women than of men. If duty drove him he would go where the devil drags most people, and Rene Drucquer was not by any means the first man or woman whose life has been wrecked, wasted, and utterly misled by a blind devotion to duty.

When throwing himself upon Christian Vellacott, no thought of possible danger to his own person had restrained or caused him a moment's hesitation. His blind faith in the righteousness of his cause was, however, on the wane. This disciple of St. Ignatius might have lived a true and manly life three hundred years earlier when his master trod the earth, but the march of intellect had trodden down the "Constitutions" years before Rene Drucquer came to study them. An ignoramus and a zealot who lived nearly four centuries ago can be no guide or help to men of the present day, and this young priest was overshadowed by the saddest doubt that comes to men on earth—the doubt of his own Creed.

While Christian Vellacott was assisting the sailors he glanced occasionally towards the kneeling priest, and on the narrow, intelligent face he read a truth that never was forgotten. He saw that Rene Drucquer was unconscious of his surroundings—unmindful of the fact that he was on board a disabled vessel at the mercy of the wild wind. His whole being was absorbed in prayer: this priest remembered only that the soul of the great, rough, disfigured man was winging its serene way to the land where no clouds are. Christian was not an impressionable man—journalism had killed all that—nor, it is to be feared, did he devote much thought to religion; but he recognised goodness when he met it. The young journalist's interest was aroused, and in that trifling incident lay the salvation of the priest. From that small beginning came the gleam of light that was to illuminate gloriously the darkness of a mistaken life.

Chance had capriciously ruled that the hand that had dislocated the Abbe's arm should set it again, and the dead sailor lying on the sticky, tarred hatch-cover had helped. The "patron" of the boat, for he it was whose head had been smashed by the spar, had held the priest's trembling, swollen shoulder while Christian's steady hands gave the painful jerk required to slip the joint back into its socket. The great, coarse lips which had trembled a little, with a true Frenchman's sympathy for suffering, were now blue and drawn; the stout, tender hands were nerveless.

The priest prayed on, while the men worked near at hand seeking to restore order, and to repair the damages made by sea and wind. They had got over their sullen, native shyness on finding that Christian could speak French like the Abbe and was almost as good a sailor as themselves. One offered him a rough blue jersey, while another placed a gold-embroidered Sunday waistcoat at his disposal, with a visible struggle between kindness of heart and economy. The first was accepted, but the waistcoat was given back with a kind laugh and an assurance that the jersey was sufficient.

The Englishman knew too well with whom he was dealing to

harbour any ill-feeling against the ignorant fishermen or even towards the Abbe Drucquer for the rough treatment he had received. The former were poor, and money never was beaten by a scruple in open combat yet. The latter, he rightly presumed, was only obeying a mandate he dared not dispute. The authority was to him Divine, the command came from one whom he had sworn to look up to and obey as the earthly representative of his Master.

At length the deck was cleared, and order reigned on board, though the mainsail could not be set until the weather moderated.

Then Hoel Grall came up to the young Englishman and said:

"Monsieur, let us carry the 'patron' down below. It is not right for the dead to lie there in this wind and storm."

"I am willing," answered Christian, looking towards the spot where the dead man lay.

"Then, perhaps—Monsieur," began the Breton with some hesitation.

"Yes," answered Christian encouragingly, "what is it?"

"Perhaps Monsieur will speak to—to the Abbe. It is that we do not like to disturb him in prayer."

The young Englishman bowed his head with characteristic decision.

"I will do so," he said gravely. Then he crawled across the deck and touched Rene Drucquer's shoulder. The priest did not look up until the touch had been repeated.

"Yes," he murmured; "yes. What do you want?"

Christian, guessed at the words, for in the tumult of the gale he could not hear them.

"Is it not better to take him below?" he shouted.

Then for the first time did the priest appear to remember that this was not one of the sailors.

"I beg your pardon," he said, rising from his knees. "You are right; it is better. But I am afraid the men will not assist me. They are afraid of touching the dead when they are afloat."

"I will help you," said Christian simply, "and that man also, I think, because he proposed it."

With a motion of the head he indicated Hoel Grall, upon whom the command of the little vessel had now devolved. The man was better educated than his companions, and spoke French fluently, but in the Breton character super- stition is so deeply rooted that generations of education will scarcely eradicate it.

The priest looked into the Englishman's face with a gentle wonder in his eyes, which were shadowy with the fervour of his recent devotions. The two men were crouching low upon the deck, grasping the black rail with their left hands; the water washed backwards and forwards around their feet.

It was the first time they had seen each other face to face in open daylight, and their eyes met quietly and searchingly as they swayed from side to side with the heavy lurching of the ship. The Englishman spoke first.

"You must leave it to us," he said calmly. "You could do

nothing in this heavy sea with your one arm!"

The gentle blue eyes were again filled with wonder, and presently the priest's intellectual face relaxed into a shadowy smile, which did not affect his thin red lips.

"You are very good," he murmured simply.

Christian did not hear this remark. He had turned away to call Grall towards him, and was about to move towards the body lying on the hatch, when the priest called him back.

"Monsieur," he said.

"Yes."

"Tell me," continued Rene Drucquer quickly, as if in doubt, "are you Christian Vellacott?"

"Of course!"

The priest looked relieved, and at the same time he appeared to be making an effort to restrain himself, as if he had been betrayed into a greater show of feeling than was desirable. When he at length spoke in reply to the Englishman's obvious desire for some explanation of the strange question, his voice was singularly cold, and modulated in such a manner as to deprive it of any expression, while his eyes were fixed on the deck.

"You are not such as I expected," he said.

Christian looked down at him with straightforward keenness, and he saw the priest's eyelids move uneasily beneath his gaze. Mixing with many men as he had done, he had acquired a certain mental sureness of touch, like that of an artist with his brush when he has handled many subjects and many effects. He divined that Rene Drucquer had been led to expect a violent, head strong man, and he could not restrain a smile as he turned away. Before going, however, he said:

"At present it is a matter of saving the ship, and our lives. My own affairs can wait, but when this gale is over you may rest assured they shall have my attention."

CHAPTER XX

WINGED

Beyond this one allusion to their respective positions, Christian was silent regarding his captivity. After the gale subsided the weather took a turn for the better, and clear skies by day and night rendered navigation an easy matter.

With characteristic daring the young Englishman had decided to offer no resistance and to seize no opportunities of escape until the termination of the voyage. The scheme half-formed within his mind was to see the voyage through, and effect his escape soon after landing in France. It was not without a certain adventurous fascination, and in the meantime there was much to interest him in his surroundings. If this young Abbe was a typical member of the Society of Jesus, he was worth studying. If this simplicity was an acquired cloak to deeper thought, it was worth penetrating, and if the man's entire individuality had been submerged in the mysterious system followed in the College of Jesuits, it was no waste of time to seek for the real man beneath the cultivated suavity that hid all feeling.

The more the two young men saw of each other the closer grew their intimacy, and with growing intimacy the domination of the stronger individuality was more marked in

Henry Seton Merriman

its influence.

To the frail and nervous priest this young Englishman was a new experience; his vitality and calm, straightforward manner of speech were such as the Abbe had never met with before. Such men and better men there were and are in the Society of Jesus, otherwise the power of the great Order would not be what it is; but Rene Drucquer had never come in contact with them. According to the wonderful code of laws laid down by its great founder (who, in other circumstances, might have prepared the world for the coming of such a man as Napoleon the First), the education of the young is entrusted to such brethren as are of slower parts; and from these honest, but by no means intelligent, men the young Abbe had learnt his views upon mankind in general. The creed they taught without understanding it themselves was that no man must give way to natural impulses; that he must restrain and quell and quench himself into a machine, without individuality or impulse, without likes or dislikes; that he must persistently perform such duties as are abhorrent to him, eat such food as nauseates him, and submit to the dictates of such men as hate him. And these, forsooth, are the teachings of one who, in his zealous shortsightedness, claims to have received his inspiration direct from the lips of the Great Teacher.

Rene Drucquer found himself in the intimate society of a man who said what he thought, acted as he conceived best, and held himself responsible, for word or deed, to none on earth. It was his first mission after a long and rigorous training. This was the first enemy of the Holy Church against whom he had been sent to fight, armed with the immeasurable power of the greatest brotherhood the world has ever known, protected by the shadow of its blessing; and there was creeping into the young priest's heart a vague and terrible suspicion that there might be two sides to the question. All the careful years of training, all the invisible meshes of the vast net that had been gathering its folds round him since he had first donned the dress of a Probationer of the College of Jesuits, were powerless to restrain the flight of a pure and guileless heart to the height of truth. Despite the countless one-sided and ingenious arguments instilled into his eager young mind in guise of mental armour against the dangers of the world, Rene Drucquer found himself, at the very first contact with the world, unconvinced that he was fighting upon the righteous side.

Brest had been left behind in a shimmering blue haze. Ahead lay the grim Pointe de Raz, with its short, thick-set lighthouse facing the vast Atlantic. Out to sea, in the fading glory of sunset, lay the long, low Ile-de-Sein, while here and there black rocks peeped above the water. The man holding the tiller was a sardine fisher, to whom every rock, every ripple, of these troubled waters was familiar. Fearlessly he guided the yawl close round by the high cliff—the westernmost point of Europe—but with the sunset the wind had dropped and the sails hung loosely, while the broad bows glided onwards with no sound of parted water.

The long Atlantic roll was swinging lazily in, and the yawl rose to it sleepily, with a long, slow movement. The distant roar of the surf upon the Finisterre coast rose in the peaceful atmosphere like a lullaby. The holy calm of sunset, the hush of lowering night, and the presence of the only man who had ever drawn him with the strange, unaccountable bond that we call sympathy, moved the heart of the young priest as it had never been moved before by anything but religious fervour.

For the first time he spoke of himself. The solitary heart suddenly broke through the restraining influence of a mistaken education, and unfolded its sad story of a misread existence. Through no fault of his own, by no relaxation of supervising care on the part of his teachers, the Jesuit had run headlong into the very danger which his Superior had endeavoured to avoid. He had formed a friendship. Fortunately the friend was a *man*, otherwise Rene Drucquer were lost indeed.

"I should think," he said musingly, "that no two lives have ever been so widely separated as yours and mine, and yet our paths have met!"

Vellacott took the cigarette from his lips. It was made of a vile tobacco, called "Petit Caporal," but there was nothing better to be had, and he was in the habit of making the best of everything. Therefore he blew into the air a spiral column of thin blue smoke with a certain sense of enjoyment before replying. He also was looking across the glassy expanse of water, but his gaze was steady and thoughtful, while his companion's eyes were dreamy and almost vacant. The light shone full upon his face, and a physician—or a mother— would have noticed, perhaps, that there was beneath his eyes a dull shadow, while his lips were dry and somewhat drawn.

"Yes," he said at length, with grave sympathy, "we have drifted together like two logs in a torrent."

The young priest changed his position, drawing in one leg and clasping his hands round his knee. The movement caused his long black garment to fall aside, displaying the dark purple stockings and rough shoes. The hands clasped round his knee were long and white, with peculiarly flat wrists.

"One log," he said vaguely, "was bound for a certain goal, the other was drifting."

Vellacott turned slowly and glanced at his companion's face.

The smoke from the bad cigarette drifted past their heads to windward. He was not sure whether the priest was speaking from a professional point of view, with reference to heresy and the unknown goal to which all heretics are drifting, or not. Had Rene Drucquer been a good Jesuit, he would have seen his opportunity of saying a word in season. But this estimable desire found no place in his heart just then.

"Your life," he continued in a monotone, "is already mapped out—like the voyage of a ship traced across a chart. Is it not so? I have imagined it like that."

Vellacott continued to smoke for some moments in silence. He sat with his long legs stretched out in front of him, his back against the rail, and his rough blue jersey wrinkled up so that he could keep one hand in his pocket. The priest turned to look at him with a sudden fear that his motives might be misread. Vellacott interpreted his movement thus, for he spoke at once with a smile on his face.

"I think it is best," he said, "not to think too much about it. From what experience I have had, I have come to the humiliating conclusion that men have very little to do with the formation of their own lives. A ship-captain may sit down and mark his course across the chart with the greatest accuracy, the most profound knowledge of wind and current, and the keenest foresight; but that will have very little effect upon the actual voyage."

"But," argued the priest in a low voice, "is it not better to have an end in view—to have a certain aim, and a method, more or less formed, of attaining it?"

"Most men have that," answered Christian, "but do not know that they have it!"

"*You* have?"

Christian smoked meditatively. A month ago he would have said "Yes" without a moment's hesitation.

"And you know it, I think," added the priest slowly. He was perfectly innocent of any desire to extract details of his companion's life from unwilling lips, and Christian knew it. He was convinced that, whatever part Rene Drucquer had attempted to play in the past, he was sincere at that moment, and he divined that the young Jesuit was weakly giving way to a sudden desire to speak to some fellow-being of his own life—to lay aside the strict reserve demanded by the tenets of the Society to which he was irrevocably bound. In his superficial way, Christian Vellacott had studied men as well as letters, and he was not ignorant of the influence exercised over the human mind by such trifling circumstances as moonshine upon placid water, distant music, the solemn hush of eventide, or the subtle odour of a beloved flower. If Rene Drucquer was on the point of committing a great mistake, he at least would not urge him on towards it, so he smoked in silence, looking practical and unsympathetic.

The priest laughed a little short, deprecating laugh, in which there was no shadow of mirth.

"I have not," he said, rubbing his slim hands together, palm to palm, slowly, "and—I know it."

"It will come," suggested the Englishman, after a pause.

The priest shook his head with a little smile, which was infinitely sadder than tears. His cold silence was worse than an outburst of grief; it was like the keen frost that comes before snow, harder to bear than the snow itself. Presently he moved slightly towards his companion so that their arms were touching, and in his soft modulated voice, trained to conceal emotion, he told his story.

"My friend," he said, intertwining his fingers, which were very restless, "no man can be the worse for hearing the story of another man's life. Before you judge of me, listen to what my life has been. I have never known a friend or relation. I have never had a boy companion. Since the age of thirteen, when I was placed under the care of the holy fathers, I have never spoken to a woman. I have been taught that life was given us to be spent in prayer; to study, to train ourselves, and to follow in the footsteps of the blessed Saint Ignatius. But how are we who have only lived half a life, to imitate him, whose youth and middle-age were passed in one of the most vicious courts of Europe before he thought of turning to holy things? How are we, who are buried in an atmosphere of mystic religion, to cope with sin of which we know nothing, and when we are profoundly ignorant of its evil results? These things I know now, but I did not suspect them when I was in the college. There all manliness, and all sense of manly honour, were suppressed and insidiously forbidden. We were taught to be spies upon each other, to cringe servilely to our superiors, and to deal treacherously with such as were beneath us. Hypocrisy—innate, unfathomable hypocrisy—was instilled into our minds so cunningly that we did not recognise it. Every movement of the head or hands, every glance of the eyes, and every word from the lips was to be the outcome—not of our own hearts—but of a law laid down by the General himself. It simply comes to this: we are not men at all, but machines carefully planned and fitted together, so as to render sin almost an impossibility. When tempted to sin we are held back, not by the fear of God, but by the thought that discovery is almost certain, and that the wrath of our Superior is withheld by no scruple of human kindness.... But remember, I knew nothing of this before I took my vows. To me it was a glorious career. I became an enthusiast. At last the time came when I was eligible; I offered myself to the Society, and was accepted. Then followed a period of hard work; I learned Spanish and Italian, giving myself body and soul to the work. Even the spies set to watch me day and night, waking and sleeping, feeding and fasting, could but confess that I was sincere. One day the Provincial sent for me—my mission had come. I was at last to go forth into the world to do the work of my Master. Trembling with eagerness, I went to his room; the Provincial was a young man with a beautiful face, but it was like the face of the dead. There was no colour, no life, no soul, no heart in it. He spoke in a low, measured voice that had neither pity nor love.

"When that door closed behind me an hour later the scales had fallen from my eyes. I began to suspect that this great edifice, built not of stones but of men's hearts, was nothing less than an unrighteous mockery. With subtle, double-meaning words, the man whom I had been taught to revere as the authorised representative of Our Lord, unfolded to me my duties in the future. The work of God, he called it; and to do this work he placed in my hands the tools of the devil. What I suspected then, I know now."

The young Englishman sat and listened with increasing interest. His cigarette had gone out long before.

"And," he said presently, in his quiet, reassuring voice, which seemed to infer that no difficulty in life was quite insurmountable—"And, if you did not know it then, how have you learnt it now?"

"From you, my friend," replied the priest earnestly, "from you and from these rough sailors. They, at least, are men. But you have taught me this."

Christian Vellacott made no answer. He knew that what his companion said was true. Unconsciously, and with no desire to do so, he had opened this young zealot's eyes to what a man's life may be. The tale was infinitely sad, but with characteristic promptitude the journalist was already seeking a remedy without stopping to think over the pathos of this mistaken career.

Presently Rene Drucquer's quick, painful tones broke the silence again, and he continued his story.

"He told me," he said, "that in times gone by we had ruled the Roman Catholic world invisibly from the recesses of kings' cabinets and queens' boudoirs. That now the power has left us, but that the Order is as firm as ever, nearly as rich, and quite as intelligent. It lies like a huge mill, perfect but idle, waiting for the grist that will never come to be crushed between its ruthless wheels. He told me that the sway over kings and princes has lapsed with the growth of education, but that we hold still within our hands a lever of greater power, though the danger of wielding it is proportionately greater to those who would use it. This power is the People. Before us lies a course infinitely more perilous than the sinuous paths trodden by the first followers of St. Ignatius as they advanced towards power. It lies on the troubled waters; it leads over the restless, mobile heads of the people."

Again the priest ceased speaking. There was a strange thrill of foreboding in his voice, which, however, had never been raised above a monotone. The two men sat side by side, as still as the dead. They gazed vacantly into the golden gates of the west, and each in his own way thought over these things. Assuredly the Angel of Silence hung over that little vessel then, for no sound from earth or sea or sky came to wake those two thinkers from their reverie.

At last the Englishman's full, steady tones broke the hush.

"This," he said, "has not been learnt in two days. You must have known it before. If you knew it, why are you what you are? You never have been a real Jesuit, and you never will be."

"I swore to the Mother of God—I am bound...."

"By an oath forced upon you!"

"No! By an oath I myself begged to take!"

This was the bitterest drop in the priest's cup. Everything had been done of his own free will—at his own desire. During eleven years a network of perfidy had been cunningly woven around him, mesh after mesh, day after day. As he grew older, so grew in strength the warp of the net. Thus, in the fulness of time, everything culminated to the one great end in view. Nothing was demanded (for that is an essential rule), everything must be offered freely, to be met by an apparently hesitating acceptance. Constant dropping wears the hardest stone in time.

"But," said Vellacott, "you can surely represent to your Provincial that you are not fitted for the work put before you."

"My friend," interrupted the priest, "we can represent nothing. We are supposed to have no natural inclinations. All work should be welcome, none too difficult, no task irksome."

"You can volunteer for certain services," said Vellacott.

The priest shrugged his shoulders.

"What services?" he asked.

The Englishman looked at him for some seconds in the fading light. In his quick way he had already found a remedy, and he was wondering whether he should propose it or hold his peace. He was not afraid of incurring responsibility. The young Jesuit had appealed to him, and there was a way out of the difficulty. Christian felt that things could not be made worse than they were. In a moment his mind was made up.

"As you know," he said, "the Society has few friends and a multitude of enemies. I am afraid I am an enemy; but there is one redeeming point in the Jesuit record which we are all bound to recognise, and I recognise it unhesitatingly. You have done more to convert the heathen than the rest of the Christian Church put together. Whatever the motive has been, whatever the results have proved to be, the missionary work is unrivalled. Why do you not offer yourself for that?"

As he asked the question Christian glanced at his companion's face. He saw the sad eyes light up suddenly with a glow that was not of this dull earth at all; he saw the thin, pure face suddenly acquire a great and wondrous peace. The young priest rose to his feet, and, crossing the deck, he stood holding with one hand to the tarred rigging, his back turned towards the Englishman, looking over the still waters.

Presently he returned, and laying his thin hand upon Christian's shoulder, he said, "My friend, you have saved me. In the first shock of my disillusion I never thought of this. I think—I think there is work for me yet."

CHAPTER XXI

TRUE TO HIS CLOTH

With the morning tide, the *Deux Freres* entered Audierne harbour. The rough sailors crossed themselves as they looked towards the old wooden cross upon the headland, facing the great Atlantic. They thought of the dead "patron" in the little cabin below, and the joyous young wife, whose snowy head-dress they could almost distinguish upon the pier among the waiters there.

Both Christian Vellacott and the Abbe were on deck. They had been there the whole night. They had lain motionless side by side upon the old sail. Day vanished, night stole on, and day came again without either having closed his eyes or opened his lips.

They now stood near the steersman, and looked upon the land with an interest which only comes after heavy weather at sea. To the Englishman this little fishing-port was unknown, and he did not care to ask. The vessel was now dropping up the river, with anchor swinging, and the women on the pier were walking inland slowly, keeping pace and waving a greeting from time to time in answer to a husband's shout.

"That is she, Monsieur L'Abbe," said Hoel Grall, with a peculiar twitch of his coarse mouth, as if from pain. "That is she with the little child!"

Rene Drucquer bowed his head, saying nothing. The *Deux Freres* slowly edged alongside the old quay in her usual berth above the sardine boats. A board was thrown across from the rail to the quay, and the priest stepped ashore alone. He went towards the smiling young wife without any hesitation; she stood there surrounded by the wives of the sailors on board the *Deux Freres*, with her snowy coiffe and spotless apron, holding her golden-haired child by the hand. All the women curtsied as the priest approached, for in these western provinces the Church is still respected.

"My daughter," said the Abbe, "I have bad news for you."

She smiled still, misunderstanding his calmness.

"Ah, mon pere," she said, "it is the season of the great winds now. What a long voyage it has been! And you say it is a bad one. My husband is no doubt in despair, but another voyage is sure to be better; is it not so? I have not seen Loic upon the deck, but then my sight is not good. I am not from Audierne, mon pere, but from inland where we cannot see so far."

The priest changed colour; no smile came into his face in response to hers. He stepped nearer, and placed his hand upon her comely arm.

"It has been a very bad voyage for your poor husband," he said. "The Holy Virgin give you comfort."

Slowly the colour vanished from the woman's round checks. Her soft, short-sighted eyes filled with a terrible, hopeless dismay as she stared at the young priest's bowed head. The women round now began to understand, and they crossed themselves with a very human prayer of thankfulness that their husbands and brothers had been spared.

"Loic is dead?" she said, in a rasping voice. For some moments she stood motionless, then, in obedience to some strange and unaccountable instinct, she began turning up the sleeves of her rough brown dress, as if she were going to begin some kind of manual work.

"The Holy Virgin comfort you, my daughter; and you, my little one," said the priest, as he stooped to lay his hand upon the golden head of the child.

"Loic is dead! Loic is dead!" spread from mouth to mouth.

"That comes from having ought to do with the priests," muttered the customs officer, beneath his heavy moustache. He was an old soldier, who read the newspapers, and spoke in a loud voice on Sunday evenings in the Cafe de l'Ouest.

The Abbe heard the remark, and looked at the man, but said nothing. He remembered that no Jesuit must defend himself.

The girl-widow stepped on board the untidy vessel in a mechanical, dreamy way. She dragged the little trotting child almost roughly after her. Christian Vellacott stood at the low cabin door. He was in the dress of a Probationer of the Society of Jesus, which he had assumed at the request, hesitatingly made, of Rene Drucquer, and for the very practical reason that he had nothing else to wear except a torn dress-coat and Hoel Grall's Sunday garments.

"Bless me, mon pere," lisped the little one, stopping in front of him.

"Much good will a blessing of mine do you, little one," he muttered in English. Nevertheless, he lifted the child up and kissed her rosy cheek. He kept her by his side, letting the mother go to her dead husband alone.

When the woman came from the cabin half-an-hour later, hard-faced, and with dry, stony eyes, she found the child sitting on Christian's knee, prattling away in broken French. Tears came to her aching eyes at the sight of the happy, fatherless child; the hard Breton heart was touched at last.

The Abbe's instructions were to keep his prisoner confined under lock and key in the cabin until nightfall, when he was to be removed inland in a carriage under the surveillance of two lay-brethren. Christian, however, never for a moment doubted his ability to escape when he wished to do so, and acting upon this conviction he volunteered a promise not to attempt evasion. Dressed as he was, in the garments of a probationer, there was no necessity of awaiting nightfall, as there was nothing unusual about him to attract attention. Accordingly the departure from the *Deux Freres* was fixed for midday. In the meantime the young Englishman found himself the object of unremitting attention on the part of two smooth-faced individuals who looked like domestic servants. These two men had come on board at the same moment that the Abbe stepped ashore, and Christian noticed that no word of greeting or recognition passed between them and Rene Drucquer. This was to him a further proof of the minuteness of organisation which has characterised the Order since Ignatius Loyola wrote down his wonderful "Constitutions," in which no trifle was too small to be unworthy of attention, no petty dramatic effect devoid of significance. Each man appeared to have received his instructions separately, and with no regard to those of his companion.

In the meantime, however, the journalist had not been

wasting his time. Although he still looked upon the whole affair as a very good farce, he had not forgotten the fact that his absence must necessarily have been causing endless anxiety in England. During the long night of wakefulness he had turned over in his mind every possible event at St. Mary Western since his sudden disappearance. Again and again he found himself wondering how they would all take it, and his conclusions were remarkably near to the truth. He guessed that Mr. Bodery would, sooner or later, be called in to give his opinion, and he sincerely hoped that the course taken would be the waiting tactics which had actually been proposed by the editor of the *Beacon*.

In this hope he determined to communicate with Sidney Carew, and having possessed himself of a blank Customs Declaration Form, he proceeded to write a letter upon the reverse side of it. In this he told his friend to have no anxiety, and, above all, to institute no manner of search, because he would return to England as soon as his investigations were complete. The letter was written in guarded language, because Christian had arrived at the conclusion that the only means he had of despatching it was through the hands of Rene Drucquer. The crew of the *Deux Freres* were not now allowed to speak with him. He possessed no money, and it would have been folly to attempt posting an unstamped letter addressed to England in a little place like Audierne.

Accordingly, as they were preparing to leave the vessel (the care of poor Loic having been handed over to the village cure), Christian boldly tendered his request.

"No, my friend, I cannot do it," replied the Abbe promptly.

"Read it yourself," urged Christian. "No harm can possibly come of it. My friend will do exactly as I tell him. In fact, it will be to your benefit that it should go."

Still the Jesuit shook his head. Suddenly, however, in the midst of an argument on the part of the Englishman, he gave in and took the letter.

"Give it to me," he said; "I will risk it."

Christian watched him place the letter within the breast of his "soutane," unread. The two lay-brethren were noting every movement.

Presently the priest removed his broad-brimmed hat and passed through the little doorway into the dimly lighted cabin where the dead sailor lay. He left the door ajar. After glancing at the dead man's still face he fell upon his knees by the side of the low bunk, and remained with bowed head for some moments. At last he rose to his feet and took the Englishman's letter from his breast. The envelope was unclosed, and with smooth, deliberate touch he opened the letter and read it by the light of the candle at the dead man's head, of which the rays were to illuminate the wandering soul upon its tortuous way. The priest read each word slowly and carefully, for his knowledge of English was limited. Then he stood for some seconds motionless, with arms hanging straight, staring at the flame of the candle with weary, wondering eyes. At last he raised his hand and held the flimsy paper in the flame of the candle till it was all burnt away. The charred remains fluttered to the ground, and one wavering flake of carbonised paper sank gently upon the dead man's throat, laid bare by the hand of his frenzied wife.

"He said that I was not a Jesuit," murmured the priest, as he burnt the envelope, and across his pale face there flitted an unearthly smile.

Scarcely had the thin smoke mingled with the incense-laden air when Christian pushed open the door. The two men looked their last upon the rigid face dimly illuminated by the light of the wavering candles, and then turned to leave the ship.

The carriage was waiting for them on the quay, and Christian noticed that the two men who had been watching him since his arrival at Audierne were on the box. Rene Drucquer and himself were invited to enter the roomy vehicle, and by the way in which the door shut he divined that it was locked by a spring.

At the village post-office the carriage stopped, and, one of the servants having opened the door, the priest descended and passed into the little bureau. He said nothing about the letter addressed to Sidney Carew, but Christian took for granted that it would be posted. Instead of this, however, the priest wrote a telegram announcing the arrival of the *Deux Freres*, which he addressed to "Morel et Fils, Merchants, Quimper."

"Hoel Grall asked me to despatch this," he said quietly, as he handed the paper to the old postmaster.

After this short halt the carriage made its way rapidly inland. Thus they travelled through the fair Breton country together, these two strangely contrasting men brought together by a chain of circumstances of which the links were the merest coincidences. Christian Vellacott did not appear to chafe against his confinement. He took absolutely no notice of the two men whose duty it was to watch his every movement. The spirit of adventure, which is not quite educated out of us Englishmen yet, was very strong in him, and the rapid movement through an unknown land to an unknown goal was not without its healthy fascination. He lay back in the comfortable carriage and sleepily watched the flying landscape. Withal he noticed by the position of the sun the direction in which he was being taken, and despite many turns and twists he kept his bearings fairly well. The carriage had left the high road soon after crossing the bridge above Audierne, and was now going somewhat heavily over inferior thoroughfares.

The sun had set before Vellacott awoke to find that they were still lumbering on. He had, of course, lost all bearing now, but he soon found that they had been journeying eastward since leaving the coast.

A halt was made for refreshment at a small hillside village which appeared to be mainly inhabited by women, for the men were all sailors. The accommodation was of the poorest, but bread was procurable, and eggs, meat being an unknown luxury in the community.

In the lowering light they journeyed on again, sometimes on the broad post-road, sometimes through cool and sombre forests. Many times when Christian spoke kindly, or performed some little act of consideration, the poor Abbe was on the point of disclosing his own treason. Before his eyes was the vision of that little cabin. He saw again the dancing flame of the paper in his hand, throwing its moving light upon the marble features of that silent witness as the charred fragments fluttered past the still face to the ground. But as the stone is worn by the dropping water, so at last is man's better nature overcome by persistent undermining when the work is carried out by men chosen as possessing "a mind self-possessed and tranquil, delicate in its perceptions, sure in its intuitions, and capable of a wide comprehension of various subjects." What youthful nature could be strong enough to resist the cunning pressure of influences wielded thus? So Rene Drucquer carried the secret in his heart until circumstances rendered it unimportant.

Man is, after all, only fallible, and those to whom is given the privilege of accepting or refusing candidates for admission to the great Society of Jesus had made a fatal error in taking Rene Drucquer. Never was a man more unfitted to do his duty in that station of life in which he was placed. His religious enthusiasm stopped short of fanaticism; his pliability would not bend so low as duplicity. All this the young journalist learnt as he penetrated further into the sensitive depths of his companion's gentle temperament. The priest was of those men to whom love and brotherly affection are as necessary as the air they breathe. His wavering instincts were capable of being hardened into convictions; his natural gifts (and they were many) could be raised into talents; his life, in fact, could have been made a success by one influence—the love of a woman—the one influence that was forbidden: the single human acquirement that must for ever be beyond the priest's reach. This Christian Vellacott felt in a vague, uncertain way. He did not know very much about love and its influence upon a man's character, these questions never having come under his journalistic field of inquiry; but he had lately begun to wonder whether man's life was given to him to be influenced by no other thoughts than those in his own brain—whether there is not in our existence a completing area in the development of character.

Looking at the matter from his own personal point of view—from whence even the best of us look upon most things—he was of the opinion that love stands in the path of the majority of men. This had been his view of the matter for many years; probably it was the reflection of his father's cynically outspoken opinion, and a well-grown idea is hard to uproot.

Brought up, as he had been, by a pleasure-seeking and somewhat cynical man, and passing from his care into the busy and practical journalistic world, it was only natural that he should have acquired a certain hardness of judgment which, though useful in the world, is not an amiable quality. He now felt the presence of a dawning charity towards the actions of his fellow-men. A month earlier he would have despised Rene Drucquer as a weak and incapable man; now there was in his heart only pity for the young priest.

Soon after darkness had settled over the country the carriage descended into a deep and narrow valley through which ran a rapid river of no great breadth. Here the driver stopped, and the two travellers descended from the vehicle. The priest exchanged a few words in a low voice with one of the servants who had leapt down from the box, and then turning to Vellacott he said in a curt manner—

"Follow me, please."

The Englishman obeyed, and leaving the road they turned along a broad pathway running at the side of the water. Christian noticed that they were going upstream. Presently they reached a cottage, and a woman came from the open doorway at their approach. Without any greeting or word of welcome she led the way down some wooden steps to the ferry-boat. As she rowed them across, the journalist took note of everything in his quick, keen way. The depth of the water, rapidity of current, and even the fact that the boat woman was not paid for her services.

"Are we near our destination?" he asked in English when he saw this.

"We have five minutes more," replied the priest in the same language.

On landing, they followed another small path for some distance, down-stream. It was a quiet moss-grown path, with poplar trees on either side, and appeared to be little used. Suddenly the young priest stopped. There was the trunk of an elm tree lying on the inside of the path, evidently cut for the purpose of making a rough seat.

"Let us sit here a few minutes," said Rene.

Christian obeyed. He sat forward and stretched his long legs out.

"I am aching all over," he said impatiently; "I wonder what it means!"

The priest ignored the remark entirely.

"My friend," he said presently, "a few minutes more and my care of you ceases. This journey will be over. For me it has been very eventful. In these few days I have learnt more than I did during all the long years of my education, and what I have learnt will never be forgotten. Without breathing one word of religion you have taught me to respect yours; without uttering a single complaint you have made me think with horror and shame of the part I have played in this affair. I dare ... scarcely hope that one day you will forgive me!"

Christian raised his hand slowly to his forehead. The gleam of the sleek, smooth water flowing past his feet made him giddy. He wondered vaguely if the strange, dull feeling that was creeping over his senses was the result of extreme fatigue.

"You speak as if we were never going to meet again," he said dreamily.

The priest did not answer for some moments. His slim hands were tightly clasped upon his knees.

"It is probable," he said at length, "that such will be the case. If our friendship is discovered it is certain!"

"Then our friendship must not be discovered," said the practical Englishman.

"But, my friend, that would be deceit—duplicity!"

"A little duplicity, more or less, cannot matter much," replied Christian, in a harder voice.

The priest looked up sharply, half fearing that his own treachery in the matter of the letter was suspected. But his companion remained silent, and the darkness prevented the expression of his face from being seen.

"And," continued the Englishman, after a long pause, "I am to be left here?"

There was a peculiar ring of weary indifference in his tone, as if it mattered little where he was left. The priest noticed it and remembered it later.

"I know nothing, my friend. I have but to obey my orders."

"And close your mind against thought?"

"I cannot prevent the thoughts from coming into my mind," replied the priest gently, "but I can keep them prisoners when they have entered."

He rose suddenly, and led the way along the river bank. Had Christian's manner been more encouraging he would have told him then and there about the letter.

As they passed along the narrow footpath, the dim form of a

man rose from behind the log of wood upon which they had been sitting. It was one of the lay brethren who had accompanied them from Audierne. Contrary to Rene Drucquer's whispered instructions, he had followed them after quitting the carriage, and had crept up behind the poplars unheard and unsuspected. He came, however, too late. Unconsciously, Christian had saved his companion.

CHAPTER XXII

GREEK AND GREEK

When they had walked about a hundred yards farther on, the footpath was brought to a sudden termination by a house built across it to the water's edge. In this lay the explanation of its scanty use and luxuriant growth of moss.

It was not a dark night, and without difficulty the priest found the handle of a bell, of which, however, no sound reached their ears. The door, cut deep in the stone, was opened after a short delay by a lay brother who showed no signs of rigid fasting. Again Christian noticed that no greeting was exchanged, no word of explanation offered or expected. The lay brother led the way along a dimly lighted corridor, in which there were doors upon each side at regular intervals. There was a chill and stony feeling in the atmosphere.

At the end of the corridor a gleam of light shone through a half-open door upon the bare stone floor. Into this cell Christian was shown. Without even noticing whether the priest followed him or not, he entered the tiny room and threw himself wearily upon the bed. Although it was an intensely hot night he shivered a little, and as he lay he clasped his head with either hand. His eyes were dull and lifeless, and the colour had entirely left his cheeks, though his lips were red and moist. He took no notice of his surroundings, which, though simple and somewhat bare, were not devoid of comfort.

In the meantime, Rene Drucquer had followed the door-keeper up a broad flight of stairs to a second corridor which was identical with that below, except that a room took the place of this small entrance-lobby and broad door. Thus the windows of this room were immediately above the river, which rendered them entirely free from overlookers, as the land on the opposite side was low and devoid of trees.

The lay brother stopped in front of the door of this apartment, and allowed the young priest to pass him and knock at the door with his own hands. The response from within was uttered in such a low tone that if he had not been listening most attentively Rene would not have heard it. He opened the door, which creaked a little on its hinges, and passed into the room alone.

In front of him a man dressed in a black soutane was seated at a table placed before the window. The only lamp in the room, which was long and narrow, stood on the table before him, so that the light of it was reflected from his sleek black head disfigured by a tiny tonsure. As Rene Drucquer advanced up the room, the occupant raised his head slightly, but made no attempt to turn round. With a quick, unobtrusive movement of his large white hand he moved the papers on the table before him, so that no written matter remained exposed to view. Upon the table were several books, and on the right-hand side of the plain inkstand stood a beautifully carved stone crucifix, while upon the left there was a small mirror no larger than a carte-de-visite. This was placed at a slight angle upon a tiny wire easel, and by raising his eyes any person seated at the table could at once see what was passing in the room behind him—the entire apartment, including the door, being reflected in the mirror.

Though seated, the occupant of this peculiarly constructed room was evidently tall. His shoulders, though narrow, were very square, and in any other garment than a thin soutane his slightness of build would scarcely have been noticeable. His head was of singular and remarkable shape. Very narrow from temple to temple, it was quite level from the summit of the high forehead to the spot where the tonsure gleamed whitely, and the length of the skull from front to back was abnormal. The dullest observer could not have failed to recognise that there was something extraordinary in such a head, either for good or evil.

The Abbe Drucquer advanced across the bare stone floor, and took his stand at the left side of the table, within a yard of his Provincial's elbow. Before taking any notice of him, the Provincial opened a thick book bound in dark morocco leather, of which the leaves were of white unruled paper, interleaved, like a diary, with blotting paper. The pages were numbered, although there was, apparently, no index attached to the volume. After a moment's thought, the tall man turned to a certain folio which was partially covered by a fine handwriting in short paragraphs. Then for the first time he looked up.

"Good evening," he said, in full melodious voice. As he raised his face the light of the lamp fell directly upon it. There was evidently no desire to conceal any passing expression by the stale old method of a shaded lamp. The face was worthy of the head. Clean-cut, calm, and dignified; it was singularly fascinating, not only by reason of its beauty, which was undeniable, but owing to the calm, almost superhuman power that lay in the gaze of the velvety eyes. There was no keenness of expression, no quickness of glance, and no seeking after effect by mobility of lash or lid. When he raised his eyes, the lower lid was elevated simultaneously, which peculiarity, concealing the white around the pupil, imparted an uncomfortable sense of inscrutability. There was no expression beyond a vague sense of velvety depth, such as is felt upon gazing for some space of time down a deep well.

"Good evening," replied Rene Drucquer, meeting with some hesitation the slow, kindly glance.

The Provincial leant forward and took from the tray of the inkstand a quill pen. With the point of it he followed the lines written in the book before him.

"I understand," he said, in a modulated and business-like tone, "that you have been entirely successful?"

"I believe so."

The Provincial turned his head slightly, as if about to raise his eyes once more to the young priest's face, but after remaining a moment in the same position with slightly parted lips and the pen poised above the book, he returned to the written notes.

"You left," he continued, "on Monday week last. On the Wednesday evening you ... carried out the instructions given to you. This morning you arrived at Audierne, and came into the harbour at daybreak. Your part has been satisfactorily performed. You have brought your prisoner with all expedition. So—" here the Provincial raised the pen from the book with a jerk of his wrist and shrugged his shoulders almost imperceptibly, "so—you have been entirely successful?"

Although there was a distinct intention of interrogation in the tone in which this last satisfactory statement was made, the young priest stood motionless and silent. After a pause, the other continued in the same kind, even voice:

"What has not been satisfactory to you, my son?"

"The 'patron' of the boat, Loic Plufer, was killed by the breaking of a rope, before we were out of sight of the English coast."

"Ah! I am sorry. Had you time—were you enabled to administer to him the Holy Rites?"

"No, my father. He was killed at one blow."

The Provincial laid aside his pen and leant back. His soft eyes rested steadily on the book in front of him.

"Did the accident have any evil effect upon the crew!" he asked indifferently.

"I think not," was the reply. "I endeavoured to prevent such effect arising, and—and in this the Englishman helped me greatly."

Without moving a muscle the Provincial turned his eyes towards the young priest. He did not look up into his face, but appeared to be watching his slim hands, which were moving nervously upon the surface of his black soutane.

"My son," he said smoothly. "As you know, I am a great advocate for frankness. Frankness in word and thought, in subordinate and superior. I have always been frank with you, and from you I expect similar treatment. It appears to me that there is still something unsatisfactory respecting your successfully executed mission. It is in connection with this Englishman. Is it not so?"

Rene Drucquer moved a little, changing his attitude and clasping his hands one over the other.

"He is not such as I expected," he replied after a pause.

"No," said the Provincial meditatively. "They are a strange race. Some of them are strong—very strong indeed. But most of them are foolish; and singularly self-satisfied. He is intelligent, this one; is it not so?"

"Yes, I think he is very intelligent."

"Was he violent or abusive?"

"No; he was calm and almost indifferent."

For some moments the Provincial thought deeply. Then he waved his hand in the direction of a chair which stood with its back towards the window at the end of the table.

"Take a seat, my son," he said, "I have yet many questions to ask you. I am afraid I forgot that you might be tired."

"Now tell me," he continued, when Rene had seated himself, "do you think this indifference was assumed by way of disarming suspicion and for the purpose of effecting a speedy escape?"

"No!"

"Did you converse together to any extent?"

"We were naturally thrown together a great deal; especially

after the death of the 'patron.' He was of great assistance to me and to Hoel Grall, the second in command, by reason of his knowledge of seamanship."

"Ah! He is expert in such matters?"

"Yes, my father."

A further note was here added to the partially-filled page of the manuscript book.

"Of what subjects did he speak? Of religion, our Order, politics, himself and his captivity?"

"Of none of those."

The Provincial leant back suddenly in his chair, and for some minutes complete silence reigned in the room. He was evidently thinking deeply, and his eyes were fixed upon the open book with inscrutable immobility. Once he glanced slowly towards Rene Drucquer, who sat with downcast eyes and interlocked fingers. Then he pressed back his elbows and inhaled a deep breath, as if weary of sitting in one position.

"I have met Englishmen," he said speculatively, "of a type similar—I think—to this man. They never spoke of religion, of themselves or of their own opinion; and yet they were not silent men. Upon most subjects they could converse intelligently, and upon some with brilliancy; but these subjects were invariably treated in a strictly general sense. Such men *never* argue, and never appear to be highly interested in that of which they happen to be speaking.... They make excellent listeners...." Here the speaker stopped for a moment and passed his long hand downwards across his eyes as if the light were troubling his sight; in doing so he glanced again towards the Abbe's fingers, which were now quite motionless, the knuckles gleaming like ivory.

"... And one never knows quite how much they remember and how much they forget. Perhaps it is that they hear everything ... and forget nothing. Is our friend of this type, my son?"

"I think he is."

"It is such men as he who have made that little island what it is. They are difficult subjects; but they are liable to sacrifice their opportunities to a mistaken creed they call honour, and therefore they are not such dangerous enemies as they otherwise might have been."

The Provincial said these words in a lighter manner, almost amounting to pleasantry, and did not appear to notice that the priest moved uneasily in his seat.

"Then," he continued, "you have learnt nothing of importance during the few days you have passed with him?"

"Nothing, my father."

"Did he make any attempt to communicate with his friends?"

"He wrote a letter which he requested me to post."

The Provincial leant forward in his chair and took a pen in his right hand, while he extended his left across the table towards his companion.

"I burnt it," said Rene gently.

"Ah! That is a pity. Why did you do that?"

"I had discretion!" replied the young priest, with quiet determination.

The Provincial examined the point of his pen critically, his perfectly formed lips slightly apart.

"Yes," he murmured reflectively. "Yes, of course, you had discretion. What was in the letter?"

"A few words in English, telling his friends to have no anxiety, and asking them particularly to institute no search, as he would return home as soon as he desired to do so."

"Ah! He said that, did he? And the letter was addressed to—"

"Mr. Carew."

"Thank you."

The Provincial made another note in the manuscript book. Then he read the whole page over carefully and critically. His attitude was like that of a physician about to pronounce a diagnosis.

"And," he said reflectively, without looking up, "was there nothing noticeable about him in any way? Nothing characteristic of the man, I mean, and peculiar. How would you describe him, in fact?"

"I should say," replied Rene Drucquer, "that his chief characteristic is energy; but for some reason, during these last two days this seems to have slowly evaporated. His resistance on Wednesday night was very energetic—he dislocated my arm, and reset it later—and when the vessel was in danger he was full of life. Later this peculiar indifference of manner came over him, and hour by hour it has increased in power. It almost seems as if he were anxious to keep away from England just now."

The Provincial raised his long white finger to his upper lip. It was the action of a man who is in the habit of tugging gently at his moustache when in thought, and one would almost have said that the smooth-faced priest had at no very distant period worn that manly ornament. His finger passed over the shaded skin with a disagreeable, rasping sound.

"That does not sound very likely," he said slowly. "Have you any tangible reason, to offer in support of this theory?"

"No, my father. But the idea came to me, and so I mention it. It seemed as if this desire came to him upon reflection, after the ship was out of danger, and the indifference was contemporaneous with it."

The Provincial suddenly closed the book and laid aside his pen.

"Thank you, my son!" he said, in smooth, heartless tones, "I will not trouble you any more to-night. You will need food and rest. Good night, my son. You have done well!"

Rene Drucquer rose and gravely passed down the long room. Before he reached the door, however, the clear voice of his superior caused him to pause for a moment.

"As you go down to the refectory," he said, "kindly make a request that Mr. Vellacott be sent to me as soon as he is refreshed. I do not want you to see him before I do!"

When the door had closed behind Rene Drucquer the Provincial rose from his seat and slowly paced backwards and forwards from the door to the table. Presently he drew aside the curtain which hid a small recess near the door, whore a simple bed and a small table were concealed. With a brush he smoothed back his sleek hair, and, dipping the ends of his fingers into a basin of water, he wiped them carefully. Thus he prepared to receive Christian Vellacott.

He returned to his chair and seated himself somewhat wearily. Although there were but few papers on the table, he had three hours' hard work before him yet. He leant back, and again, that singular gesture, as if to stroke a moustache that was not there, was noticeable.

"I have a dull presentiment," he muttered reflectively, "that we have made a mistake here. We have gone about it in the wrong way, and if there is blame to be attached to any one, Talma is the man. That temper of his is fatal!"

After a pause he heaved a weary sigh, and stretched his long arms out on either side, enjoying a free and open yawn.

"Ah me!" he sighed, "what an uphill fight this has become, and day by day it grows harder. Day by day we lose power; one hold after another slips from our grasp. Perhaps it means that this vast organisation is effete—perhaps, after all, we are dying of inanition, and yet—yet it should not be, for we have the people still.... Ah! I hear footsteps. This is our journalistic friend, no doubt. I think he will prove interesting."

A moment later someone knocked softly at the door. There was a slight shuffling of feet, and Christian Vellacott entered the room alone. There was a peculiar dull expression in his eyes, as if he were suffering pain, mental or physical. After glancing at the mirror, the Provincial rose and bowed formally with his hand upon the back of his chair. As the Englishman came forward the Jesuit glanced at his face, and with a polite motion of the hand he said:

"Sir, take the trouble of seating yourself," speaking in French at once, with no apology, as if well aware that his companion knew that language as perfectly as his own.

"Thank you," replied Christian. He drew the chair slightly forward as he seated himself, and fixed his eyes upon the Jesuit's face. Through the entire interview he never removed his gaze, and he noticed that until the last words were spoken those soft, deep eyes were never raised to his.

"I suppose," said the Jesuit at length, almost humbly, "that we are irreconcilable enemies, Mr. Vellacott?"

The manner in which this was spoken did not bear the slightest resemblance to the cold superiority with which Rene Drucquer had been treated.

The Englishman sat with one lean hand resting on the table and watched. He knew that some reply was expected, but in face of that knowledge he chose to remain silent. It was a case of Greek meeting Greek. The inscrutable Provincial had met a foeman worthy of his steel at last. His strange magnetic influence threw itself vainly against a will as firm as his own, and he felt that his incidental effects, dramatic and conversational, fell flat. Instantly he became interested in Christian Vellacott.

"I need hardly remind a man of your discrimination, Mr. Vellacott," he continued tentatively, "that there are two sides to every question."

The Englishman smiled and moved slightly in his chair, drawing in his feet and leaning forward.

"Implying, I presume," he said lightly, "that in this particular question you are on one side and I upon the other."

"Alas! it seems so."

Vellacott leant back in his chair again and crossed his legs.

"In my turn," he said quietly, "I must remind you, monsieur, that I am a journalist."

The Provincial raised his eyebrows almost imperceptibly and waited for his companion to continue. His silence and the momentary motion of his eyebrows, which in no way affected the lids, expressed admirably his failure to see the connection of his companion's remark.

"Which means," Christian went on to explain, "that my place is not upon either side of the question, but in the middle. I belong to no party, and I am the enemy of no man. I do not lead men's opinions. It is my duty to state facts as plainly and as coldly as possible in order that my countrymen may form their own judgment. It may appear that at one time I write upon one side of the question; the next week I may seem to write upon the other. That is one of the misfortunes of my calling."

"Then we are not necessarily enemies," said the Jesuit softly.

"No—not necessarily. On the other hand," continued Christian, with daring deliberation, "it is not at all necessary that we should be friends."

The Jesuit smiled slightly—so slightly that it was the mere ghost of a smile, affecting the lines of his small mouth, but in no way relieving the soft darkness of his eyes.

"Then we are enemies," he said. "He whose follower I am, said that all who are not with Him are against Him."

The Englishman's lips closed suddenly, and a peculiar stony look came over his face. There was one subject upon which he had determined not to converse.

"I am instructed," continued the Provincial, with a sudden change of manner from pleasant to practical, "to ask of you a written promise never to write one word either for or against the Society of Jesus again. In exchange for that promise I am empowered to tender to you the sincere apologies of the Society for the inconvenience to which you may have been put, and to assist you in every way to return home at once."

A great silence followed this speech. A small clock suspended somewhere in the room ticked monotonously, otherwise there was no sound audible. The two men sat within a yard of each other, each thinking, of the other in his individual way, from his individual point of view, the Jesuit with downcast eyes, his companion watching his immobile features.

At length Christian Vellacott's full and quiet tones broke the spell.

"Of course," he said simply, "I refuse."

The Provincial rose from his seat, pushing it back as he did so.

"Then I will not detain you any longer. You are no doubt fatigued. The lay brother waiting outside will show you the room assigned to you, and at whatever time of day or night you may wish to see me, remember that I am at your service."

Christian rose also. He appeared to hesitate, and then to grasp the table with both hands to assist himself. He stood for a moment, and suddenly tottered forward. Had not the

Provincial caught him he would have fallen.

"My head turns," he mumbled incoherently.

"What is the matter? ... what is the matter?"

The Jesuit slipped his arm round him—a slight arm, but as hard and strong as steel.

"You are tired," he said sympathetically, "perhaps you have a little touch of fever. Come, I will assist you to your room."

And the two men passed out together.

CHAPTER XXIII

STRICKEN DOWN

In later days Christian Vellacott could bring back to his memory no distinct recollection of that first night spent in the monastery. There was an indefinite remembrance of the steady, monotonous clang of a bell in the first hours, doubtless the tolling of the matins, calling the elect to prayer at midnight.

After that he must have fallen into a deep, lethargic sleep, for he never heard the distant strains of the organ and the melodious chanting of gruff voices. The strange, unquiet melody hovered over him in the little cell, following him as he glided away from earth upon the blessed wings of sleep, and haunted his restless dreams.

The monks were early astir next morning, for the sweet smell of drying hay filled the air, and the second crop of the fruitful earth lay waiting to be stacked. With tucked-up gowns and bared arms the sturdy devotees worked with rake and pitchfork. No whispered word passed between them; none raised his head to look around upon the smiling landscape or search in the cloudless sky for the tiny lark whose morning hymn rippled down to them. Each worked on in silence, tossing the scented hay, his mind being no doubt filled with thoughts above all earthly things.

Near at hand lay a carefully-kept vegetable garden of large dimensions. Here grew in profusion all nourishing roots and herbs, but there was no sign of more luscious fruits. Small birds hopped and fluttered here and there unheeded and unmolested, calling to each other joyously, and the warming air was alive with the hum of tinier wings.

In the midst of this walked man—the lord of all—humbly, silently, with bowed head and unadmiring eyes—man whose life was vouchsafed for the enjoyment of all these things.

A little square patch of sunlight lay on the stone floor of the small cell allotted to Christian Vellacott. The thick oak door deadened the sounds of life in the monastery, such as they were, and the strong, laboured breathing of the young Englishman alone broke the chill silence.

Christian lay, all dressed, on the narrow bed. His eyes were half closed, and the ruddy brown of his cheeks had faded into an ashy grey. His clenched hands lay numbly at his side. Through his open, swollen lips meaningless words came in a hoarse whisper.

Presently the door opened with a creaking sound, but the sleeper moved no limb or feature. Rene Drucquer entered the cell and ran quickly to the bedside. Behind, with more dignity and deliberation, followed the sub-prior of the monastery. The young priest had obtained permission from his Provincial to see Christian Vellacott for a few moments before his hurried departure for India. Thus Rene had received his mission sooner than he had hoped for. The astute and far-seeing Provincial had from the beginning intended that Rene Drucquer should be removed from harm's way without delay once his disagreeable mission to St. Mary

Western was performed.

"My father," exclaimed the young priest in alarm, "he is dying!"

The venerable sub-prior bent his head over the bed. He was a tall, spare man, with very sunken cheeks, and a marvellous expression of placid contentment in his eyes such as one never finds in the face of a young monk. He was very learned in medicines, and in the administration of such simple herbs as were required to remedy the illnesses within the monastery walls. Perhaps some of his patients died when they might have lived under more skilled treatment, but it is a short and easy step from life to death within a comfortless cell, and his bony hands were as tender over his sick brethren as those of a woman.

He felt the Englishman's pulse and watched his ashen face for some moments, touching the clammy forehead softly, while Rene Drucquer stood by with a great sickening weight of remorse and fear upon his heart. Then the sub-prior knelt stiffly down, and placed his clean-shaven lips near to Christian's ear.

"My son," he said, "do you hear me?"

Christian breathed less heavily, as if he were listening to some far-off sound, but never moved a feature. Presently he began to murmur incoherently, and the sub-prior bent his ear to listen.

"Much good would a blessing of mine do you, Hilda," observed Christian into the reverend ear. The old gentleman raised his cadaverous head and looked somewhat puzzled. Again he listened.

"Look after Aunt Judy—she cannot last long," murmured the young Englishman in his native tongue, which was unknown to the monk.

"It is fever," said the sub-prior presently—"one of those terrible fevers which kill men as the cold kills flies!"

No thought seemed to enter the monk's mind of possible infection. He knelt upon the cold floor with one bare and bony arm beneath the sick man's head, while the other lay across his breast. He was looking intently into the veiled eyes, inhaling the very breath of the swollen lips.

"Will he die, my father?" asked Rene Drucquer in a whisper; his face was as pale as Vellacott's.

"He is in the hands of the good God," was the pious answer. The tall monk rose to his feet and stood before the bed thinking. He rubbed his bony hands together slowly. Through the tiny window a shaft of sunlight poured down upon his grizzled head, and showed up relentlessly the deep furrows that ran diagonally down from his cheek-bone to his chin.

"You must watch here, my son," he continued, "while I inform the Father-Provincial of this."

The venerable sub-prior was no Jesuit, and perhaps he would have been just as well pleased had the Provincial elected to live elsewhere than in the monastery. But the Prior—an old man of ninety, and incapable of work or thought—was completely in the power of the Society.

When he found himself alone with the Englishman, Rene Drucquer sat wearily upon a small wooden bench, the only form of seat provided, and leaned his narrow face upon his hands.

Henry Seton Merriman

The prospect that he saw before him as he sat staring vacantly at the floor of the little cell was black enough. He saw no possible outlet, and he had not the courage to force his way through the barriers erected all round him. It must be remembered that he was a Roman Catholic, and over a sincere disciple of the Mother Church the power of the Jesuits is greater than man should ever be allowed to exercise. The slavery that England fought against so restlessly is nothing to it, for mental bondage is infinitely heavier than physical service. He had determined to accept the Provincial's offer of missionary work in Asia, but the sudden horror of realising that he was a Jesuit, and could never be anything else than a Jesuit for the rest of his days, was fresh upon him. He was too young yet to find consolation in the thought that he at all events could attempt to steer a clear, unsullied course through the shoals and quicksands that surround a priest's existence, and he was too old to buoy himself up with the false hope that he might, despite his Jesuit's oath, do some good work for his Church. His awakening had been rendered more terrible by the brilliancy of the dreams which it had interrupted.

He had not looked upon Christian Vellacott as a victim hitherto, for the bravest receive the least sympathy, and the young Englishman's cool way of treating his reverse of fortune had repelled pity or commiseration. But now all that was changed. Whatever this sickness might prove to be, Rene Drucquer felt that the blame of it lay at his own door. If Christian Vellacott were to die, he, Rene Drucquer, was in the eyes of God a murderer, for he had forcibly brought him to his death. This was an unpleasant reflection for a young devotee whose inward soul was full of human kindness; and the presence of the strong man who lay gasping for breath upon the narrow, comfortless bed was not reassuring.

It was only natural that those thoughts, coupled with the

realisation of the aimlessness of his own existence, should have bred in the young Jesuit's heart a dull fire of antagonism against the man who was in immediate authority over him, and when the Provincial noiselessly entered the cell a few minutes later, he felt a sudden thrill of misgiving at the thought that his feelings were sacred to none—that this man with his deep, inscrutable eyes could read the face of his very soul like an open book.

In this, Rene Drucquer was right. The Provincial was fully aware of the presence of this spirit of antagonism, and, moreover, he knew that it extended to the taciturn sub-prior who accompanied him. But this knowledge in no way disturbed him. The spirit of antagonism had met him in every turn of life. It was so familiar that he had learned to despise it. Hitherto he had never failed in any undertaking, and he had never been turned aside from the execution of his purpose by the fear of incurring the enmity of men. Such minds as this make their mark in the line of life which they take up, and if they do not happen to win the love of their fellow-beings, they get on remarkably well without it.

The Provincial came into the cell with a singular noiselessness of motion. His pale face expressed neither surprise nor annoyance, and his eyes rested upon the form of the sick man with no sign of apprehension. He approached, and with his long white finger touched Christian's wrist. For a few moments he watched the uneasy movements of his flushed face, and then he turned aside, without, however, leaving the bedside. Here again there seemed to be no fear or thought of infection.

The sub-prior stood behind him with clasped hands, while Rene, who had risen from his seat, was near at hand.

"This man, my father," said the Provincial coldly, "must not die. You must take every care, and spare no expense or trouble. If it is necessary you can have doctors from Nantes. I will bear every expense, and I shall be grieved to hear of his death!"

Then he turned to leave the cell. He was a busy man, and his visit had already lasted nearly three minutes.

Rene Drucquer stepped forward hurriedly. He was between his superior and the door, so that he was in a position to command attention.

"My father," he pleaded, "may I nurse him?"

The Provincial raised his eyebrows almost imperceptibly; then he waved his hand, commanding the young priest to stand aside.

"No," he said softly, "you must leave for Nantes in half-an-hour," and he passed out into the noiseless corridor.

CHAPTER XXIV

BACK TO LIFE

One mellow autumnal evening, when the sunlight reflected from the white monastery walls upon the fruit trees climbing there was still warm and full of ripening glow, the Provincial was taking his post-prandial promenade.

It is, perhaps, needless to observe that he was alone. No one ever walked with the Provincial. No footstep ever crushed the gravel in harmony with his gliding tread. Perhaps, indeed, no one had ever walked with him thus, in the twilight, since a fairy, dancing form had moved in the shadow of his tall person, and footsteps lighter than his own had vainly endeavoured to keep time with his longer limbs. But that was in no monastery garden; and the useful, vegetable producing enclosure bore little resemblance to the chateau terrace. In those days it may be that there was a gleam of life in the man's deep, velvety eyes—perhaps, indeed, a moustache adorned the short, twisted lip where the white fingers rasped so frequently now.

The pious monks were busy with their evening meal, and the Provincial was quite alone in the garden. All around him the leaves glowed ruddily in the warm light. Everywhere the fruits of earth were ripe and full with mature beauty; but the solitary walker noted none of these. He paced backwards and forwards with downcast eyes, turning slowly and indifferently as if it mattered little where he walked. The merry blackbirds in the hay field adjoining the garden called to each other continuously, and from a hidden rookery came the voice of the dusky settlers, which is, perhaps, the saddest sound in all nature's harmonies. But the Jesuit resolutely refused to listen. Once, however, he stopped and stood motionless for some seconds, with his head turned slightly to meet the distant cry; but he never raised his eyes, which were deep and lifeless in their gaze. It may be that there was a rookery near that southern chateau, where he once had walked in the solemn evening hour, or perhaps he did not hear that sound at all though his ear was turned towards it.

It would be hard indeed to read from the priest's still features the thoughts that might be passing through his powerful brain; but the strange influence of his being was such as makes itself felt without any spoken word. As he walked there with his long hands clasped behind his back, his peculiarly shaped head bent slightly forward, and his perfect lips closely pressed, no one could have looked at him without feeling instinctively that no ordinary mind was busy beneath the tiny tonsure—that no ordinary soul breathed there for weal or woe, seeking after higher things in the right way or the wrong. The man's cultivated repose of manner, his evident intellectuality, and his subtle strength of purpose visible in every glance of his eyes, betrayed that although his life might be passed in the calm retreat of a monastery, his soul was not there. The man was never created to pass his existence in prayerful meditation; his mission was one of strife and contention amidst the strong minds of the age. One felt that he was living in this quiet Breton valley for a purpose; that from this peaceful spot he was dexterously handling wires that caused puppets—aye, puppets with golden crowns—to dance, and smirk, and bow in the farthest corners of the earth.

Presently the Jesuit heard footsteps upon the gravel at the far side of the garden, but he did not raise his head. His interest in the trivial incidents of everyday life appeared to be quite dead.

"Softly, softly!" said a deep, rough voice, which the Provincial recognised as that of the sub-prior; then he raised his eyes slightly and looked across the garden, without, however, altering his pace.

He saw there Christian Vellacott walking by the side of the hard-faced old monk with long, hesitating strides, like a man who had forgotten how to use his legs. It was exactly six weeks since the young journalist had passed through that garden with Rene Drucquer, and those weeks had been to him a strange and not unpleasant dream. It seemed as if the man lying upon that little bed was in no way connected with the wiry, energetic Christian Vellacott of old. As he lay there semi-somnolent and lazily comfortable from sheer weakness, his interest in life was of a speculative description, as if he looked on things from afar off. Nothing seemed to matter much. There was an all-pervading sense of restful indifference as to whether it might be night or day, morning, noon, or evening. All responsibility in existence seemed to have left him: his ready pride of self-dependence had given way to a gentle obedience, and the passage from wakefulness to sleep was very sweet.

Through all those dreamy hours he heard the soft rustle of woollen garments and the suppressed shuffle of sandalled feet. Whenever he opened his heavy eyes he discerned vaguely in the dim light a grey, still form seated upon the plain wooden bench at his bedside. Whenever he tried to change his position upon the hard bed and his weary bones refused their function, strong, hard hands were slipped beneath him and kind assistance freely given. As a rule, it was the tall sub-prior who ministered to the sick man, fighting the dread fever with all his simple knowledge; his hands smoothed oftenest the tossed pillow; but many clean-shaven, strong, and weary faces were bowed over the bed during those six weeks, for there was a competition for the post of sick-nurse. The monks loved to feel that they were performing some tangible good, and not spending their hours over make-believe tasks like a man-of-warsman in fine weather.

One frequent visitor, however, Christian Vellacott never saw beneath his lazy lashes. The Provincial never entered that little cell unless he was positively informed that its inmate was asleep. The inscrutable Jesuit seemed almost to be ashamed of the anxiety that he undoubtedly felt respecting the sick man thus thrown upon his hands by a peculiar chain of incidents. He spoke coldly and sarcastically to the sub-prior whenever he condescended to mention the subject at all; but no day passed in which he failed to pay at least one visit to the little cell at the end of the long, silent corridor.

"Softly, softly!" said the old sub-prior, holding out his bony hand to stay his companion's progress, "you are too ambitious, my son."

Christian laughed in a low, weak voice, and raised his head to look round him. The laugh ceased suddenly as he caught sight of the Provincial, and across the potato-bed the two strong men looked speculatively into each other's eyes in the peaceful twilight. The Jesuit's gaze fell first, and with a dignified bow he moved gently away.

"I am stronger than I look, my father," said Christian, turning to his companion. Then they walked slowly on, and presently rested upon a wooden bench built against the monastery wall.

The young Englishman leaned back and watched the Provincial, who was pacing backwards and forwards where they had first seen him. The old monk sat with clasped hands, and gravely contemplated the gravel beneath his feet. Thus they waited together within the high, whitewashed walls, while the light faded from the western sky. Three types, as strangely contrasted as the student of human kind could wish to see: the old monk with his placid bloodless face and strong useless arms—a wasted energy, a mere monument to mistaken zeal; and the younger men so widely severed by social circumstances, and yet resembling each other somewhat in heart and soul. Each had a strong individuality—each a great and far-reaching vitality. Each was, in his way, a power in the world, as all strong minds are; for in face of what may be said (and with apparent justice) respecting chance and mere good fortune, good men must come to the top among their fellows. They must—and most assuredly they do. As in olden days the doughtiest knights sought each other in the battlefield to measure steel, so in these later times the ruling intellects of the day meet and clear a circle round them. The Provincial was a power in the Society of Jesus; perhaps he was destined one day to be General of it; and Christian Vellacott had suddenly appeared upon the field of politic strife, heralding his arrival with two most deadly blows dealt in masterly succession. From the first they were sure to come together, sooner or later; and now, when they were separated by nothing more formidable than a bed of potatoes, they were glancing askance and longing to be at each other. But it could not be. Had the sub-prior left the garden it would have made no difference. It was morally impossible that those two men could speak what they were thinking, for one of them was a Jesuit.

The Provincial, however, made the first move, and the Englishman often wondered in later days what his intention might have been. He walked on to the northern end of the garden, where a few thick-stemmed pear trees were trained against the wall. The fruit was hanging in profusion, for it was not consumed in the monastery but given to the poor at harvest-time. The Provincial selected a brown, ripe pear, and broke it delicately from the tree without allowing his fingers to come in contact with the fruit itself. Then he turned and walked with the same lazy precision towards the two other occupants of the garden. At his approach the sub-prior rose from his seat and stood motionless with clasped hands; there was a faint suggestion of antagonism in his attitude, which was quite devoid of servility. Christian, however, remained seated, raising his keen grey eyes to the Provincial's face with a quiet self-assertion which the Jesuit ignored.

"I am glad, Monsieur, to see you restored to health," he said coldly to Christian, meeting his gaze for a moment.

The Englishman bowed very slightly, and there was a peculiar expressiveness in the action which betrayed his foreign education, but the cool silence with which he waited for the Provincial to speak again was essentially British. The Jesuit moved and glanced slowly beneath his lowered eyelids towards the motionless figure of the sub-prior. He was too highly bred to allow himself to be betrayed into any sign of embarrassment, and too clever to let the Englishman see that he was hesitating. After a momentary pause he turned gravely to the sub-prior, and said:

"Will you allow your patient, my brother, to taste of our fruit? it is ripe and wholesome."

Then, without awaiting a reply, he presented the pear to Vellacott. It was a strange action, and no doubt there was some deep intention in it. The Jesuit must have known, however, from Rene Drucquer's report, and from his own observations, that Christian Vellacott was of too firm a mould to allow his feelings to be influenced by a petty action of this description, however sincere and conciliatory might have been the spirit in which it was conceived. Perhaps he read the Englishman's character totally wrong, although his experience of men must have been very great; or perhaps he really wished to conciliate him, and took this first step with the graceful delicacy of his nation, with a view to following it up.

With a conventional word of thanks, Vellacott took the pear and set it down upon the bench at his side. Whatever the Jesuit's intention might have been, it was frustrated by his quiet action. It would have been so easy to have said a few words of praise regarding the fruit, and it was only natural to have begun eating it at once; but Vellacott read a deeper meaning in all this, and he chose a more difficult course. It was assuredly harder to keep silence then than to talk, and a weaker-minded man would have thanked the Provincial with effusion. The manner in which Vellacott laid the fruit upon the bench, his quiet and deliberate silence, conveyed unmistakably and intentionally that the Provincial's society was as unwelcome as it was unnecessary. There was nothing to be done but take the hint; and in the lowering twilight the solitary, miserable man moved reluctantly away. With contemplative hardness of heart the Englishman watched him go; there was no feeling of triumph in his soul—neither, however, was there pity. The Jesuit had chosen his own path, he had reached his goal, and that most terrible thirst—the thirst for power—was nearly slaked. If at times—at the end of a long day of hard mental work, when men's hearts are softened by weariness and lowering peace—he desired something else than power, some little touch of human sympathy perhaps, his was the blame if no heart responded to his own. Christian Vellacott sat and wondered dreamily, with the nonchalance of a man who has been at the very gates of death, if power were worth this purchase-money.

The sub-prior had seated himself again, and with his strong hands meekly clasped he waited. He knew that something was passing which he could not understand: his dull instincts told him vaguely that between these two strong men there was war-fare, dumb, sullen, and merciless; but unused as he was to the ways of men, unlearned in the intricacies of human thoughts, he could not read more.

"You have not told me yet, my father," said Vellacott, "how long I have been ill."

"Six weeks, my son," replied the taciturn monk.

"And it was very bad?"

"Yes, very bad."

Christian slowly rubbed his thin hands together. His fingers were moist and singularly white, with a bleached appearance about the knuckles. His face was thin, but not emaciated, his long jaw and somewhat pronounced chin were not more bony than of old, but the expression of his mouth was quite changed; his lips were no longer thrust upward with a determined curve, and a smile seemed nearer at hand.

"I have a faint recollection of being very tenderly nursed and cared for; generally by you, I think. No doubt you saved my life."

The sub-prior moved a little, and drew in his feet.

"The matter was not in my hands," he said quietly.

The Englishman, with some tact, allowed this remark to pass in acquiescent silence.

"Did you ever think that ... I was not ... going back to England?" he asked presently, in a lighter tone, though the thought of returning home brought no smile to his face.

The sub-prior did not reply at once. He appeared to be thinking deeply, for he leaned forward in an unmonastic attitude with his knees apart, his elbows resting upon them, and his hands clasped. He gazed across the prosaic potato-bed with his colourless lips slightly apart.

"One night," he began meditatively, "I went to sit with you after the bell for matins had been rung. From midnight till three o'clock you never moved. Then I gave you some cordial, and as I stooped over you the candle flickered a little; there were strange shadows upon your face, but around your lips there was a deeper shade. I had seen it once before, on my brother's face when he lay upon the hard Paris pavement with a bullet in his lungs, and his breath whistling through the orifice as the wind whistles round our walls in winter. I held the candle closer to your face, and as I did so, a hand came over my shoulder and took it from my fingers. The Father Provincial had come to help me. He said no word, but set the candle down upon the bed, and I held you up while he administered the cordial drop by drop, as a man oils a cartwheel."

"Ah!" said Christian slowly and suggestively, "*he* was there!"

The monk made no reply. He sat motionless, with a calm, acquired silence, which might have meant much or nothing.

"Did he come often?" inquired the Englishman.

"Very often."

"I never saw him."

This, again, was met with silence. Presently the sub-prior continued his narrative.

"When daylight came at last," he said, "the shadow had left your lips. I think that night was the worst; it was then that you were nearer ... nearer than at any other time."

Christian Vellacott was strong enough now to take his usual interest in outward things. With the writer's instinct he went through the world looking round him, always studying men and things, watching, listening, and storing up experience. The Provincial interested him greatly, but he did not dare to show his curiosity; he hesitated to penetrate the darkness that surrounded the man's life, past, present, and future. In a minor degree the taciturn sub-prior arrested his attention. The old monk was in a communicative humour, and the Englishman led him on a little without thinking much about the fairness of it.

"Did your brother die?" he asked sympathetically.

"He died," was the reply. "Yes, my son, he died—died cursing the tyrant's bullet in his lungs. He threw away his life in a vain attempt to alter human nature, to set straight that which is crooked and cannot be set straight. He sought to bring about at once that which cometh not until the lion shall eat straw like an ox. See, my son, that you do not attempt the same."

"I think," said Christian, after a pause, "that we all try a little, and perhaps some day a great accumulation of little efforts will take place. You, my father, have tried as well!"

The monk slowly shook his head, without, however, any great display of conviction.

"I was not always a monk," he said, as if seeking to excuse a bygone folly.

It was nearly dark now. The birds were silent, and only the whispering of the crisp, withering leaves broke the solemn hush of eventide. The two men sat side by side without speaking. They had learnt to know each other fairly well during the last weeks—so well that between them silence was entirely restful. At length Christian moved restlessly. He had reached that stage of convalescence where a position becomes irksome after a short time. It was merely a sign of returning strength.

"Where is the Abbe Drucquer," he asked abruptly.

"He left us some time ago," was the guarded reply.

"He spoke of going abroad," said Christian, deliberately ignoring the sub-prior's tone.

"The Father Provincial told me that the Abbe had gone abroad—to India—to spread there the Holy Light to such as are still in darkness."

The young journalist thought that he detected again a faint suggestion of antagonism in the sub-prior's voice. The manner in which the information was imparted was almost an insult to the Provincial. It was a repetition of his words, given in such a manner that had the speaker been a man of subtle tongue it would have implied grave doubt.

Christian was somewhat surprised that Rene Drucquer should have attained his object so quickly. He never suspected that he himself might have had much to do with it, that it had been deemed expedient to remove the young priest beyond the possible reach of his influence, because he was quite unconscious of this influence. He did not know that its power had affected Rene Drucquer, and that some reflection of it had even touched the self-contained Provincial—that it was even now making this old sub-prior talk more openly than was prudent or wise. He happened to be taking the question from a very different point of view.

CHAPTER XXV

BACK TO WORK

Day by day Christian Vellacott recovered strength. The enforced rest, and perhaps also the monastic peacefulness of his surroundings, contributed greatly towards this. In mental matters as in physical we are subject to contagion, and from the placid recluses, vegetating unheeded in the heart of Brittany, their prisoner acquired a certain restfulness of mind which was eminently beneficial to his body. Life inside those white walls was so sleepy and withal so pleasant that it was physically and mentally impossible to think and worry over events that might be passing in the outer world.

Presently, however, Christian began to feel idle, which is a good sign in invalids; and soon the days became long and irksome. He began to take an increased interest in his surroundings, and realised at once how little he knew of the existence going on about him. Though he frequently passed, in the dim corridors and cloisters, a silent, grey-clad figure, exchanging perhaps with him a scarcely perceptible salutation, he had never spoken with any other inmates of the monastery than the Provincial and the sub-prior.

He noticed also that the watchful care of the nurse had imperceptibly glided into that of a warder. He was never allowed out of his cell unless accompanied by the sub-prior—in fact, he was a state prisoner. His daily walks never extended beyond the one path near the potato bed, or backwards and forwards at the sunny end of the garden, where the huge pears hung ripely. From neither point was any portion of the surrounding country visible, but the Provincial could not veil the sun, and Christian knew where lay the west and where the east.

No possible opportunity for escape presented itself, but the Englishman was storing up strength and knowledge all the while. He knew that things would not go on for long like this, and felt that the Provincial would sooner or later summon him to the long room at the end of the corridor upon the upper floor.

This call came to him three weeks after the day when the two men had met in the garden—nine weeks after the English-man's captivity had commenced.

"My son," said the sub-prior one afternoon, "the Father Provincial wishes to speak with you to-day at three."

Christian glanced up at the great monastery clock, which declared the time to be a quarter to three.

"I am ready," he said quietly. There was no tremor in his voice or light in his eyes, and he continued walking leisurely by the side of the old monk; but a sudden thrill of pleasant anticipation warmed his heart.

A little later they entered the monastery and mounted the stone stairs together. As they walked along the corridor the clock in the tower overhead struck three.

"I will wait for you at the foot of the stairs," said the monk slowly, as if with some compunction. Then he led the way to the end of the corridor and knocked at the door. He stood back, as if the Provincial were in the habit of keeping knockers waiting. Such was, at all events, the case now, and some minutes elapsed before a clear, low voice bade him enter.

The monk opened the door and stood back against the wall for Christian to pass in. The Provincial was seated at the table near the window, which was open, the afternoon being sultry although the autumn was nearly over. At his left hand stood the small Venetian mirror which enabled him to see who was behind him without turning round.

As Christian crossed the room the Provincial rose and bowed slightly, with one of his slow, soft glances. Then he indicated the chair at the left-hand side of the table, and said, without looking up:

"Be good enough—Mr. Vellacott."

When they were both seated the Provincial suddenly raised his eyes and fixed them upon the Englishman's face. The action was slightly dramatic, but very effective, and clearly showed that he was accustomed to find the eyes of others quail before his. Christian met the gaze with a calmness more difficult to meet than open defiance. After a moment they turned away simultaneously.

"I need scarcely," said the Provincial, with singular sweetness of manner, which, however, was quite devoid of servility, "apologise to you, Monsieur, for speaking in French, as it is almost your native language."

Christian bowed, at the same time edging somewhat nearer to the table.

"There are one or two matters," continued the Jesuit, speaking faster, "upon which I have been instructed to treat with you; but first I must congratulate you upon your restoration to health. Your illness has been very serious... I trust that you have had nothing to complain of... in the treatment which you have received at our hands."

Christian, while sitting quite motionless, was making an exhaustive survey of the room.

"On the contrary," he said, in a conventional tone which, in comparison to his companion's manner, was almost brutal, "it is probably owing to the care of the sub-prior that I am alive at the present moment, and—"

He stopped suddenly; an almost imperceptible motion of the Jesuit's straight eyebrows warned him.

"And...?" repeated the Provincial, interrogatively. He leant back in his chair with an obvious air of interest.

"And I am very grateful—to him."

"The reverend father is a great doctor," said the Jesuit lightly. "Excuse me," he continued, rising and leaning across the table, "I will close the window; the air from the river begins to grow cool."

The journalist moved slightly, looking over his shoulder towards the window; at the same moment he altered, with his elbow, the position of the small mirror standing upon the table. Instead of reflecting the whole room, including the door at the end, it now reproduced the blank wall at the side opposed to the curtained recess where the bed was placed.

"And now, Mr. Vellacott," continued the Jesuit, reseating

himself, "I must beg your attention. I think there can be no harm in a little mutual frankness, and—and it seems to me that a certain allowance for respective circumstances can well be demanded."

He paused, and opening the leather-bound manuscript book, became absorbed for a moment in the perusal of one of its pages.

"From your pen," he then said, in a businesslike monotone, "there has emanated a serious and hitherto unproved charge against the Holy Society of Jesus. It came at a critical moment in the political strife then raging in France; and, in proportion to the attention it attracted, harm and calumny accrued to the Society. I am told that your motives were purely patriotic, and your desire was nothing beyond a most laudable one of keeping your countrymen out of difficulties. Before I had the pleasure of seeing you I said, 'This is a young journalist who, at any expense, and even at the sacrifice of truth, wishes to make a name in the world and force himself into public attention.' Since then I have withdrawn that opinion."

During these remarks the Provincial had not raised his eyes from the table. He now leant back in the chair and contemplated his own clasped hands. Christian had listened attentively. His long, grave face was turned slightly towards the Provincial, and his eyes were perhaps a little softer in their gaze.

"I endeavoured," he said, "some weeks ago, to explain my position."

The Jesuit inclined his head. Then he raised his long white finger to his upper lip, stroking the blue skin pensively.

Henry Seton Merriman

Presently he raised his eyes to the Englishman's face, and in their velvety depths Christian thought he detected an expression which was almost pleading. It seemed to express a desire for help, for some slight assistance in the performance of a difficult task. He never again looked into those eyes in all his life, but the remembrance of them remained in his heart for many years after the surrounding incidents had passed away from memory and interest. He knew that the Soul looking forth from that pale and heartless face was of no ordinary mould or strength. In later years, when they were both grey-haired men whose Yea or No was of some weight in the world—one speaking with the great and open voice of the Press, the other working subtly, dumbly, secretly—their motives may have clashed once more, their souls may have met and touched, as it were, over the heads of the People, but they never looked into each other's eyes again.

The Provincial moved uneasily.

"It has been a most unfortunate business," he said gently, and after a pause continued more rapidly, with his eyes upon the book. "I am instructed to lay before you the apologies of the Society for the inconvenience to which you have been put. Your own sense of justice will tell you that we were bound to defend ourselves in every way. You have done us a great injury, and, as is our custom, we have contradicted nothing. The Society of Jesus does not defend itself in the vain hope of receiving justice at the hands of men. I am now in a position to inform you again that you are at liberty—free to go where you will, when you will—and that any sum you may require is at your disposal to convey you home to England ... on your signing a promise never to write another word for private or public circulation on the subject of the Holy Order of Jesus, or to dictate to the writing of another."

"I must refuse," said Christian laconically, almost before the words had left the Jesuit's lips. "As I explained before, I am simply a public servant; what I happen to know must ever be at the public disposal or I am useless."

A short silence followed this remark. When at length the Provincial spoke his tone was cold and reserved.

"Of course," he said, "I expected a refusal—at first. I am instructed to ask you to reconsider your refusal and to oblige me, at the end of a week, with the result of your meditations. If it remains a refusal, another week will be accorded, and so on."

"Until—?"

The Jesuit closed the book upon the table in front of him and with great care altered its position so that it lay quite squarely. He raised his eyebrows slightly and glanced sideways towards the Englishman. At that moment the bell began summoning the devotees to their evening meal, its deep tone vibrating weirdly through the bare corridors.

"Until you accept," suggested he softly.

Christian looked at him speculatively. The faintest suspicion of a smile hovered for a moment in his eyes, and then he turned and looked out of the window.

"I hope, Monsieur," continued the Jesuit, "that when I have the pleasure of seeing you—a week hence—your health will be quite re-established!"

"Thank you!"

"And in the meantime I shall feel honoured by your asking for anything you may require."

"Thank you!" answered Christian again. He was still looking over his shoulder, down at the brown river which ran immediately below the window.

"Please excuse my rising to open the door for you," said the Provincial, with cool audacity, "but I have a few words to write before joining our brethren at their evening repast."

Christian turned and looked at him vaguely. There was a peculiar gleam in his eyes, and he was breathing heavily. Then he rose and, as he passed the Jesuit, bowed slightly in acknowledgment of his grave salutation. He walked quickly down the length of the room, which was not carpeted, and opened the door, closing it again with some noise immediately. But he never crossed the threshold. To the man sitting at the table it was as if the Englishman had left the room, closing the door after him.

Presently the Provincial glanced at the mirror, from mere habit, and found that it was displaced. He re-arranged it thoughtfully, so that the entire room was included in its field of reflection.

"I wonder," he said aloud, "when and why he did that!"

Then he returned to his writing. In a few minutes, however, he rose and pushed back his chair. With his hands clasped behind his back he stood and gazed fixedly out of the window. Beneath him the brown water glided past with curling eddy and gleaming ripple, while its soft murmur was the only sound that broke the pathetic silence surrounding this lonely man. His small and perfectly formed face was quite expressionless; the curve of his thin lips meant nothing; all the suppressed vitality of his being lay in those deep, soft eyes over which there seemed to be a veil. Presently he turned, and with lithe, smooth steps passed down the long room and out of the door.

Instantly Christian Vellacott came from his hiding-place within the recess. He ran to the window and opened it noiselessly. A moment later he was standing upon the stone sill. The afternoon sun shone full upon his face as he stood there, and showed a deep red flush on either cheek. Slowly he stooped forward, holding with one hand to the woodwork of the window while he examined critically the surface of the water. Suddenly he threw his arms forward and like a black shadow dived noiselessly, passing into the depth without a splash. When he rose to the surface he turned to look at the monastery. The Provincial's window was the only outlet directly on to the river.

The stream was rapid, and after swimming with it for a short time he left the water and lay down to recover his breath under the friendly cover of some bushes. There he remained for some time, while the short October twilight closed over the land. A man just dragged from the jaws of death, he lay in his wet clothes where he first found shelter without even troubling to move his limbs from the pools of water slowly accumulating. Already the monastery was a thing of the past. With the rapid forethought of his generation he was already looking to the future. He knew too well the spirit of the people in France to fear pursuit. The monks never ventured beyond their own walls except on ostentatious missions of charity. The machinations of the Society of Jesus were less to be feared in France than in England, and he had only to take his story to the nearest sub-prefecture to raise a storm of popular opinion in his favour. But this was not his project. With him, as in all human plans, his own personal feelings came before the possible duty he owed to the public. He lay beneath the bramble undergrowth, and speculated as to what might have taken place subsequent to his disappearance. At that moment the fortunes of the *Beacon* gave him no food for thought. What Mr. Bodery and his subordinate might, or might not, think found no interest in his mind. All his speculations were confined to events at St. Mary Western, and the outcome of his meditations was that when the friendly cover of darkness lay on the land he rose and started to walk briskly across the well-tilled country towards the north.

That portion of Brittany which lies along the northern coast is a pastoral land where sleep occupies the larger half of man's life. Although it was only evening, an hour when Paris and London recover, as it were, from the previous night's vigil and brighten up into vigour, the solitary Englishman passed unheeded through the squalid villages, unmolested along the winding roads. Mile after mile of scanty forest land and rich meadow were left behind, while, except for a few heavily-breathing cattle, he met no sign of life. At last he came upon a broader road which bore unmistakable signs of military workmanship in its construction, and here he met, and passed with laconic greeting, a few peasant women returning with empty baskets from some neighbouring market; or perhaps a "cantonnier" here and there, plodding home with "sabots" swinging heavily and round shoulders bent beneath the burden of his weighty stone-breaking implements.

Following the direction of this road his course was now towards the north-east, with more tendency to the eastward than he desired, but there was no choice. About eight o'clock he passed through a small village, which appeared to be already wrapped in stupid slumber such as attends the peasant's pillow. A cock crowed loudly, and in reply a dog barked with some alarm, but Christian was already beyond the village upon the deserted high road again.

He now began to feel the weakening effect of his illness; his legs became cramped, and he frequently rested at the roadside. The highway was running still more to the eastward now, and Christian was just beginning to consider the advisability of taking to the country again, when it joined a broader road cut east and west. Here he stopped short, and, raising his head, stood quite still for some moments.

"Ah!" he muttered. "The sea. I smell the sea."

He now turned to the left, and advanced along the newly-discovered road towards the west. As he progressed the pungent odour of seaweed refreshed him and grew stronger every moment. Suddenly he became aware that although high land lay upon his left hand there was to his right a hollow darkness without shadow or depth. No merry plash of waves came to explain this; the smell of the sea was there, but the joyous tumble of its waters was not to be heard. The traveller stooped low and peered into the darkness. Gradually he discerned a distant line of horizon, and to that point there seemed to stretch a vast dead sheet of water without light or motion. Upon his ears there stole a soft bubbling sound, varied occasionally by a tiny ripple. Suddenly a flash of recollection appeared to pass through the watcher's mind, and he muttered an exclamation of surprise as he turned towards the east and endeavoured to pierce the gloom. He was right. Upon the distant line of horizon a jagged outline cut the sky. It was like the form of a huge tooth jutting out from the softer earth. Such is Mont St. Michel standing grandly alone in the midst of a shallow, sullen sea. The only firm thing among the quaking sands, the only stone for miles around.

"The Bay of Cancale!" reflected Christian. "If I keep to the westward I shall reach St. Malo before ten o'clock!"

And he set off with renewed vigour. From his feet there

stretched away to the north a great dead level of quicksand, seething, bubbling, and heaving in the darkness. The sea, and yet no sea. Neither honest land nor rolling water.

CHAPTER XXVI

SIGNOR BRUNO

Silas Lebrun, captain and part-owner of the brig *Agnes and Mary* of Jersey, was an early riser. Moreover, the old gentleman entertained peculiar views as to the homage due to Morpheus. He made no elaborate toilet before entering the presence of that most lovable god. Indeed he always slept in his boots, and the cabin-boy had on several occasions invited the forecastle hands to believe that he neither removed the ancient sealskin cap from his head nor the wooden pipe from his lips when slumber soothed his senses; but this statement was always set aside as unauthenticated.

In person the ancient sailor was almost square, with short legs and a body worthy of promotion to something higher. His face was wrinkled and brown, like the exterior of that incomprehensible fruit the medlar, which is never ripe till it is bad, and then it is to be avoided. A yellow-grey beard clustered closely round a short chin, and when perchance the sealskin cap was absent yellow-grey hair of a similar hue completed the circle, standing up as high from his brow as fell the beard downward from his chin. A pair of intensely blue eyes, liquid always with the milk of human kindness, rendered the hirsute medlar a pleasant thing to look at.

Henry Seton Merriman

The *Agnes and Mary* was ready for sea, her cargo of potatoes, with a little light weight in the way of French beans and eggs, comfortably stowed, and as Captain Lebrun emerged from what he was pleased to call his "state-room" with the first breath of a clear morning he performed his matinal toilet with a certain sense of satisfaction. This operation was simple, consisting merely in the passage of four very brown fingers through the yellow-grey hair, and a hurried dispersal of the tobacco ash secreted in his beard.

The first object that met the mariner's astonished gaze was the long black form of a man stretched comfortably upon the cabin locker. The green mud adhering to the sleeper's thin shoes showed that he had climbed on board at low tide when the harbour was dry.

Captain Lebrun gazed meditatively at the intruder for some moments. Then he produced a powerfully-scented pipe of venerable appearance, which had been, at various stages of its existence, bound in a seaman-like manner with pieces of tarred yarn. He slowly filled this object, and proceeded to inform it in a husky voice that he was "blowed." The pipe was, apparently, in a similar condition, as it refused absolutely to answer to the powerful suction applied to it.

He then seated himself with some difficulty upon the corner of the low table, and examined the sleeper critically.

"Poor devil," he again said, addressing himself to his pipe. "He's one of them priest fellows.—Hi, mister!" he observed, raising his voice.

Christian Vellacott woke up at once, and took in the situation without delay. He was not of those who must go through terrible contortions before regaining their senses after sleep.

"Good morning, Captain!" he observed pleasantly.

"Oh—yourn't a parlee voo, then!"

"No, I'm an Englishman."

"Indeed. Then you'll excuse me, but what in the name of glory are you doing here?"

Christian sat up and looked at his muddy shoes with some interest.

"Well, the truth is that I am bolting. I want to get across to England. I saw where you hailed from by your rig, and clambered on board last night. It seemed to me that when an Englishman is in a hole he cannot do better than go to a fellow-countryman for help."

Captain Lebrun made a mighty effort to force a passage through his pipe, and was rewarded by a very high-pitched squeak.

"Ay!" he said doubtfully. "But what sort of hole is it? Nothing dirty, I'm hopin'. Who are yer? Why are ye runnin' away, and who are ye runnin' from?"

Though a trifle blunt the sailor's manner was not unfriendly, and Christian laughed before replying.

"Well," he said, "to tell you the whole story would take a long time. You remember perhaps there was a row, about two months ago, respecting some English rifles found in Paris?"

"Of course I remember that; we had a lot o' trouble with the Customs just then. The thing was ferreted out by a young newspaper fellow!"

Christian rubbed his hands slowly together. He was terribly anxious to hear the sequel.

"I am that newspaper fellow," he said, with a quick smile.

Captain Lebrun slowly stood up. He contemplated his pipe thoughtfully, then laying it upon the table he turned solemnly towards Christian, and held out a broad brown hand which was covered with scales in lieu of skin.

"Shake hands, mister?" he said.

Christian obliged him.

"And now," he said quickly, "I want to know what has happened since—since I left England. Has there been a great row? Has ... has anybody wondered where I was?"

The old sailor may have had his suspicions. He may have guessed that Christian Vellacott had not left England at the dictates of his own free will, for he looked at him very kindly with his liquid blue eyes, and replied slowly:—

"I couldn't say that *nobody* hasn't been wonderin' where ye was, but—but there's been nothing in the papers!"

"That is all right! And now will you give me a passage, Captain?"

"Course I will! We sail about eleven this morning. I'm loaded and cleared out. But I should like you to have a change o' clothes. Can't bear to see ye in them black things. It makes me feel as if I was talkin' to a priest."

"I should like nothing better," replied Christian, as he rose and contemplated his own person reflectively.

"Come into my state-room then. I've got a few things of my own, and a bit of a slop-chest: jerseys and things as I sell to the men."

The Captain's wardrobe was of a marine character and somewhat rough in texture. He had, however, a coat and waistcoat of thick blue pilot-cloth which fitted Christian remarkably well, but the continuations thereof were so absurdly out of keeping with the young fellow's long limbs as to precipitate the skipper on to the verge of apoplexy. When he recovered, and his pipe was re-lighted, he left the cabin and went forward to borrow a pair of the required articles from Tom Slake, an ordinary seaman of tall and slim proportions. In a short time Christian Vellacott bore the outward semblance of a very fair specimen of the British tar, except that his cheeks were bleached and sunken, which discrepancy was promptly commented upon by the blunt old sailor.

Secrecy was absolutely necessary, so Tom, of the long legs, was the only person to whom Christian's presence was made known; and he it was who (in view of a possible berth as steward later on) was entrusted with the simple culinary duties of the vessel.

Breakfast, as served up by Tom, was of a noble simplicity. A long shiny loaf of yesterday's bread, some butter in a saucer—which vessel was deemed entirely superfluous in connection with cups—brown sugar in an old mustard-tin, with portions of yellow paper adhering to it, and solid slices of bacon brought from the galley in their native frying-pan. Such slight drawbacks, however, as there might have been in the matter of table-ware disappeared before the sense of kindly hospitality with which Captain Lebrun poured the tea into a cracked cup and a borrowed pannikin, dropping in the sugar with careful judgment from his brown fingers. Such defects as there might have lurked in the culinary art as carried on in the galley vanished before the friendly solicitude with which Tom tilted the frying-pan to pour into Christian's plate a bright flow of bacon-fat cunningly mingled with cinders.

When the meal had been duly despatched Captain Lebrun produced his pipe and proceeded to fill it, after having extracted from its inward parts the usual high-toned squeak.

Christian leant back against the bulkhead with his hands buried deeply in Tom's borrowed pockets. He felt much more at home in pilot cloth than in cashmere.

"There is one more thing I should like to borrow," he said.

"Ay?" repeated the captain interrogatively, as he searched in his waistcoat-pocket for a match.

"Ay, what is it?"

"A pipe. I have not had a smoke for two months."

The Captain struck a light upon his leg.

"I've got one somewhere," he replied reassuringly; "carried it for many years now, just in case this one fell overboard or got broke."

Tom, who happened to be present, smiled audibly behind a hand which was hardly a recommendation for the coveted berth of steward, but Christian looked at the battered pipe with sympathetic gravity.

At ten o'clock the *Agnes and Mary* warped out of harbour and dropped lazily down the Rance, setting sail as she went. Christian had spent most of the morning in the little cabin smoking Captain Lebrun's reserve pipe, and seeking to establish order among the accounts of the ship. The accounts were the *bete noire* of the old sailor's existence. Upon his own confession he "wasn't no arithmetician," and Christian found, upon inspecting his accounts, no cause to contradict this ambiguous statement.

When the *Agnes and Mary* was clear of the harbour he went on deck, where activity and maritime language reigned supreme. The channel was narrow and the wind light, consequently the little brig drifted more or less at her own sweet will. This would have been well enough had the waterway been clear of other vessels, but the Jersey steamer was coming in, with her yellow funnel gleaming in the sunlight, her mail-flag fluttering at her foremast, and her captain swearing on the bridge, with the whistle-pull in his hand.

Seeing that the *Agnes and Mary* had no steerage way, the captain stopped his engines for a few minutes, and then went ahead again at half-speed. This brought the vessels close together, and, as is the invariable custom in such circumstances, the two crews stared stonily at each other. On the deck were one or two passengers enjoying the morning air after a cramped and uncomfortable night. Among these was an old man with a singularly benign expression; he was standing near the after-wheel, gazing with senile placidity towards St. Malo. As the vessels neared each other, however, he walked towards the rail, and stood there with a pleasant smile upon his face, as if ready to exchange a greeting with any kindred soul upon the *Agnes and Mary*.

Christian Vellacott, seated upon the rail of the after-deck, saw the old man and watched him with some interest—not, however, altering his position or changing countenance. The vessels moved slowly on, and, in due course, the two men were opposite to each other, each at the extreme stern of his ship.

Then the young journalist removed Captain Lebrun's spare pipe from his lips, and leaning sideways over the water, called out:

"Good morning, Signor Bruno!"

The effect of this friendly greeting upon the benevolent old gentleman was peculiar. He grasped the rail before him with both hands, and stared at the young Englishman. Then he stamped upon the deck with a sudden access of fury.

"Ah!" he exclaimed fiercely, while a tiger-like gleam shone out from beneath his smooth white brows. "Ah! it is you!"

Christian swung his legs idly, and smiled with some amusement across the little strip of water.

Suddenly the old man plunged his hand into the breast-pocket of his coat. He appeared to be tugging wildly at some article which was caught in the lining of his clothes, when a remarkable change came over his face. A dull red colour flew to his cheeks, and his eyes gleamed ruddily, as if shot with blood. Then without a word he fell forward with his breast against the painted rail, remained there a second, and as the two ships passed away from each other, rolled over upon his back on the clean deck, grasping a pistol in his right hand.

Christian Vellacott sat still upon the rail, swinging one leg, and smiling reflectively. He saw the old man fall and the other passengers crowd round him, but the *Agnes and Mary* had now caught the breeze and was moving rapidly out to sea, where the sunlight danced upon the water in little golden bars.

"Apperlexy!" said a voice in the journalist's ear. He turned and found Captain Lebrun standing at his side looking after the steamer. "Apperlexy!"

"Do you think so?" asked Christian.

"I do," was the reply, given with some conviction. "I seen a man fall just like that; he was a broad-built man wi' a thick neck, and in a moment of excitement he fell just like that, and died a'most at once. Apperlexy they said it was."

"It seemed to come over him very suddenly, did it not?" said Christian absently.

"Ay, it did," said the captain. "Ye seemed to know him!"

Christian turned and looked his companion full in the face. "I have met him twice," he said quietly. "He was in England for some years, I believe; a political refugee, he called himself."

By sea and land Captain Lebrun had learnt to devote an exclusive attention to his own affairs, allowing other men to manage theirs, well or ill, according to their fancy. He knew that Christian Vellacott wished to tell him no more, and he was content that it should be so, but he had noticed a circumstance which, from the young journalist's position, was probably invisible. He turned to give an order to the man at the wheel, and then walked slowly and with some difficulty (for Captain Lebrun suffered, in a quiet way, agonies from rheumatism) back towards his passenger.

"Seemed to me," he said reflectively, as he looked upwards to see if the foretopsail was shivering, "as if he had something in his hand when a' fell."

Christian followed the Captain's gaze. The sails were now filling well, and there was an exhilarating sound of straining cordage in the air while the vessel glided on. The young journalist was not an impressionable man, but he felt all these things. The sense of open freedom, the gentle rise and fall of the vessel, the whirring breeze, and the distant line of high land up the Rance towards Dinant—all these were surely worth hearing, feeling, and seeing; assuredly, they added to the joy of living.

"Something in his hand," he repeated gravely; "what was it?"

Captain Lebrun turned sideways towards the steersman, and made a little gesture with his left hand. A wrinkle had appeared in one corner of the foretopsail. Then he looked round the horizon with a sailor's far-seeing gaze, before replying.

"Seemed to me," he mumbled, without taking his pipe from his lips, "that it was a revolver."

Then the two men smoked in silence for some time. The little vessel moved steadily out towards the blue water, passing a lighthouse built upon a solitary rock, and later a lightship, with its clean red hull gleaming in the sunlight as it rose and fell lazily. So close were they to the latter that the man watching on deck waved his hand in salutation.

Still Vellacott had vouchsafed no reply to Captain Lebrun's strange statement. He sat on the low rail, swinging one leg monotonously, while the square little sailor stood at his side with that patient maritime reflectiveness which is being slowly killed by the quicker ways of steam.

"My calling brings me into contact with a rum lot of people," said the young fellow at last, "and I suppose all of us make enemies without knowing it."

With this vague elucidation the little skipper was forced to content himself. He gave a grunt of acquiescence, and walked forward to superintend the catheading of the anchor.

CHAPTER XXVII

IN THE RUE ST. GINGOLPHE AGAIN

One would almost have said that the good citizen Jacquetot was restless and disturbed. It was not that the little tobacco shop left aught to be desired in the way of order, neither had the tobacconist quitted his seat at the window-end of the counter. But he was not smoking, and at short intervals he drew aside the little red curtain and looked out into the quiet Rue St. Gingolphe with a certain eagerness.

The tobacconist was not in the habit of going to meet things. He usually waited for them to come to him. But on this particular evening of September in a year which it is not expedient to name, he seemed to be looking out into the street in order that he might not be taken by surprise in the event of an arrival. Moreover he mopped his vast forehead at unnecessarily frequent intervals, just as one may note a snuff-taker have recourse to that solace more frequently when he is agitated than when a warm calm reigns within his breast.

"So quiet—so quiet," he muttered, "in our little street—and in the others—who knows? It would appear that they have their shutters lowered there."

He listened intently, but there was no sound except the clatter of an occasional cart or the distant whistle of a Seine steamer.

Then the tobacconist returned to the perusal of the *Petit Journal.* Before he had skimmed over many lines, he looked up sharply and drew aside the red curtain. Yes! It was some one at last. The footsteps were hurried and yet hesitating— the gait of a person not knowing his whereabouts. And yet the man who entered the shop a moment later was evidently the same who had come to the citizen Jacquetot when last we met him.

"Ah!" exclaimed the tobacconist. "It is you!"

"No," replied the other. "It is not. I am not the citizen...Morot— I think you call it."

"But, yes!" exclaimed the fat man in amazement. "You are that citizen, and you are also the Vicomte d'Audierne."

The new-comer was looking round him curiously; he stepped towards the curtained door, and turned the handle.

"I am," he said, "his brother. We are twins. There is a resemblance. Is this the room? Yes!"

"Yes, monsieur. It is! But never was there such a resemblance."

The tobacconist mopped his head breathlessly.

"Go," said the other, "and get a mattress. Bring it and lay it on this table. My brother is wounded. He has been hit."

Jacquetot rose laboriously from his seat. He knew now that

this was not the Vicomte d'Audierne. This man's method was quite different. He spoke with a quiet air of command, not doubting that his orders would be obeyed. He was obviously not in the habit of dealing with the People. The Vicomte d'Audierne had a different manner of speaking to different people—this man, who resembled him so strangely, gave his orders without heeding the reception of them.

The tobacconist was essentially a man of peace. He passed out of a small door in the corner of the shop, obeying without a murmur, and leaving the new-comer alone.

A moment later the sound of wheels awoke the peaceful stillness of the Rue St. Gingolphe. The vehicle stopped, and at the same instant the man passed through the little curtained doorway into the room at the back of the shop, closing the door after him.

The gas was turned very low, and in the semi-darkness he stood quite still, waiting. He had not long to wait; he had scarcely closed the door when it was opened again, and some one entered rapidly, closing it behind him. Then the first comer raised his arm and turned up the gas.

Across the little table, in the sudden flood of light, two men stood looking at each other curiously. They were so startlingly alike, in height and carriage and every feature, that there was something weird and unpleasant in their action—in their silence.

"Ah!" said the last comer. "It is thou. I almost fired!"

And he threw down on the table a small revolver.

"Why have you done this?" continued the Vicomte d'Audierne. "I thought we agreed sixteen years ago that the world was big enough to contain us both without meeting, if we exercised a little care."

"She is dead," replied the brother. "She died two years ago— the wife of Prangius—what does it matter now?"

"I know that—but why did you come?"

"I was ordered to Paris by the General. I was near you at the barricade, and I heard the bullet hit you. Where is it?"

The Vicomte looked down at his hand, which was pressed to his breast; the light of the gas flickered, and gleamed on his spectacles as he did so.

"In my chest," he replied. "I am simply dripping with blood. It has trickled down my legs into my boots. Very hot at first—and then very cold."

The other looked at him curiously, and across his velvety eyes there passed that strange contraction which has been noted in the glance of the Vicomte d'Audierne.

"I have sent for a mattress," he said. "That bullet must come out. A doctor is following me; he will be here on the instant."

"One of your Jesuits?"

"Yes—one of my Jesuits."

The Vicomte d'Audierne smiled and winced. He staggered a little, and clutched at the back of a chair. The other watched him without emotion.

"Why do you not sit down?" he suggested coldly. "There are none of your—*People*—here to be impressed."

Again the Vicomte smiled.

"Yes," he said smoothly, "we work on different lines, do we not? I wonder which of us has dirtied his hands the most. Which of the two—the two fools who quarrelled about a woman. Ha? And she married a third—a dolt. Thus are they made—these women!"

"And yet," said the Jesuit, "you have not forgotten."

The Vicomte looked up slowly. It seemed that his eyelids were heavy, requiring an effort to lift them.

"I do not like to hear the rooks call—that is all," he said.

The other turned away his soft, slow glance, the glance that had failed to overcome Christian Vellacott's quiet defiance—

"Nor I," he said. "It makes one remember."

There was a short silence, and then the Jesuit spoke—sharply and suddenly.

"Sit down, you fool!" he said. "You are fainting."

The Vicomte obeyed, and at the same moment the door opened and the tobacconist appeared, pushing before him a mattress.

The Jesuit laid aside his hat, revealing the tonsure gleaming whitely amidst his jetty hair, and helped to lay the mattress upon the table. Then the two men, the Provincial and the tobacconist of the Rue St. Gingolphe, lifted the wounded aristocrat gently and placed him upon the improvised bed. True to his blood, the Vicomte d'Audierne uttered no sound of agony, but as his brother began to unbutton the butcher's blouse in which he was disguised he fainted quietly. Presently the doctor arrived. He was quite a young man, with shifting grey eyes, and he saluted the Provincial with a nervous obsequity which was unpleasant to look upon. The deftness with which he completed the task of laying bare the wound was notable. His fingers were too clever to be quite honest. When, however, he was face to face with the little blue-rimmed orifice that disfigured the Vicomte's muscular chest, the expression of his face—indeed his whole manner—changed. His eyes lost their shiftiness—he seemed to forget the presence of the great man standing at the other side of the table.

While he was selecting a probe from his case of instruments the Vicomte d'Audierne opened his eyes.

"Ah!" said the doctor, noting this at once. "You got this on the Boulevard?"

"Yes."

"How did you get here?" He was feeling the wounded man's pulse now.

"Cab."

"All the way?"

"Of course."

"Who carried you into this room?" asked the doctor, returning to his case of instruments.

"No one! I walked." The doctor's manner, quick and nonchalant, evidently aggravated his patient.

"Why did you do that?"

He was making his preparations while he spoke, and never looked at the Vicomte.

"In order to avoid attracting attention."

This brought the doctor's glance to his face, and the result was instantaneous. The young man started, and into his eyes there came again the shifty expression, as he looked from the face of the patient to that of the Provincial standing motionless at the other side of the table. He said nothing, however, and returned with a peculiar restraint to his preparations. It is probable that his silence was brought about by the persistent gaze of two pairs of deep velvety eyes which never left his face.

"Will Monsieur take chloroform," he asked, unfolding a clean pocket-handkerchief, and taking from his waistcoat pocket a small phial.

"No!"

"But—I beg of you—"

"It is not necessary," persisted the Vicomte calmly.

The doctor looked across to the Provincial and made a hopeless little movement of the shoulders, accompanied by an almost imperceptible elevation of the eyebrows.

The Jesuit replied by looking meaningly at the small glass-stoppered bottle.

Then the doctor muttered:

"As you will!"

He had laid his instruments out upon the mattress—the gas was turned up as high as it would go. Everything was ready. Then he turned his back a moment and took off his coat, which he laid upon a chair, returning towards the bed with one hand behind his back.

Quick as thought, he suddenly darted forward and pressed the clean handkerchief over the wounded man's mouth and nose. The Vicomte d'Audierne gave a little smothered exclamation of rage, and raised his arms; but the Jesuit was too quick for him, and pinned him down upon the mattress.

After a moment the doctor removed the handkerchief, and the Vicomte lay unconscious and motionless, his delicate lips drawn back in anger, so that the short white teeth gleamed dangerously.

"It is possible," said the surgeon, feeling his pulse again, "that Monsieur has killed himself by walking into this room."

Like a cat over its prey, the young doctor leant across the mattress. Without looking round he took up the instruments he wanted, knowing the order in which they lay. He had been excellently taught. The noiseless movements of his white fingers were marvellously dexterous—neat, rapid, and finished. The evil-looking instruments gleamed and flashed beneath the gaslight. He had a peculiar little habit of wiping each one on his shirt-sleeve before and after use, leaving a series of thin red stripes there.

After the lapse of a minute he raised his head, wiped something which he held in his fingers, and passed it across to the Provincial.

"That is the bullet, my father," he said, without ceasing his occupation, and without raising his eyes from the wounded man.

"Will he live?" asked the Jesuit casually, while he examined the bullet.

"If he tries, my father," was the meaning reply.

The young doctor was bandaging now, skilfully and rapidly.

"This would be the death of a dog," said the Provincial, as if musing aloud; for the surgeon was busy at his trade, and the tobacconist had withdrawn some time before.

"Better than the life of a dog," replied the Vicomte, in his smoothly mocking way, without opening his eyes.

It was very easy to blame one woman, and to cast reflections upon the entire sex. If these brothers had not quarrelled about that woman, they would have fallen out over something else. Some men are so: they are like a strong spirit—light and yet potent—that floats upon the top of all other liquids and will mingle with none.

It would seem that these two could not be in the same room without quarrelling. It was only with care that (as the Jesuit had coldly observed) they could exist in the same world without clashing. Never was the Vicomte d'Audierne so cynical, so sceptical, as in the presence of his brother. Never was Raoul d'Audierne so cold, so heartless, so Jesuitical, as when meeting his brother's scepticism.

Sixteen years of their life had made no difference. They were as far apart now as on one grey morning sixteen years ago, when the Vicomte d'Audierne had hurried away from the deserted shore of the Cote du Nord, leaving his brother lying upon the sand with an ugly slit in his neck. That slit had healed now, but the scar was always at his throat, and in both their hearts.

True to his training, the Provincial had not spoken the truth when he said that he had been ordered to Paris. There was only one man in the world who could order him to do anything, and that man was too wise to test his authority. Raoul d'Audierne had come to Paris for the purpose of seeing his brother—senior by an hour. There were many things of which he wished to speak, some belonging to the distant past, some to a more recent date. He wished to speak of Christian Vellacott—one of the few men who had succeeded in outwitting him—of Signor Bruno, or Max Talma, who had died within pistol range of that same Englishman, a sudden, voiceless death, the result of a terrible access of passion at the sight of his face.

But this man was a Jesuit and a d'Audierne, which latter statement is full of import to those who, having studied heredity, know that wonderful *inner* history of France which is the most romantic story of human kind. And so Raoul d'Audierne—the man whose power in the world is like that of the fires burning within the crust of the earth, unseen, immeasurable—and so he took his hat, and left the little room behind the tobacconist's shop in the Rue St. Gingolphe—beaten, frustrated.

CHAPTER XXVIII

THE MAKING OF CHRISTIAN VELLACOTT

"Money," Captain Lebrun was saying emphatically, as the *Agnes and Mary* drifted slowly past Gravesend pier on the rising tide. "Hang money! Now, I should think that you make as much of it in a month as I do in a year. You're a young man, and as far as I know ye, ye're a successful one. Life spreads out before you like a clean chart. I'm an old 'un—my time is nearly up. I've lived what landsmen call a hard life, and now I'm slowly goin' home. Ay, Mr. Vellacott, goin' home! And you think that with all your manifold advantages you're a happier man than me. Not a bit of it! And why? 'Cause you belong to a generation that looks so far ahead that it's afraid of bein' happy, just for fear there's sorrow a comin'. Money, and lookin' ahead, that's what spoils yer lives nowadays."

The skipper emphasised these weighty observations by expectorating decisively into the water, and walked away, leaving Christian Vellacott with a vaguely amused smile upon his face. It is just possible that Silas Lebrun, master and owner of the *Agnes and Mary*, was nearer the mark than he thought.

An hour later, Vellacott was walking along the deserted

embankment above Westminster, on the Chelsea side of the river. It was nine o'clock, for which fact Big Ben solemnly gave his word, far up in the fog. The morning was very dark, and the street lamps were still alight, while every window sent forth a gleam suggestive of early autumnal fires.

Turning up his own street he increased his pace, realising suddenly that he had not been within his own doors for more than four months. Much might have happened in that time—to change his life, perhaps. As he approached the house he saw a strange servant, an elderly woman, on her knees at the steps, and somehow the sight conveyed to his mind the thought that there was something waiting for him within that peaceful little house. He almost ran those last few yards, and sprang up the steps past the astonished woman without a word of explanation.

The gas in the narrow entrance-hall was lighted, and as he threw aside his cap he perceived a warm gleam of firelight through the half-open door of the dining-room. He crossed the carpeted hall, and pushed open that door.

Near the little breakfast-table, just under the gas, stood Hilda Carew. In *his* room, standing among *his* multifarious possessions, in the act of pouring from *his* coffee-pot. She was dressed in black—he noticed that. Instead of being arranged high upon her head, her marvellous hair hung in one massive plait down her back. She looked like a tall and beautiful school-girl. He had not seen her hair like that since the old days when he had been as one of the Carews.

As he pushed open the door, she looked up; and for a moment they stood thus. She set down the coffee-pot, carefully and symmetrically, in the centre of the china stand provided for its reception—and the colour slowly left her face.

"You have come back at last!" she said quite monotonously. It sounded like a remark made for the purpose of filling up an awkward silence.

Then he entered the room, and mechanically closed the door behind him. She noticed the action, but did not move. He passed round the table, behind Aunt Judy's chair, and they shook hands conventionally.

"Yes," he said almost breathlessly; "I am back; you do not seem elated by the fact."

Suddenly she smiled—the smile that suggested, in some subtle way, a kitten.

"Of course—I am glad ... to see you."

In a peculiar dreamy way she began to add milk to the coffee. It seemed as if this were mere play-acting, and not real life at all.

"How is it that you are here?" he asked, with a broken, disjointed laugh. "You cannot imagine how strange an effect it was ... for me ... to come in and see you ... here—of all people."

She looked at him gravely, and moved a step towards him.

"Aunt Judy is dead!" she explained; "and Aunt Hester is very ill. Mother is upstairs with them—her—now. I have just come from the room, where I have been since midnight."

She stopped, raised her hand to her hair as if recollecting something, and stood looking sideways out of the window.

"There is something about you this morning," he said, with a concentrated deliberation, "that brings back the old Prague days. I suppose it is that I have not seen your hair as you have it to-day—since then."

She turned quite away from his hungry gaze, looking out of the window.

After a pause she broke the silence—with infinite tact—not speaking too hurriedly.

"It has been a terrible week," she said. "Mother heard from Mr. Bodery that they were very ill; so we came. I never dreamt that it was so bad when you spoke of them. Five years it has been going on?"

"Yes; five years. Thank you for coming, but I am sorry you should have seen it."

"Why?"

"Every one should keep guard over his own skeleton."

She was looking at him now.

"You look very ill," she said curtly. "Where have you been?"

"I was kidnapped," he said, with a short laugh, "and then I got typhoid. The monks nursed me."

"You were in a monastery?"

"Yes; in Brittany."

She was idly arranging the cups and saucers with her left hand, which she seemed desirous of bringing under his notice; but he could look at nothing but her face.

Henry Seton Merriman

"Then," she said, "it would have been impossible to find you?"

"Quite," he replied, and after a pause he added, in a singularly easy manner, "Tell me what happened after I disappeared."

She did not seem to like the task.

"Well—we searched—oh! Christian, it was horrid!"

"I wondered," he said, in a deep, soft voice, "whether you would find it so."

"Yes, of course, we *all* did."

This did not appear to satisfy him.

"But you," he persisted, "you, yourself—what did you think?"

"I do not know," she answered, with painful hesitation. "I don't think I thought at all."

"Then what did you do, Hilda?"

"I—oh, we searched. We telegraphed for Mr. Bodery, who came down at once. Then Fred rode over, and placed himself at Mr. Bodery's disposal. First he went to Paris, then to Brest. He did everything that could be done, but of course it was of no avail. By Mr. Bodery's advice everything was kept secret. There was nothing in the newspapers."

She stopped suddenly, and there was a silence in the room. He was looking at her curiously, still ignoring that little left hand. Only one word of her speech seemed to have attached itself to his understanding.

"Fred?" he said. "Fred Farrar?"

"Yes—my husband!"

He turned away—walked towards the door, and then returned to the hearthrug, where he stood quite still.

"I suppose it was a quiet wedding," he said in a hard voice, "on my account; eh?"

"Yes," she whispered. He waited, but she added nothing.

Then suddenly he laughed.

"I have made a most extraordinary mistake!" he said, and again laughed.

"Oh, don't" she exclaimed.

"Don't what?"

"Laugh."

He came nearer to her—quite near, until his sleeve almost touched her bowed head.

"I thought—at St. Mary Western—that you loved *me*."

She seemed to shrink away from him.

"What made me think so, Hilda?"

She raised her head, and her eyes flashed one momentary appeal for mercy—like the eyes of a whipped dog.

"Tell me," he said sternly.

"It was," she whispered, "because *I* thought so myself."

"And when I was gone you found out that you had made a mistake?"

"Yes; he was so kind, so *brave*, Christian—because he knew of my mistake."

Christian Vellacott turned away, and looked thoughtfully out of the window.

"Well," he said, after a pause, "so long as you do not suffer by it—"

"Oh—h," she gasped, as if he were whipping her. She did not quite know what he meant. She does not know now.

At last he spoke again, slowly, deliberately, and without emotion.

"Some day," he said, "when you are older, when you have more experience of the world, you will probably fall into the habit of thanking God, in your prayers, that I am what I am. It is not because I am good ... perhaps it is because I am ambitious—my father, you may remember, was considered heartless; it may be *that*. But if I were different—if I were passionate instead of being what the world calls cold and calculating—you would be ... your life would be—" he stopped, and turning away he sat down wearily in Aunt Judy's armchair. "You will know some day!" he said.

It is probable that she does know now. She knows, in all likelihood, that her husband would have been powerless to save her from Christian Vellacott—from herself—from that

Love wherein there are no roses but only thorns.

And in the room above them Aunt Hester was dying. So wags the world. There is no attention paid to the laws of dramatic effect upon the stage of life. The scenes are produced without sequence, without apparent rhyme or reason; and Chance, the scene-shifter, is very careless, for comedies are enacted amid scenic effects calculated to show off to perfection the deepest tragedy, while tragedies are spoilt by their surroundings.

The doctor and Mrs. Carew stood at the bedside, and listened to the old woman's broken murmurings. Into her mind there had perhaps strayed a gleam of that Light which is not on the earth, for she was not abusing her great-nephew.

"Ah, Christian," she was murmuring, "I wish you would come. I want to thank you for your kindness, more especially to Aunt Judy. She is old, and we must make allowances. I know she is aggravating. It happened long ago, when your father was a little boy—but it altered her whole life. I think women are like that. There is something that only comes to them once. I am feeling far from well, nephew Vellacott. I think I should like to see a doctor. What does Aunt Judy think? Is she asleep?"

She turned her head to where she expected to find her sister, and in the act of turning her eyes closed. She slumbered peacefully. The two sisters had slept together for seventy years—seventy long, monotonous years, in which there had been no incident, no great joy, no deep sorrow—years lost. Except for the natural growth and slow decay of their frames, they had remained stationary, while around them children had grown into men and women and had passed away.

Presently Aunt Hester opened her eyes, and they rested on

the vacant pillow at her side. After a pause she slowly turned her head, and fixed her gaze upon the doctor's face. He thought that the power of speech had left her, but suddenly she spoke, quite clearly.

"Where is my sister Judith?" she asked.

There are times when the truth must be spoken, though it kill.

"Your sister died yesterday," replied the doctor.

Aunt Hester lay quite still, staring at the ceiling. Her shrivelled fingers were picking at the counter-pane. Then a gleam of intelligence passed across her face.

"And now," she said, "I shall have a bed to myself. I have waited long enough."

Aunt Hester was very human, although the shadow of an angel's wing lay across her bed.

*   *   *   *   *

It was many years later that Christian Vellacott found himself in the presence of the Angel of Death again. A telegram from Havre was one day handed to him in the room at the back of the tall house in the Strand, and the result was that he crossed from Southampton to Havre that same night.

As the sun rose over the sea the next morning, its earliest rays glanced gaily through the open port-hole of a cabin in a large ocean steamer, still panting from her struggle through tepid Eastern seas.

In this little cabin lay the Jesuit missionary, Rene Drucquer, watching the moving reflections of the water, which played ceaselessly on the painted ceiling overhead. He had been sent home from India by a kind-hearted army surgeon; a doomed man, stricken by a climatic disease in which there was neither hope nor hurry. When the steamer arrived in the Seine it was found expedient to let the young missionary die where he lay. The local agent of the Society of Jesus was a kind-hearted man, and therefore a faithless servant. He acceded to Rene Drucquer's prayer to telegraph for Christian Vellacott.

And now Vellacott was actually coming down the cabin stairs. He entered the cabin and stood by the sick man's bed.

"Ah, you have come," said the Frenchman, with that peculiar tone of pathetic humour which can only be rendered in the language that he spoke.

"But how old! Do I look as old as that, I wonder? And hard—yes, hard as steel."

"Oh no," replied Vellacott. "It may be that the hardness that was once there shows now upon my face—that is all."

The Frenchman looked lovingly at him, with eyes like the eyes of a woman.

"And now you are a great man, they tell me."

Vellacott shrugged his shoulders.

"In my way," he admitted. "And you?"

"I—I have taught."

"Ah! and has it been a success?"

"In teaching I have learnt."

Vellacott merely nodded his head.

"Do you know why I sent for you?" continued the missionary.

"No."

"I sent for you in order to tell you that I burnt that letter at Audierne."

"I came to that conclusion, for it never arrived."

"I want you to forgive me."

Vellacott laughed.

"I never thought of it again," he replied heartily.

The priest was looking keenly at him.

"I did not say 'thou,' but '*you*,'" he persisted gently.

Vellacott's glance wavered; he raised his head, and looked out of the open port-hole across the glassy waters of the river.

"What do you mean?" he inquired.

"I thought," said Rene Drucquer, "there might be some one else—some woman—who was waiting for news."

After a little pause the journalist replied.

"My dear Abbe," he said, "there is no woman in the whole

world who wants news of me. And the result is, as you kindly say, I am a great man now—in my way."

But he knew that he might have been a greater.

Choose from Thousands of 1stWorldLibrary Classics By

A. M. Barnard
Ada Leverson
Adolphus William Ward
Aesop
Agatha Christie
Alexander Aaronsohn
Alexander Kielland
Alexandre Dumas
Alfred Gatty
Alfred Ollivant
Alice Duer Miller
Alice Turner Curtis
Alice Dunbar
Allen Chapman
Alleyne Ireland
Ambrose Bierce
Amelia E. Barr
Amory H. Bradford
Andrew Lang
Andrew McFarland Davis
Andy Adams
Angela Brazil
Anna Alice Chapin
Anna Sewell
Annie Besant
Annie Hamilton Donnell
Annie Payson Call
Annie Roe Carr
Annonaymous
Anton Chekhov
Archibald Lee Fletcher
Arnold Bennett
Arthur C. Benson
Arthur Conan Doyle
Arthur M. Winfield
Arthur Ransome
Arthur Schnitzler
Arthur Train
Atticus
B.H. Baden-Powell
B. M. Bower
B. C. Chatterjee
Baroness Emmuska Orczy
Baroness Orczy
Basil King
Bayard Taylor
Ben Macomber
Bertha Muzzy Bower
Bjornstjerne Bjornson

Booth Tarkington
Boyd Cable
Bram Stoker
C. Collodi
C. E. Orr
C. M. Ingleby
Carolyn Wells
Catherine Parr Traill
Charles A. Eastman
Charles Amory Beach
Charles Dickens
Charles Dudley Warner
Charles Farrar Browne
Charles Ives
Charles Kingsley
Charles Klein
Charles Hanson Towne
Charles Lathrop Pack
Charles Romyn Dake
Charles Whibley
Charles Willing Beale
Charlotte M. Braeme
Charlotte M. Yonge
Charlotte Perkins Stetson
Clair W. Hayes
Clarence Day Jr.
Clarence E. Mulford
Clemence Housman
Confucius
Coningsby Dawson
Cornelis DeWitt Wilcox
Cyril Burleigh
D. H. Lawrence
Daniel Defoe
David Garnett
Dinah Craik
Don Carlos Janes
Donald Keyhoe
Dorothy Kilner
Dougan Clark
Douglas Fairbanks
E. Nesbit
E. P. Roe
E. Phillips Oppenheim
E. S. Brooks
Earl Barnes
Edgar Rice Burroughs
Edith Van Dyne
Edith Wharton

Edward Everett Hale
Edward J. O'Biren
Edward S. Ellis
Edwin L. Arnold
Eleanor Atkins
Eleanor Hallowell Abbott
Eliot Gregory
Elizabeth Gaskell
Elizabeth McCracken
Elizabeth Von Arnim
Ellem Key
Emerson Hough
Emilie F. Carlen
Emily Bronte
Emily Dickinson
Enid Bagnold
Enilor Macartney Lane
Erasmus W. Jones
Ernie Howard Pie
Ethel May Dell
Ethel Turner
Ethel Watts Mumford
Eugene Sue
Eugenie Foa
Eugene Wood
Eustace Hale Ball
Evelyn Everett-green
Everard Cotes
F. H. Cheley
F. J. Cross
F. Marion Crawford
Fannie E. Newberry
Federick Austin Ogg
Ferdinand Ossendowski
Fergus Hume
Florence A. Kilpatrick
Fremont B. Deering
Francis Bacon
Francis Darwin
Frances Hodgson Burnett
Frances Parkinson Keyes
Frank Gee Patchin
Frank Harris
Frank Jewett Mather
Frank L. Packard
Frank V. Webster
Frederic Stewart Isham
Frederick Trevor Hill
Frederick Winslow Taylor

Friedrich Kerst
Friedrich Nietzsche
Fyodor Dostoyevsky
G.A. Henty
G.K. Chesterton
Gabrielle E. Jackson
Garrett P. Serviss
Gaston Leroux
George A. Warren
George Ade
Geroge Bernard Shaw
George Cary Eggleston
George Durston
George Ebers
George Eliot
George Gissing
George MacDonald
George Meredith
George Orwell
George Sylvester Viereck
George Tucker
George W. Cable
George Wharton James
Gertrude Atherton
Gordon Casserly
Grace E. King
Grace Gallatin
Grace Greenwood
Grant Allen
Guillermo A. Sherwell
Gulielma Zollinger
Gustav Flaubert
H. A. Cody
H. B. Irving
H.C. Bailey
H. G. Wells
H. H. Munro
H. Irving Hancock
H. R. Naylor
H. Rider Haggard
H. W. C. Davis
Haldeman Julius
Hall Caine
Hamilton Wright Mabie
Hans Christian Andersen
Harold Avery
Harold McGrath
Harriet Beecher Stowe
Harry Castlemon
Harry Coghill
Harry Houidini

Hayden Carruth
Helent Hunt Jackson
Helen Nicolay
Hendrik Conscience
Hendy David Thoreau
Henri Barbusse
Henrik Ibsen
Henry Adams
Henry Ford
Henry Frost
Henry James
Henry Jones Ford
Henry Seton Merriman
Henry W Longfellow
Herbert A. Giles
Herbert Carter
Herbert N. Casson
Herman Hesse
Hildegard G. Frey
Homer
Honore De Balzac
Horace B. Day
Horace Walpole
Horatio Alger Jr.
Howard Pyle
Howard R. Garis
Hugh Lofting
Hugh Walpole
Humphry Ward
Ian Maclaren
Inez Haynes Gillmore
Irving Bacheller
Isabel Cecilia Williams
Isabel Hornibrook
Israel Abrahams
Ivan Turgenev
J.G.Austin
J. Henri Fabre
J. M. Barrie
J. M. Walsh
J. Macdonald Oxley
J. R. Miller
J. S. Fletcher
J. S. Knowles
J. Storer Clouston
J. W. Duffield
Jack London
Jacob Abbott
James Allen
James Andrews
James Baldwin

James Branch Cabell
James DeMille
James Joyce
James Lane Allen
James Lane Allen
James Oliver Curwood
James Oppenheim
James Otis
James R. Driscoll
Jane Abbott
Jane Austen
Jane L. Stewart
Janet Aldridge
Jens Peter Jacobsen
Jerome K. Jerome
Jessie Graham Flower
John Buchan
John Burroughs
John Cournos
John F. Kennedy
John Gay
John Glasworthy
John Habberton
John Joy Bell
John Kendrick Bangs
John Milton
John Philip Sousa
John Taintor Foote
Jonas Lauritz Idemil Lie
Jonathan Swift
Joseph A. Altsheler
Joseph Carey
Joseph Conrad
Joseph E. Badger Jr
Joseph Hergesheimer
Joseph Jacobs
Jules Vernes
Julian Hawthrone
Julie A Lippmann
Justin Huntly McCarthy
Kakuzo Okakura
Karle Wilson Baker
Kate Chopin
Kenneth Grahame
Kenneth McGaffey
Kate Langley Bosher
Kate Langley Bosher
Katherine Cecil Thurston
Katherine Stokes
L. A. Abbot
L. T. Meade

L. Frank Baum
Latta Griswold
Laura Dent Crane
Laura Lee Hope
Laurence Housman
Lawrence Beasley
Leo Tolstoy
Leonid Andreyev
Lewis Carroll
Lewis Sperry Chafer
Lilian Bell
Lloyd Osbourne
Louis Hughes
Louis Joseph Vance
Louis Tracy
Louisa May Alcott
Lucy Fitch Perkins
Lucy Maud Montgomery
Luther Benson
Lydia Miller Middleton
Lyndon Orr
M. Corvus
M. H. Adams
Margaret E. Sangster
Margret Howth
Margaret Vandercook
Margaret W. Hungerford
Margret Penrose
Maria Edgeworth
Maria Thompson Daviess
Mariano Azuela
Marion Polk Angellotti
Mark Overton
Mark Twain
Mary Austin
Mary Catherine Crowley
Mary Cole
Mary Hastings Bradley
Mary Roberts Rinehart
Mary Rowlandson
M. Wollstonecraft Shelley
Maud Lindsay
Max Beerbohm
Myra Kelly
Nathaniel Hawthrone
Nicolo Machiavelli
O. F. Walton
Oscar Wilde

Owen Johnson
P.G. Wodehouse
Paul and Mabel Thorne
Paul G. Tomlinson
Paul Severing
Percy Brebner
Percy Keese Fitzhugh
Peter B. Kyne
Plato
Quincy Allen
R. Derby Holmes
R. L. Stevenson
R. S. Ball
Rabindranath Tagore
Rahul Alvares
Ralph Bonehill
Ralph Henry Barbour
Ralph Victor
Ralph Waldo Emmerson
Rene Descartes
Ray Cummings
Rex Beach
Rex E. Beach
Richard Harding Davis
Richard Jefferies
Richard Le Gallienne
Robert Barr
Robert Frost
Robert Gordon Anderson
Robert L. Drake
Robert Lansing
Robert Lynd
Robert Michael Ballantyne
Robert W. Chambers
Rosa Nouchette Carey
Rudyard Kipling
Saint Augustine
Samuel B. Allison
Samuel Hopkins Adams
Sarah Bernhardt
Sarah C. Hallowell
Selma Lagerlof
Sherwood Anderson
Sigmund Freud
Standish O'Grady
Stanley Weyman
Stella Benson
Stella M. Francis

Stephen Crane
Stewart Edward White
Stijn Streuvels
Swami Abhedananda
Swami Parmananda
T. S. Ackland
T. S. Arthur
The Princess Der Ling
Thomas A. Janvier
Thomas A Kempis
Thomas Anderton
Thomas Bailey Aldrich
Thomas Bulfinch
Thomas De Quincey
Thomas Dixon
Thomas H. Huxley
Thomas Hardy
Thomas More
Thornton W. Burgess
U. S. Grant
Upton Sinclair
Valentine Williams
Various Authors
Vaughan Kester
Victor Appleton
Victor G. Durham
Victoria Cross
Virginia Woolf
Wadsworth Camp
Walter Camp
Walter Scott
Washington Irving
Wilbur Lawton
Wilkie Collins
Willa Cather
Willard F. Baker
William Dean Howells
William le Queux
W. Makepeace Thackeray
William W. Walter
William Shakespeare
Winston Churchill
Yei Theodora Ozaki
Yogi Ramacharaka
Young E. Allison
Zane Grey

www.ingramcontent.com/pod-product-compliance
Lightning Source LLC
Chambersburg PA
CBHW021311250626
47155CB00002B/476